D1196860

Technological Change, INDUSTRIAL RESTRUCTURING AND Regional Development

Edited by

ASH AMIN and JOHN GODDARD

University of Newcastle Upon Tyne

London
ALLEN & UNWIN
Boston   Sydney

© A. Amin, J. B. Goddard and contributors, 1986
This book is copyright under the Berne Convention. No reproduction without permission. All rights reserved

Allen & Unwin (Publishers) Ltd,
40 Museum Street, London WC1A 1LU, UK

Allen & Unwin (Publishers) Ltd,
Park Lane, Hemel Hempstead, Herts HP2 4TE, UK

Allen & Unwin Inc.,
8 Winchester Place, Winchester, Mass. 01890, USA

Allen & Unwin (Australia) Ltd,
8 Napier Street, North Sydney, NSW 2060, Australia

First published in 1986

British Library Cataloguing in Publication Data

Technological change, industrial restructuring and
regional development.
1. Technological innovations—Economic aspects—
Great Britain   2. Great Britain—Economic
conditions—1945–   —Regional disparities
I. Amin, Ash   II. Goddard, J. B.
338'.06   HC260.T4
ISBN 0-04-338131-6

Library of Congress Cataloging in Publication Data

Main entry under title:
    Technological change, industrial restructuring, and
regional development.
"This book has its origins in a workshop organized by the Centre
for Urban and Regional Development Studies (CURDS) at the
University of Newcastle upon Tyne in March 1984"—p.
Includes bibliographies and index.
1. Great Britain—Economic conditions—1945–   —Regional
disparities—Congresses.   2. Technological innovations—
Economic aspects—Great Britain—Congresses.   3. Industrial
organization—Great Britain—Regional disparities—Congresses.
I. Amin, Ash.   II. Goddard, J. B.
III. University of Newcastle upon Tyne.
Centre for Urban and Regional Development Studies.
HC256.6.T45 1986   338.941   85-22902
ISBN 0-04-338131-6 (alk. paper)

Set in 10 on 11 point Bembo by Paston Press, Norwich
and printed in Great Britain by Blackmore Press Ltd, Dorset.

Preface

This book has its origins in a workshop organized by the Centre for Urban and Regional Development Studies (CURDS) at the University of Newcastle upon Tyne in March 1984. The workshop, which was funded by the Economic and Social Research Council (ESRC), addressed the issue of technical change in the context of industrial and economic restructuring and regional development in the United Kingdom.

The purpose of the workshop and therefore also of this book was to open up a dialogue between regional analysts, economists and sociologists of different persuasions, with a view to furthering our understanding of how new technologies can and do influence regional development. We felt that one way of achieving this objective was to bring together different disciplines and diverse analytical traditions. Such an exercise can go some way towards overcoming the narrowness of issues and perspectives which dominates much of the existing literature on technical change and spatial development, exemplified by, in the case of some economists, a failure to consider the social consequences of new technology; or in the case of some regional analysts, a failure to consider non-regional economic and social processes; or in the case of some specialists in technology policy, a failure to give sufficient attention to the real social and economic determinants of the generation and diffusion of new technology.

The problems in the literature are not simply connected with disciplinary boundaries. Extending the boundaries alone will not resolve the problems. This is because there are substantive analytical deficiencies, above all in the mainstream and policy literature, which in our opinion call for debate of a more rigorous and theoretical nature within each discipline. In the field of regional development studies, there is some urgency for such a debate because the hopes of many have been pinned on new technologies as a feasible solution for the regions where the present economic crisis has reached almost dramatic proportions. This book attempts to set out the terms for such a debate by bringing together the work of scholars from different disciplines and research traditions. We hope that this exercise of presenting different perspectives on technology can act as a stimulus for more active discussion within both the academic and non-academic communities.

We would like to end this preface by expressing our gratitude to a number of people. The writing of the editorial introduction has been

iii

greatly facilitated by the written comments on each of the papers in this book. We are therefore grateful to the following eleven discussants whose names are listed in accordance with the sequence of chapters:

Ed Sciberras, The Technical Change Centre, London
Doug Watts, Department of Geography, Sheffield University
Ian Clarke, The Work Organization Research Centre, Aston University
Rod Coombes, Department of Management Sciences, Manchester University
Stephen Davies, School of Economic and Social Studies, University of East Anglia
John Metcalfe, Department of Economics, Manchester University
David Gleave, The Technical Change Centre, London
Richard Meegan, CES Ltd, London
Bert Nicholson, The Small Business Research Trust, London
Al Rainnie, Department of Occupational Studies, Newcastle Polytechnic
David Keeble, Department of Geography, Cambridge University.

Although the workshop was not primarily concerned with public policy issues it did conclude with a discussion of policy and some of the points from that debate are included in the introductory chapter. We are grateful to those policymakers that led this debate, namely

Paul Waldchen, European Commission
David Rees, Department of Trade and Industry
Judith Marquand, Manpower Services Commission
Victor Hausner, Policy Studies Institute

Our thanks are also due to all the other participants of the conference for their helpful comments and to the following members of CURDS for preparing detailed transcripts of the lively debates which followed the papers: Neil Alderman, Mike Coombes, Judith Eversley, Andrew Gillespie, David Gibbs, Anne Green, Ray Oakey and David Owen.

Finally, we would like to thank Judith Houston for dealing with the administrative arrangements for the conference, and also John Rowlands for preparing the artwork for the book.

Ash Amin
John Goddard

Newcastle upon Tyne, *March 1985*

Acknowledgements

The following individuals and organizations have kindly given permission for the reproduction of figures and tables (numbers in parentheses):

Manpower Serevices commission (8.5); Counter Information Services (8.6); figures and tables in Chapter 9 reproduced from *New technology and the future of work and skills* (P. Marstrand, ed.) by permission of Francis Pinter Ltd, and the British Association for the Advancement of Science; Roy Rothwell (12.1–3); Table 4.4 reproduced from *Multinational investment strategies in the British Isles* (Hood & Young) by permission of the Controller, Her Majesty's Stationery Office; Croom Helm (Tables 10.1 & 7).

Contents

List of tables

x

1 The internationalization of production, technological change, small firms and regional development: an overview

A. AMIN and J. B. GODDARD

Introduction

Widening regional disparities have been one of the key characteristics of the current long recession, particularly within the United Kingdom. The lagging peripheral regions whose economies have been based on sectors developed in the 19th century (e.g. coal, steel, textiles, heavy engineering) have been joined by other more prosperous and central regions specializing in the industries of the early 20th century (e.g. motor vehicles, other consumer durables, chemicals), as these sectors have begun to suffer the consequences of de-industrialization and job loss. Much of this job loss in both types of region has occurred in large corporations which have been eliminating excess capacity in the UK and/or switching investment overseas. Regional disparities have been exacerbated because at the same time a limited number of areas have experienced some growth in output and employment due to the rise of new technology-based industries and services, many associated with the emergence of microelectronics technology, with much of this growth taking place in new and small businesses or within the limited number of multinational enterprises operating in this field.

As these tendencies have emerged, the instruments that policymakers have traditionally used to tackle problems of regional industrial decline have become less and less effective. General capital subsidies to attract new and potentially mobile investment in large firms to greenfield sites in lagging regions have no longer produced the desired jobs as the long established relationship between new investment, output and employment growth has broken down in

1

most sectors. In these circumstances policymakers have turned to the promotion of new and small high technology firms and the attraction of high technology investment as the new means of promoting regional development. Recommendations are being made for areas to develop science parks, to provide advanced telecommunication services, to provide venture capital and other services for small high technology firms, to support research into new products and processes and to stimulate the diffusion of new technology amongst local firms. The assumption which underlies these policies is that what is happening due to the operation of market forces in the growth areas can be reproduced through public intervention in the crisis regions.

As is so often the case such policy initiatives have run ahead of the research and critical debate which should underpin them. One of the purposes of this book is to add a note of caution to the chorus of optimistic expectation concerning the contribution of new technologies and small firms to the solution of regional problems as manifested in the shortfall of employment opportunities. Many of the contributions in the volume are therefore not directly concerned with regional policies, but they are included in this volume because of the need to place the sorts of initiatives regional policymakers are pursuing in the context of a broader debate about the role of large and small firms and technological change in economic development and job generation. Such a debate poses a number of questions for the regions which need to be borne in mind when considering the various contributions. Some of the questions are set out below:

(a) How central is technical innovation for a sustained economic recovery? Undoubtedly, new technologies can significantly raise the rate of capital accumulation by strengthening competitiveness, raising productivity and reducing costs. However, might there not be other forms of restructuring which could achieve the same economic effects? Do we have to abandon the traditional sectors which fail to innovate their technologies?

(b) Do new technologies represent jobless growth? They have been used as labour-saving devices; they have helped firms to become more footloose and locate production abroad; they have generated new mental skills, but at the cost of many manual ones. In other words how far are the economic benefits of new technology at odds with the aims of improving the quality and quantity of employment? Do high unemployment regions need new technologies? Or can new products in existing industries create sufficient employment to offset the decline elsewhere?

(c)   What sort of growth has really occurred in the so-called 'high-tech' regions? Have Scotland and Wales had the same employment, income and spin-off effects as the 'M4 corridor' in the South East, or are they simply experiencing a new form of dependent development in the hands of the high-tech multi-nationals?

(d)   Is the idea that all regions can benefit from new technology simply a zero-sum game? Critics of those economic theories which assume or postulate the possibility of equilibrium (with or without State intervention), would argue that it is not possible for all the regions to develop at the same rate or from the same thing. According to this view, disequilibrium is structurally built into the workings of the capitalist economy. The constant drive to raise profits, the anarchy of the market and the inability to plan production in consonance with the market all lead to uneven development between and within different branches of production and between individual firms. This uneven development entails uneven spatial development by virtue of the fact that the conditions for accumulation are unevenly distributed in geographical space. Hence, in the instance of high-tech industries, some areas will attract investments and growth (the M4 corridor), some will only attract externally controlled investments and limited growth, and others will not experience investments or growth. Even if government intervention does succeed in modifying the regional distribution of investments, the laws of competition will see to the take-over or closure of the less competitive firms, with related regional consequences.

(e)   Can small and medium-sized firms in different technology spectrums make a real contribution to self-sustained economic growth in the regions? Can such firms make any significant contribution to employment? If the current recession has exacerbated the tendency for capital to be concentrated and centralized into the hands of the more powerful corporations which set the tune in the market, is it realistic to think that smaller firms can develop or survive in such a context? Alternatively, are there some old and new product markets in which the terms of competition are more favourable? Such firms could be developed in the lesser developed regions. Nevertheless, are they not susceptible to merger and take-over bids from larger corporations, causing thereupon problems of dependence for the region?

(f)   Leaving aside issues related to the economics of the small firm, are there not important social and political questions concerning industrial relations in the small firm? Many small firms manage to survive in the market through minimizing labour costs and by maximizing labour exploitation. Substandard working conditions, employment insecurity and anti-union practices are often the hallmark of such firms. How desirable in that case are policies aimed at generating the growth of small firms in the regions? Alternatively, is it not dangerous to generalize that all small firms have a poor social record? Are there not sectors in which such firms can thrive without having to squeeze labour?

(g) In an economy such as that of the UK, dominated by large and multinational corporations, is it not an *a priori* task to analyse the use and impact of new technologies by such firms, before developing abstract models of regional development from abstract notions of technology? How general are the following observations: that automation and product diversification are a means by which the large corporation enhances its market power; that innovations in the labour process are a direct attack on organized labour; that computerized information technologies are making capital more and more footloose? If these observations are correct, can those policies which fail to influence or regulate the behaviour of the multinationals be of any use for regional development in the UK?

The contributions of this volume address, some more directly than others, the above questions and offer, in several cases, recommendations which are quite different from current policy initiatives. The first three contributions consider some of the realities and spatial implications concerning the internationalization of production. The next five contributions examine both theoretically and empirically the role of new technology in national and regional economic development. The book closes with three contributions on the sociology and economics of small firms.

The internationalization of production

The first three contributions are not directly concerned with technical change nor, with the exception of that by Young, with regional development. They are, however, extremely relevant to the two issues. Firstly, the corporate approach helps not only to examine the ways in which new technologies are being used by dominant industrial corporations, but also to place technological change appropriately in the wider arena of industrial restructuring. Corporations, in their pursuit for higher profits, have embarked on an industrial restructuring which involves a lot more than simply changes in technology. It involves, for example, changes in market behaviour and in the quantity, quality and location of employment. Technology, therefore, cannot be separated from other social and economic factors in the study of industrial and spatial change.

Secondly, the focus on corporations which operate on a multinational basis raises some interesting issues for the analysis of regional development, especially in the case of the UK manufacturing economy which is now so heavily dominated by the multinationals and so extensively integrated internationally. One implication is that growth or the lack of it in the UK regions may now be less connected with the relationship of one region to another or with each region having a distinct role within the *national* accumulation process than with a region's relationship to international capital. Another implication is that if international integration is affecting, albeit to different degrees, the *whole* of the UK economy, then the problems and prospects faced by the different regions may be converging. Finally, if regional economic development is becoming governed more and more by international forces, then it may weaken the thrust of nationally or locally based policies These are not the claims which are necessarily or directly made by the authors of the first three chapters. However, what does emerge quite clearly is the need to locate regional issues in an international context.

In chapter 2 Cowling examines the relationship between de-industrialization and the internationalization of production. He holds the multinational corporations responsible for closures and job loss in the advanced countries such as the UK: 'The combination of unified international markets and giant international firms bestriding them provides a ready mechanism for the process of de-industrialization to develop wherever the conditions for capitalist accumulation have been weakened'. Cowling argues that the latter has indeed been the case in the UK as the strength and militancy of labour have prompted the multinationals during the present recession to relocate capacity abroad into areas where workers can be paid less and exploited more freely. This attack on labour has involved not only the transfer of production to overseas subsidiaries but also subcontracting to dependent companies locally and abroad. The geographical and vertical fragmentation of production has been facilitated by new information technologies which enable the centralized and flexible control of disjointed operations.

Cowling sustains this thesis on de-industrialization by demonstrating how the erosion of production in the UK car and car component industry is directly related to the strategy of the majors (Ford, General Motors, Chrysler, Lucas, GKN, Dunlop, Automotive Products and Associated Engineering) to service the UK market from production facilities in Europe and run down domestic capacity. He rejects the view held in some neo-classical and Keynesian quarters that such an internationalization of production represents an efficient allocation of capital. In his view, it represents the opposite. It is inefficient because monopoly profits and monopoly control prevent the utilization of new resources and the maximization of output. The attack on wages is also forecast to have a deleterious impact on demand by lowering purchasing power. In other words the multinationals' productive strategies are an obstacle to growth in general, and in the case of weaker economies such as the UK they signal the gradual erosion of output, productivity and innovation in manufacturing as more and more capital is exported abroad. This process is also undemocratic because workers globally come to be paid less to do more work and because the multinationals are eroding the power of national communities to determine their own future. The paper concludes that a reversal of this state of affairs must include, in spite of the difficulties involved, binding regulation of the multinationals at local, national and EEC level.

While Cowling's interest in internationalization is to look for those factors which initiate a process of de-industrialization in certain economies, the thrust of Amin and Smith's contribution (Ch. 3) is rather different. They are more concerned with a total explanation of the current internationalization of productive capital. Amin and Smith suggest that the dominant characteristic in the current phase of internationalization is cross-investment, in the hands of the multinationals, between the 'advanced' economies and not the flight of capital from the latter to countries in the Third World and lagging regions in the developed world. This historical development, in their view, restricts the relevance of the wages/productivity thesis on de-industrialization and internationalization to a small number of sectors and countries. Instead, they place greater emphasis upon the chronic build-up of capacity and the global over-accumulation of capital during the boom years as an explanatory factor. The multinationals' response to the threat of under-consumption and over-production posed by the recession has been to internationalize production on an even wider scale in order to maintain or raise their profit rates. Rather than being a strategy to expand investment and output in individual industries, this internationalization has been a programme to restructure, involving: rationalization through closures, new openings and new production technologies; the fragmentation of the labour process on an international basis; diversification into related sectors; and, above all, the increasing penetration and control of markets in the higher income and higher demand economies. Thus, at the point of production, internationalization by the multinationals has undoubtedly involved fragmentation, but it has also meant the growing integration between sectors, both horizontally and vertically, of their activities.

Notwithstanding their differences in perspective, Amin and Smith share Cowling's view that de-industrialization in the UK is much more closely connected with the current strategies of the multinationals than is generally acknowledged and that internationalization does not augur well for self-sustaining accumulation within the UK. The latter conclusion is justified by arguing that the UK, one of the world's economies most heavily dominated by the multinationals emerges as a weak participant in a new order of accumulation operating at an international scale and in the hands of the multinationals. For the UK this means growing subservience and vulnerability to the ever-changing needs of organizations with international rather than national interests. It also implies a deterioration in the balance of payments as UK markets are serviced from abroad. More seriously, the power and control of the multinationals over production and markets severely restricts the prospects for revitalizing an independent national manufacturing base in the UK. This loss seems not to be compensated by a growth in the multinationals' output and employment in the UK for two reasons: firstly because labour inten sive and high-tech investments alike are tending to be located abroad; secondly, because the multinationals' subsidiaries in the UK are tending to occupy a restricted and subordinate position in the corporations' international division of labour. The UK therefore faces the dual problem of disinvestment and a development increasingly dependent on international capital, which raises the prospect of it becoming a lesser developed region in the international order.

Young and Stewart's analysis of the impact of inward direct investment in the UK regions (Ch. 4), takes up the regional perspective on multinationals which is absent in the first two chapters. Their contribution tends to challenge Amin and Smith's implicit suggestion that internationalization is presenting the UK regions with a homogeneous set of problems. Furthermore, in being more concerned with corporate spatial hierarchies than with international capital mobility and by focusing on incoming rather than outgoing investment, this contribution is less pessimistic about the multinationals than the two which precede it.

Young and Stewart argue that debate in the UK on the benefits of foreign direct investment (FDI) has tended to be either too selective or too narrow in its choice of criteria for assessing the behaviour and impact of the multinationals. They propose a much wider analytical framework which is outlined in Figure 4.1. The chapter draws upon a wealth of empirical evidence from both primary and secondary sources to demonstrate that on a number of counts there are significant regional variations in the behaviour of foreign-owned subsidiaries. The bulk of the evidence is drawn from a joint survey with Neil Hood on 140 US and European affiliates in the chemical and the mechanical and electrical industries located in the South East of England, the Assisted Areas of the UK, and Ireland. The survey, which considers a wide range of locational and performance factors (enumerated in Fig. 4.2), suggests that the differences between subsidiaries operating in the South East, Eire and the UK 'assisted areas' are more distinctive than those to be found between the 'assisted areas.' The latter occupy, to varying degrees, an inter-mediate position between the plants in the South East and those in Ireland. The plants in the South East are characterized by a more complex division of tasks in production and offer greater benefits to the domestic economy in terms of both the quality and stability of employment and linkages. The branch plants in Ireland are smaller, more labour intensive, less skilled and export oriented. In explaining these differences, the authors give considerable weight to the level and nature of regional policy instruments together with the peripherality of the areas.

The chapter concludes that, for the UK as a whole, the benefits of inward investment have been uneven. Foreign manufacturing pre-sence in the 'assisted areas' has been beneficial to employment in the case of the 'greenfield' investments, but also threatens to reinforce problems of dependent development. The authors are optimistic about the ability of government schemes to influence the character of subsidiaries in the regions and suggest that improvements could be made by devoting more policy attention towards negotiating local transfer agreements with the multinational corporations on equity, technology and management. They concede, however, that 'raising the status and decision-making authority of subsidiaries remains the major but intractable problem at regional level'.

In the light of the intense problems for regional development posed by the growing internationalization of capital and the difficul-ties of attracting mobile investment with a high technological con-tent to lagging regions, researchers and policymakers have turned to indigenous development in general and technological innovation in particular, as an alternative development strategy. The next five chapters consider the extent to which new technologies can stimulate growth in a national and regional context and seek to examine the development challenges posed by such strategies.

New technology

In Chapter 5 Freeman is optimistic about the potential contribution of technological change to stimulating an upswing in economic activity. Freeman derives his inspiration from the work of Schumpeter who, writing in and about the depressed 1930s, drew attention to the need to look at economic change in a long run historical perspective. Such an approach highlights the role of new opportunities for investment, profits, growth and employment arising from new technologies. However, the whole process implies considerable economic and social disequilibrium. Radical innovations are likely to occur only in a few enterprises and to be concentrated in a limited number of branches of the economy; these innovations may subsequently diffuse into a wide range of other industries and give rise to technological revolutions when this diffusion process transforms the inter-industry input–output matrix through creating totally new branches and destroying others. The role of information technology as a product, process and managerial innovation in a wide range of sectors, including its potential ability to create totally new services, suggests that it alone amongst contemporary innovations has the capacity to bring about such a revolutionary transformation.

The work of Freeman and Soete, in contrast to that of Mensch, suggests that radical innovations do not bunch on a downswing of an economic cycle but are more randomly distributed. More significantly, the research results of Freeman and Soete suggest that the widespread diffusion of new technologies tends not only to stimulate but also to require a general upswing in economic activities. This suggests a link between the Schumpeterian technology push approach to the understanding of economic development and a Keynesian perspective which tends to emphasize the importance of aggregate effective demand. It follows that the State can play an important role in stimulating technological change through its macro-economic policies as well as its micro-economic policies designed to encourage directly the uptake of new technology.

A key feature of Freeman's analysis is the emphasis it gives to the interaction between the technological, economic and institutional systems in bringing about such revolutionary transformations. He argues that in the downswing a mis-match develops between the emerging technological capacity and what is actually realizable given existing institutional and market conditions. In the case of information technology, 'fundamental changes in the education and training system, in industrial relations, in managerial and corporate structures, managerial styles, capital markets and financial systems, the pattern of public, private and hybrid investments and the legal and political framework are all required to ensure the widespread diffusion of the new technology', Also, investment in the infrastructure of information technology, especially telecommunications is a fundamental condition for its widespread adoption.

A number of implications for regional analysis follow from Freeman's discussion. Firstly, the way in which technological revolutions induce instability in the inter-industry input–output matrix suggest that while additional economic activity may be created in the economy as a whole some enterprises in some regions may lose out at the expense of other enterprises in the same product market in other regions which fail to raise productivity through process innovation or the introduction of new and improved products. Nevertheless, it is extremely difficult to specify the timescale and geographical scale over which such processes might operate. It may therefore be more useful to concentrate on those aspects of Freeman's argument which concern the mis-match between technological and institutional capacity. The regional perspective may be helpful here, since many of the bottlenecks have a very clear geographical manifestation. Labour skills are far from mobile and are by and large developed in local labour markets, and are very much influenced by the legacy of previous rounds of industrial investment. Areas where skills developed based around heavy engineering may be unable to make the transition to electro-mechanical technologies but will need a heavy investment in training to embrace those parts of pure electronics where the emphasis is upon mental rather than physical skills. Moreover, the training capacity in local institutes of higher education is likely to reflect the needs of earlier periods and take a long time to adjust. In terms of management information, the enterprise's scanning of its business environment will be strongly conditioned by existing personal contact networks which are likely, for simple time and geographical considerations, to have a strong local orientation. Information reaching enterprises in areas dominated by outmoded technologies consequently may not embrace the latest technological knowledge. Lastly, in the context of the information technology revolution, a lack of demand for telecommunication services arising from a failure to use the ability of this technology to provide access to an international store of technological knowledge may lead to an under-investment in the infrastructure that is likely to be a necessary condition for the next upswing.

Freeman's analysis is cast largely in macro-economic terms. Thomas's contribution in Chapter 6 suggests that these macro-generalizations must have a sound basis in a micro-economic behaviour of individual enterprises. The behavioural approach suggests that macro-economic considerations constitute the environment within which individual entrepreneurs operate; likewise, the regional dimension would suggest the importance of the local industrial milieu to the innovation process within individual enterprises and workplaces.

In adopting a behavioural perspective Thomas rejects the neoclassical theory of the firm because of its failure to come to grips with uncertainty, which is a key feature of technical change in the real world. He suggests an appreciative theory which, although not so formally rigorous as the neo-classical approach, is more closely related to reality. The behavioural theory of the firm advocated by Cyert and March over twenty years ago provides the basis for such a theory; thus the innovation process may be described as a series of distinct chronological steps or points at which critical non-routine (entrepreneurial) decisions are made. These decisions can be seen as responses to, or attempts at creating, market conditions favourable to the enterprise. By inference, regions lacking entrepreneurial managers or powerful market-shaping enterprises are likely to lose out in the essentially competitive process of technological innovation.

While the behavioural approach does provide valuable retrospective insights and while it does consider the disequilibrium conditions associated with technological innovations, its chief shortcoming as compared with the neo-classical approach concerns its limited ability to make predictions about future tendencies, particularly with regard to phenomena (e.g. market structure) which only have meaning at the macro level. Schumpeter's suggestion that industries characterized by intensive innovative activity are dominated by oligopolistic large firms is open to question; while innovation may be motivated by desire for monopoly power, it does not follow that monopoly or oligopoly once achieved encourages innovation. And even if Schumpeter's view is correct, at the regional level it is clear that many adverse consequences can flow from oligopolistic or monopolistic situations – for example, the spatial division of labour within large companies will mean that only certain regions will provide the highly innovative functions or parts of the corporation.

The next three chapters concern themselves specifically with such regional issues and all provide direct empirical evidence on the regional dimension to technological change in Britain. Again following Schumpeter, Goddard, Thwaites and Gibbs draw a distinction between fundamental and incremental product innovations and the diffusion of process innovations. The link with Freeman's concern with 'institutional bottlenecks' and Thomas's with the entrepreneur is provided by their use of Schmookler's definition of the technological capacity of an economy as the accumulated body of technical knowledge weighted by the number of persons who have access to that knowledge; their inference is that the development of regions lacking, for example, a significant number of research workers in either public or private sector organizations may be hindered by limited access to advances in technology.

Goddard, Thwaites and Gibbs' empirical findings suggest that enterprises located in presently lagging regions of Britain rate poorly in many stages of the innovation process. In these regions there is an under-representation of research staff in manufacturing establishments, a finding which is particularly serious given the association they demonstrate between on-site R&D and product innovation. The poorest innovative performances are found amongst small and medium-sized enterprises. Although the branches of large firms based outside the regions record higher rates of innovation, this is dependent on the transfer of products developed elsewhere. Such branch establishments therefore add little to the technological capacity of the regions. While there are some regional lags in the adoption of advanced process technologies such as computerized numerical control of machine tools, well established process innovations are quickly adopted by enterprises in all regions since they require little in-house research capacity. Thus lagging regions suffer the job displacement effects of process innovations but do not benefit from the job-creating (or job-preserving) introduction of new products.

The authors end their contribution by suggesting that policymakers may encourage the development of their regions by promoting the adoption of new technologies amongst enterprises currently located in their areas. Such an approach is questioned in the remaining two chapters in this section. While the contribution of Schutt and Leach (Ch. 9) concentrates on the application of new technology, Sayer and Morgan (Ch. 8) examine an industry which is regarded as the basis of the information technology revolution, the electronics industry itself. Their study reveals that taken as a whole the UK electronics industry is relatively weak in an international context. While output has been increasing and employment declining less than in other parts of British manufacturing industry, the competitive position of the sector on world markets has deteriorated. There is therefore little evidence to support the view that the electronics industry itself can be the propulsive sector that will lead the national let alone the regional economy out of decline; nevertheless, an analysis confined to the current recession may represent too short a period on which to base such a pessimistic conclusion.

At the theoretical level Sayer and Morgan's chapter questions whether new technology can contribute to the development *of* a region as opposed to development *in* a region. Given the tendency for 'jobless' growth even in sectors like electronics where output is expanding, they are sceptical about the contribution of new technology to employment in lagging regions. While new technology-based industries may be leading to the development of *some* regions, Sayer and Morgan's studies of firms located in South Wales, Central Scotland and the M4 corridor lead them to question whether it is realistic to expect 'that the success of Berkshire can be reproduced in

other regions on a major scale . . . simultaneously.' The success of
this area is the product of the location preferences of entrepreneurs
who have built up

'a critical mass of highly skilled personnel . . . for which there is an
international shortage . . . access to good communications, especially
Heathrow . . . a core of government research establishments, a rural
working environment capable of sustaining elite life-styles and a
marked absence of trade-union traditions . . . what distinguishes the
M4 corridor from Central Scotland or South Wales is its elite occupational structure and dense decision-making network of activities which
have the potential for spawning (and sustaining) new firm formation to
an extent not readily apparent elsewhere'.

Notwithstanding these advantages, it is clear that they have been
produced not only by private decisions but by the uncoordinated
actions of the State – for example, concerning the location of research
facilities, the award of defence contracts, the modernization of road,
rail and air communications and strict planning controls preserving
the quality of residential environments. Development agencies in
lagging regions may take comfort in the hope that a better managed
State in which regional concerns are higher on the agenda could
reproduce some of these conditions elsewhere; they might also be
encouraged by the fact that the M4 corridor region has emerged from
a relatively backward agricultural area in less than 20 years, achieving
this transformation from the in-migration of a highly mobile elite.
Finally, Morgan and Sayer's analysis of the M4 corridor confirms the
importance in a successful region of social networks in developing
the technological capacity of the area; the extent to which such
networks can be created in lagging areas by the effort of public sector
'*animateurs*' remains an open question.

The final chapter in this section of the book examines in detail the
impact of a new production process – computer-controlled weighing
and packing – by corporations which dominate their market segment
– cereals and savoury snacks – in the UK food industry. Shutt and
Leach demonstrate how competition between the leading firms in
these markets has led to the adoption of a Japanese process innovation
with a view to reducing labour costs. One outcome of the resultant
higher productivity has been the creation of excess capacity which
has in turn necessitated production rationalization. Of interest to
regional analysts is their demonstration that there is no deterministic
association between the introduction of the technology and the form
and geographical pattern of and subsequent rationalization. Precisely
the same innovation introduced into different organizational and
labour relations situations has produced geographically different
outcomes – in the one case the concentration of production in one or

two plants, but in another its fragmentation and decentralization. Moreover, it could be argued that those geographical differences were not simply a passive consequence of the company's investment decision processes since the companies took advantage of existing operations in different geographical sites to split opposition within the workforce to the introduction of labour-displacing technology.

Such developments seem to need to be seen in a longer term historical perspective. Concentration of ownership in the food processing industry began in the 1930s but expanded dramatically in the 1950s with the introduction of convenience foods to meet the needs of households where more women were working – some of them in newly created food packing occupations. Ironically, the introduction of new technologies is now displacing woman workers, resulting in households with less income to purchase the same convenience foods. At the same time falling household incomes are leading to pressures on food manufacturers from retailers to reduce prices and this in turn may be encouraging further rounds of job-displacing investment. Falling household demand is therefore leading to process innovation rather than the product innovations associated with the increasing demand discussed earlier in connection with Freeman's analysis.

A final important feature of Shutt and Leach's analysis is that it examines the introduction of new technology from the viewpoint of labour, in outlining the impact of technological change on the labour process. The restructuring of capital described at the macro level in earlier chapters is here given a social dimension at the micro level of the individual workplace and production line. It is the scale of the job displacement which their analysis demonstrates that has led policymakers to the small firm sector as an alternative source of new employment opportunities, perhaps in the belief that the relationship between capital and labour is more human because of the close juxtaposition of employer and employee. Small firms are by definition 'locally owned', may be more innovative than larger and older businesses and therefore would form a basis for the indigenous development of a region. The final section of the book considers these possibilities.

Small firms

In recent years, there has been growing research and policy interest in the contribution of small firms to national and regional economic development. This interest is hardly surprising, given the scale of capacity reduction and job loss in large scale industry over the last fifteen years. By 1980, there were in the UK over 1 million less jobs in manufacturing firms employing more than 1000 people than in 1971. Research evidence, notably by Birch on the USA, regarding the contribution of small firms to job generation has taken this interest a step further, especially at a policy level, with the present UK government sponsoring over 100 schemes to help small businesses.

The orientation towards small firms is noticeable in the field of regional development studies, where it is felt by some that the small firm could generate self-sustaining economic growth, especially in those regions in which economic activity is dominated by externally owned enterprises. A strategy to stimulate local initiatives, if successful, could help to reduce the problems of dependence and instability caused by the larger and more footloose firms. To some extent this orientation towards small local firms has also been forced by the cutbacks in central government support for the UK regions and by the reduction in investment and employment in the large firm sector during the present long recession.

The last three chapters of the book demonstrate, however, that the issue concerning the contribution of small firms to the creation of wealth and jobs at a local or national level is far from clear. Storey argues in Chapter 10 that there are important questions related to the economic performance and survival of small firms which need to be addressed in advance of policy prescriptions. Indeed the author argues that, in the UK, public policy for small firms has developed well in advance of research findings, and that such policies threaten to be wasteful if it is found that small firms are failing to create jobs and wealth. This shortage of detailed empirical work by economists on the UK small firm sector is, in the eyes of the author, 'serious because it has helped those with an ideological commitment to small businesses to exert a disproportionate influence over public policy'. Accordingly, the first half of his chapter outlines a research agenda on the economics of the small firm which should yield a more cost–effective and efficacious basis for allocating public resources to small firms. The new agenda isolates two research priorities related to economic performance: studies monitoring the impact of macro-economic change on firms of different sizes and a detailed assessment of economic aggregates, notably the relationship between profits and the growth of the small firm in financial and employment terms.

Another important priority which should be added to the above list concerns the analysis of the real economic interface between small and large firms. The support for small firms from supply-side economists originates in the belief that such firms are strong candidates in the market because of their ability to keep down supply costs through high labour productivity, low wage costs and a more 'efficient' utilization of resources. Additionally, the small firm is seen to be the standard-bearer of competitiveness, flexibility, dynamism and innovativeness in the (preferably deregulated) market. There are, however, counter-arguments suggesting that small firms could only play a restricted role in the advanced economies. For instance, the prospects for survival may be quite narrow in a world in which the terms of both production and competition are set by the large corporations. Indeed, it could be argued that the survival of small firms is related not to a series of internal advantages but to protection from market forces arising from various contractual ties with larger institutions. Furthermore, characteristics such as competitiveness, flexibility, dynamism and innovativeness may be equally, if not more, applicable to the large firm sector. The absence of rigorous work on the interrelationships between the two sectors is likely to reinforce the dangers outlined by Storey.

The second half of Storey's paper looks at small firms from a regional perspective. The author cites evidence to demonstrate that, in the UK as a whole, the contribution of small firms to employment has been modest and that where growth has occurred it has tended to be concentrated in the more prosperous regions. Storey also suggests that national small firm policy has actually contributed to rather than reversed this regional pattern.

Curran and Stanworth in Chapter 11 accept that on face value small firms may play an important role in the present restructuring of the UK economy. Some of the promising signs for small firms include the growing tendency for larger firms to opt for smaller and more flexible production units; and burgeoning government support for small firms, including the removal of restrictions on unionization and work practices, changes in taxation, an increase in finance and support services, and renewed ideological patronage for the *petit-bourgeoisie*. The authors are, however, sceptical about the authenticity of small employers' complaints in the past about 'restrictions on their activities, and they also assert that many of the above policy changes are also likely to favour the large firm sector. This leads them to conclude that in the changing economy, 'there appears to be no good reason to suggest that the small firm will somehow change its relative position to come to occupy a far more central, let alone *the* central, role'.

The chapter's main concern, however, is not with the economics but with the industrial relations of small firms. Curran and Stanworth draw upon a wide range of literature to demolish the myth that the small firm is the haven of tension-free employer–employee relations. A more accurate description is that employers are opposed to trade unions and are quite aware that their interests diverge from those of the workforce; the quality of jobs and working conditions is generally poor; labour turnover is high and workers have very little employment stability. In other words, the distinctive features of small firms are substandard working conditions and the suppression of basic trade union and labour rights – practices which are *not* supported by the workers.

For Curran and Stanworth, therefore, small is not so beautiful from the perspective of industrial relations. The small firm is above all a *capitalist* firm, subjected to the laws of the market and bound by opposing class interests in production. This, together with the fact that the rules of the game in the economy are shaped and enforced by the larger institutions, provides the impetus for more exploitative work practices in the small firm. The suggestion therefore is that such work practices are often the basis for survival because in all other respects small firms find themselves in a weak position in the market.

One element that is missing from Curran and Stanworth's analysis is the attempt to differentiate between small firms. For example, the industrial relations in small high-tech or new product firms employing only qualified personnel may not conform to the image described by the two authors, because such firms may be able to compete without having to maximize labour exploitation. In the final chapter of the book, Oakey and Rothwell focus their attention on such high-tech small firms, although not from the perspective of their industrial relations, but their job creation potential.

Oakey and Rothwell cite evidence predominantly from the USA showing that the greatest short and long term employment growth possibilities in manufacturing lie with technologically innovative and new small firms. Such firms have had markedly higher employment growth rates than firms which are, separately or in combination, larger, older and less innovative. It is not, however, clear whether the employment figures cited by the authors are net gains or refer only to survivors; or whether the new small firms examined are truly independent operators in the market. Additionally, it is worth considering whether it is valid to compare employment growth rates between firms which are just starting up and those which have already established levels of employment beyond which it may be more convenient to raise output and sales through technical means.

The inception and growth of new technology-based small firms, however, according to the authors, is not spatially uniform but varies significantly between regions. This conclusion is drawn from Oakey's survey of employment growth within 174 small high-tech firms in the instruments and electronics engineering sectors located in South East England, Scotland and the San Francisco Bay area in California. The survey results demonstrate that although on the whole few new firms had been formed and had expanded employment by a limited number over a five year period (Table 12.10), the number of foundations and the scale of job generation had been greater in the USA than in Britain. In fact, according to the authors, 'in Britain, there is both a noticeable lack of new fast-growing high technology firms . . . and a dearth of currently large firms of the Texas Instruments type that were small thirty years ago'.

Oakey and Rothwell claim that the two distinctive factors under-lying the rapid expansion of some firms are the quality of entrep-reneurship and easy access to local venture capital. Business acumen is a necessary but not sufficient condition for success and therefore needs to be combined with the technical ability to innovate. The other advantage from which the US firms have benefited is the existence and ready availability of local private venture capital for investment, especially in R&D. The authors strongly recommend the provision of such a local service by the State for firms in the UK regions. One question which is not raised by this contribution is whether employment growth has been higher in the USA solely because the firms have been more innovative and have received better financial services. A comparison of productivity changes, macro-economic policy and market conditions in the two countries might demonstrate that the expansion of employment in the US firms may also be the result of lower productivity increases, expan-sionary government economic policy, entry into new markets at an early date and protective contracts with other larger firms or with the US State.

Some policy conclusions

This volume does not seek to provide a detailed appraisal of public policies to promote regional development through technical change and small firms. Nevertheless the various contributions do pose a number of challenges for policymakers, particularly concerning the interrelationship between national industrial policy and regional policy. The first is the need for a radical shift in national economic policy geared towards expanding output, demand and employment. The second is the need for regional policy to be an active and integral component of a much widened national industrial strategy, rather than as an appendix to the latter. The final need is for action, preferably commensurate, at EEC, national and local levels. The case for such changes is argued below.

Several of the authors in this volume tend to question the optimism policymakers have attached to the contribution of the new technol-ogy industries and small firms to national and regional development in the UK. The UK electronics industry is becoming less competitive; process innovations especially in the hands of the giant corporations have been used as labour-saving devices; the record of job-creating innovations through new products is poor because an ailing economy and major institutional barriers are preventing the full benefits of new technology from being realized; and the large corporations' appropriation of and control over major innovations threaten to restrict their diffusion across the rest of the economy. Such evidence tends to suggest that a national technology policy needs to be more widely ranging than it is at present, selecting between different technologies not only in terms of those which are more conducive for growth but also those which enhance the quantity and quality of employment. More importantly, however, the evidence makes a strong case for extensive public intervention in other areas in order to create a more conducive environment for the development and widespread diffusion of growth led by new technologies. This would include, firstly, a series of positive institutional reforms in the arenas of training, management, finance, industrial relations, etc., tailoring these more strongly to the needs and potentialities of localities; secondly, more stringent controls on takeover activity and/or technology and skill transfer agreements with the large corporations to guarantee the survival of smaller high-tech firms; and finally, direct state intervention in the procurement of goods from the growth industries.

The need for greater scrutiny and greater integration with renewed policy action in other areas of the economy is also the conclusion on UK small firm policy reached by some of the contributions. The real scepticism concerning the quantity and quality of employment growth among small firms would suggest the need for State support which in the first instance is more selective along sectoral, economic and social criteria, but which in the second instance is much more sensitive to the technical and financial requirements of selected firms. Furthermore, a salutory reminder for policymakers is that the continued success of small firms may require action which deals appropriately with the monopoly practices of large corporations which threaten the survival of small firms in the market.

The multi-disciplinary approach of this volume also brings to the fore the inadequacy of an industrial strategy which on the one hand, through lack of intervention, allows industrial decline in Britain to continue unabated and which on the other hand narrowly confines positive action to the higher-tech industries and to small firms. The scale of de-industrialization in the UK dwarfs the volume of wealth and jobs which is likely to be created, certainly in the short term, by the latter two branches of the economy, especially given the constraints they face. The contributions in this volume which analyse the activities of large corporations and the multinationals tend to attach considerable responsibility to the growth of oligopoly and to the international reorganization of production by such corporations for the decline of output and employment in the UK. The persistence of liberal policies in the financial and commodity markets, together with the relaxation of controls on the behaviour of multinational corporations, is likely to foster even more de-industrialization, which at a time of 'jobless growth' will not be compensated by sufficient employment gains arising through inward investment. If there is, as some of the contributions argue, a strong relationship between the behaviour of the multinationals, industrial decline and negative multiplier effects, this would then not only raise serious doubts about the irreversibility or the necessity of de-industrialization in the UK, but it would also suggest that it may be possible to reverse this state of affairs through the introduction of more stringent controls on the multinationals. Included among the controls would be the following: a strengthening of and adherence to anti-trust legislation; closer scrutiny of merger and acquisition activity; codes of conduct on the employment practices, pricing policies and purchasing strategies of the multinationals; regulations on production functions in branch plants; skill and technology transfer agreements; disclosure of investment intentions; and barriers on related-party imports. Clearly, the introduction of such controls runs the risk of promoting the flight of capital, but this would depend on the terms of benefits and incentives offered to the multinationals. Legislation at EEC level would undoubtedly raise the negotiating power of member governments; one encouraging step in this direction is that of the Vredeling Proposals, which are being used in negotiating for the introduction of policy in favour of greater worker participation within the multinationals.

The case for renewing growth is not simply an argument for greater public intervention, but is one which concerns a significant shift in the quality and content of macro-economic policy. There is also a suggestion among the contributions that the combination of open-door economic policies, reduced government intervention in the economy, stringent monetary regulation and the absence of a coherent and integrated industrial strategy have weakened the competitiveness of UK industry (even in the growth sectors). A reversal in national economic policy towards reflation, greater public expenditure and direct intervention in the economy is likely to strengthen competitiveness, boost demand and promote investment.

However, a shift in national or EEC economic and industrial policy is not likely to reduce regional disparities. This is a challenge posed by most of the contributions directly concerned with regional issues. Their message is that the regions are not microcosms of the national economy, but entities with differing industrial and social structures, with different forms and reasons for industrial decline and with different propensities for economic innovation and change. A renewed national industrial strategy, if kept separate from a regional policy which continues simply to ameliorate the consequences of industrial decline or promote the development of small high-technology firms, is likely in fact to widen the regional gap for three reasons: In the first place, action at a national level is most likely to favour the strongest sections of the economy which tend to be located in the more prosperous regions. Secondly, a blanket industrial strategy will not be sensitive to regionally specific problems and needs. Finally, a regional policy confined to a narrow set of initiatives will come nowhere near confronting the enormity of the economic and social problems facing the lagging regions.

In relation to the last point, the regional analyses demonstrate that the track record of the lagging regions in developing indigenous potential in the high-tech sectors has been poor, and due to the absence of just about every local factor endowment which influences location, ranging from the level of entrepreneurship and skilled personnel, industrial and ownership structure, good communications, government R&D establishments, venture capital and innovation diffusion networks to environmental factors influencing the quality of life-styles. Consequently, regional policy initiatives of the EEC designed to increase the rate of technological innovation in small and medium-sized enterprises in some regions, although a step in the right direction, address not only a small proportion of the obstacles to technological advance in lagging regions, but also a small proportion of the growth problems of such regions.

What is made apparent by this volume is firstly that regional policy should not be separated from but integrated into national and EEC policy initiatives. National policies need to take regional diversity into consideration and should contain a regional dimension. In addition to this, regional policy is in need of being extended along the lines mentioned above.

The final policy challenge raised by this volume concerns the spatial level at which policy initiatives, especially for the regions, can be effective. The fact that the arena of technological change and industrial accumulation is increasingly international suggests that public policy must also operate at this level. Initiatives within the European Commission have begun to reflect this need. One example is the Commission's ESPRIT programme aimed at promoting collaborative research on information technology on a pan-European basis as a means of resisting American and Japanese competition in this field. Another is the existence of a wide range of initiatives to create a community-wide market in information technology products and services.

At the same time, however, given the enormous diversity between localities, it is of vital importance that the task of unlocking local reserves for the economic and social development of the community should be left in the hands of local actors. The success of many of the UK metropolitan authorities in stimulating innovation is increasingly recognized. If there is a conclusion from the debate about policy it is that a regional dimension is important for both national and local development and this may not be a zero-sum game if hitherto latent potential for innovation is released. In this respect local and community-based initiatives, drawing on national programmes where these are appropriate, may provide an important way of overcoming the obstacles to change inherent in a socioeconomic system at present heavily controlled by the state and multi-national corporations.

2 The internationalization of production and de-industrialization

KEITH COWLING

We now live in an era in which production and markets are controlled by giant corporations with transnational bases. We also live in an era during which national and international controls over trade and capital flows have been progressively reduced. The resulting combination of unified international markets and giant international firms bestriding them provides a ready mechanism for the processes of de-industrialization to develop wherever the conditions for capitalist accumulation are weakened. In contrast to the earlier history of the development of monopolies and cartels around the turn of the century, when protectionism was demanded to restrict or eliminate foreign competition in domestic and colonial markets, the new period of international oligopoly – transnational monopoly capitalism – is characterized by demands on the part of the giant corporations for free trade and the supranational institutions to pursue and sanction it: a global freedom to pursue accumulation, given their own dominance within the global system and given the threat, or potential threat, of organized labour and universal suffrage at the level of the nation state. We now have a neo-imperialism of free trade in similar vein to the 19th century British imperialism of free trade (Krause & Nye 1975), but this time, rather than being of national origin, the imperialism is that of the transnationals.

This chapter will examine the implications of the evolution of dominant transnational corporations for the pattern of production and investment within and between the advanced industrial countries, and between this group of countries and the Third World. The recent history of the British economy will be examined in some detail. Then the following question will be asked – Is this a zero-sum, global game? Do the losses of the advanced industrial countries simply mirror the gains of the newly industrializing countries? It will be argued that the process of adjustment is fundamentally socially inefficient and undemocratic. Given this, forms of intervention to secure a globally more efficient and democratic outcome will be briefly discussed.

23

The new international division of labour[1]

The old international division of labour divided the world up into the
advanced industrialized countries and the backward primary producers with international trade between these groups of countries
dominating world trade. International firms, if they existed in the
production sphere, were involved in extracting primary products
from the backward countries. With the evolution of the transnational
corporation this simple dichotomy is progressively destroyed. Initially the switching of production and investment took place between
centre and periphery within the industrialized countries or to their
geographical neighbours. Thus US corporations invested in Europe
and Mexico, Western-based corporations invested in their southern
neighbours and Ireland, and, more recently, Japanese corporations
invested in South Korea and Taiwan. While such moves could be
stimulated by a myriad of causes it seems clear that an all-pervading,
general influence would be the existence of, and changes in, relative
labour costs reflecting differences in the relative power and militancy
of labour. By extension, an increasing tendency to switch production
and investment away from the advanced industrial countries to the
unindustrialized or newly industrializing countries would be
expected. This tendency would occur because of rising worker
power and militancy *generally* in the older industrial countries,
associated with the 'long boom' of the quarter-century period after
World War II, implying rising relative wages and falling relative
productivity, and because of the growth of a de-skilling technology.
The actual timing of such shifts would also depend on the innovation
and diffusion of corporate structures capable of handling such global
production patterns and of systems of communication and transportation which would facilitate it. The rapid diffusion of the multi-divi-
sional organizational structure (M-form) across the giant corporations of the capitalist world has provided an ideal environment for
the flexible switching of capital flows within the global economy.
Rather than simply delaying capitalism's early bureaucratic demise
the advent of this organizational innovation has directly contributed
to the conversion of the major corporations to their present global
status and reach. The recent revolution in information technology
has already played a significant role in the same process and will
clearly continue as a major accommodating factor.

Given the existence of flexible corporate structures, the decompos-
ition of complex processes so that only unskilled labour is needed and
an information technology which renders geographical distance
unimportant, the social and economic infrastructure of the advanced
industrial countries remains the only significant economic impediment to a wholesale transfer of industrial production to the low wage

countries. But the switching of production between the older industrialized centres and the newly emerging industrial periphery is not entirely dependent on the growth of the transnational ownership of production facilities; it can also reflect the growth of a new putting-out system, which may have a purely domestic basis, but which will often have an international one. Thus an increasingly popular device for circumventing a powerful and well organized labour force, which has evolved within the conducive atmosphere of the large plant in the older industrial areas over the 'long boom' of the postwar years up to the early to mid-1970s, has been the vertical *dis*-integration of production. More and more of the work is subcontracted out to a domestic, relatively competitive fringe or to foreign suppliers, where the producers face a less powerful and less well organized labour force. In part this may represent a first step in a process of transition where production as a whole is shifted from a region or a country with a well organized labour force to alternative locations, domestic or foreign, where this is not the case. But whatever the final form, the issue of control, within the process of production and within markets, is more fundamental than the ownership of the production units themselves. The current general promotion of small business is explicable in these terms. Rather than being a threat to the giant corporations it fits in perfectly with their strategy of moving production away from those centres where they have tended to lose control, and will in turn serve to circumscribe the power of organized labour in those production units which must of necessity, at least in the short term, remain in the old-established centres.

Increasingly the major corporations will become co-ordinating agencies for large numbers of production units, each supplying services to the dominant organization at competitive rates and paying competitive wages.[2] This represents an extension of the notion of the M-form corporation with its centralization of strategic, capital allocation decisions, coupled with the decentralization of operating/production decisions. Now strategic marketing and production decisions are being added, with small business in satellite relation with the dominant corporation, tied in with long term contracts. The dominant corporations' basic role is then to secure an allocation of production, internally *or externally,* consistent with cost minimization, while maintaining or enhancing market control. This ststem of control may include a retail sector in the same, internal or external, satellite relation with the dominant supplying corporation, or the retail sector itself may be the dominant element in the system of control. Thus the British Shoe Corporation is a dominant element in shoe retailing, has some production units of its own, but is also a major importer of shoes produced by other firms; while Marks & Spencer has long term contracts with external suppliers, British or foreign. In contrast the General Electric Company (GEC) deals directly with State corporations in its own sphere of operations but is moving towards splitting its existing M-form structure into small autonomous companies, and in its other spheres of operation it uses its own trade marks and advertising to sell goods which are to a substantial degree foreign sourced – sometimes intra-corporate and in other cases inter-firm.

The central point is that although systems will differ the aim of the giant corporation will be the control of a sector of the relevant economy so that the maximum level of profits can be squeezed from it. While the ownership of production facilities by such giants may contribute to this objective, this is generally neither necessary nor sufficient. This point can perhaps be best illustrated by the extreme strategy of industrial capital withdrawing into finance or financial capital by handing over control to workers at the point of production, if conditions for capitalist production become very difficult. Charging the appropriate rate for the use of capital, i.e. the appropriate interest rate, the income of workers could be restricted to the competitive wage. Capitalist income could be increased by the elimination of monopoly wages and/or by incorporating into the valuation of the transferred assets, and thus into interest payments, the anticipated increase in the productivity of labour arising from the co-operative organization of production. So long as the corporation retained its control of the market for the product, via long term contracts coupled with its prior investment in advertising, product differentiation and distribution networks, workers could be allowed to make all operating/production decisions, and be exploited via the market rather than directly in the sphere of production or distribution. In this context it is significant that the former owners of Triumph Motor Cycles saw no problem in handing over control of production to the workforce but baulked for more than a year over the control of the name and the marketing of the product. It is also perhaps significant that GEC got involved in the Triumph co-operative – it might seem a logical extension of its declared tendency toward the decentralization of production.

Clearly the sponsorship of workers' co-operatives by capitalist organizations – workers control for worker control – is not yet a normal response to difficulties encountered in capitalist production. The more generally observed tendency is either towards subcontracting to other capitalist organizations (or, in some cases, to individual households), at home or abroad, thus circumventing some of the difficulties which giant organizations will inevitably generate, or towards switching production and investment to new sites where labour is unorganized, has no history of large-scale organization or exists under a repressive regime. Such tendencies will be manifest within as well as between countries – between the 'frostbelt' and the 'sunbelt' within the USA, as well as between the USA and Mexico and Brazil; between the North and Midlands and the 'M4 belt' within the UK, as well as between the UK and Malaysia or Singapore. The central feature is an increasing geographical flexibility of capitalist production which allows capital to escape the clutches of organized labour and which must ultimately weaken the position of such labour in the areas of production that remain.

Globalism of this sort could of course work the other way round. Rather than moving jobs to the (unorganized) workers, domestically or internationally, (unorganized) workers could be moved to the jobs. This was the dominant pattern of the 'long boom.' The old division of labour persisted at the level of nation states but the workforce, at least in the industrial countries, was internationalized. The internationalization of production had a very specific meaning. The impediment to industrial expansion posed by relatively full employment in the advanced industrial countries was removed by substantial migrations from the periphery. But, as Adam (1975) shows, this process started to falter in the late 1960s and early 1970s due to rising wage demands, with General Motors complaining about the 'unpredictability' of the American labour market and leaders of West German corporations stressing the necessity and inevitability of international sourcing in response to the 'unjustified' wage demands of 1972–73. Adam also makes the interesting point that it is not sufficient to say that the recession-induced unemployment of that period led to the cut-back in *Gästarbeiter* because it was the growth in *external* investment which led to the jobs cut-back in West Germany. One of the underlying reasons for the switch was undoubtedly the growing resistance to immigration which in turn strengthened the position of labour in such economies. The consequence has been a growth in managed trade and a decline in managed migration.

Perhaps at this stage it would be useful to put Japanese expansionism into perspective since it is often argued that de-industrialization within the USA and Europe has been induced by the rising dominance of Japanese capital and thus the relative decline in European and American capital. In other words a new industrial division of labour may have come about, but it has not been managed or controlled by the giant corporations of the old order. Instead a new order prevails. When analysing the relative performances of national economies this may appear to be so. Japan increased its share of world industrial production and exports throughout the 1960s and 1970s while the USA and Europe in aggregate experienced declining shares. However, if we measure changes in world sales classified by the nationality of the parent company a very different picture emerges. Although Japanese industrial capital made considerable gains at the expense of particularly US capital in the 1960s, almost no further advance was achieved in the 1970s. The advance of European industrial capital since 1967 has considerably exceeded that of Japanese industrial capital and this must have been achieved by a relatively rapid expansion of foreign production. A significant part of this is undoubtedly due to the rising share of oil industry revenue, but this serves as a reminder of the dominance of European and American capital in the markets for many strategic new materials. Detailed calculations on these points are contained in Dowrick (1983).

Our conclusion must be that the de-industrialization which the West as a whole has experienced in the 1970s cannot be ascribed to Japanese expansionism. The high relative growth rate of Japanese industrial capital in the 1960s took place in a period of relative buoyancy in economic activity in the West. It seems clear that the forces of de-industrialization, which have been most obvious in Europe, have been most active during a period when European industrial capital was increasing its share of the world economy. This is entirely in line with the argument made in this contribution.

De-industrialization: the case of Britain

While there was an observed tendency for the capitalist system as a whole to enter an apparent long term downswing in the 1970s, the experience of the British economy has been an extreme one and may be at least partly related to the relatively high degree of internationalization of British capital, both industrial and financial. These strong international links and commitments imply that money capital can be readily shifted abroad so that the rate of investment within the domestic economy is retarded. This will be most obviously the case where investment abroad is used to replace the domestic sourcing of the British market by foreign sourcing, or where exports from Britain are being replaced by overseas production, but it can also apply generally as the financing of British investment tends to dry up. Although the giants will always be able to get the financing they require, newer and smaller firms will often face difficulties, and their position in the British economy, in contrast to the other European economies and the USA, will be that much more vulnerable.[3] This may help to explain why the British economy has a much weaker small firm sector than, for example, West Germany and the United States, and correspondingly, why the giant corporations in Britain tend to be much more dominant. The argument that giantism is required for dynamism and international competitiveness hardly seems to hold water when we note that the most undynamic and uncompetitive economy also possesses most of the giant firms in Europe. A recent survey published by the *Financial Times* (Rapoport 1982) reveals that no less than twenty-five of the top fifty corporations in Europe are based in Britain.

The short-run impact of the retarding of domestic investment, if uncompensated by other forms of expenditure, will be a cut-back in output and employment in Britain. The longer term impact will be that domestic productivity growth will fall relative to other economies without such international connections, which in turn will lead to lower levels of investment in new processes and products and therefore to a relative decline in internal and external demand for the output of the British economy. This leads into a process of cumulative causation. A relative decline in external demand feeds through, via a variety of mechanisms, into a relative decline in the growth of output, productivity, innovation and capital stock, which in turn leads to a further twist in the relative decline in the growth of external demand for British output. The British economy has entered the vicious circle of relative decline partly because of the special international connections of British capital, whereas, in contrast, the continental European economies and Japan, largely exploiting foreign markets from a *domestic* production base, have, as a result, entered the virtuous circle of cumulative causation, with productivity growth responding to the growth in output following external demand. Success breeds success, failure breeds failure, *at the level of the national economy,* but, as we have already seen, we should distinguish carefully between the success of national economies and the success of national capitals. However, in the British case, it could be argued that the relative demise of the national economy has gone so far as to have had a marked deleterious effect on national capital. Despite its strong and pervasive international connections, British capital's lack of a strong domestic base has probably severely damaged its future prospects.

One question which might be raised about this story is why the British state has not intervened to secure a break-out from the vicious circle of relative decline. Limited attempts have been made from time to time but they have generally floundered on their implicit unwillingness to address the root cause. As a result brief periods of expansion have been followed inevitably by sharp cut-backs; the stop-go history of the 1950s and 1960s, which finally led in the mid-1970s to a move away from Keynesian to monetarist policies as the rate of inflation increased. Given the lack of success of the British economy there was a boiling-up of worker dissatisfaction which got translated into inflationary pressure. Thus the forces which led to the lack of success, such as the international posture of British capital, inevitably led to the adoption of deflationary policies by the State, which led via an extended process of cumulative causation to further deterioration in the relative performance of the British economy and at the same time weakened the position of British capital in its global stance.

The British motor industry: a case study

The car industry in Britain has clearly been in sharp decline over the past decade, with production falling from a peak of almost 2 million in 1972 to less than 1 million in the early 1980s. However, it would be wrong to conclude that the British motor industry generally has been an unprofitable area of activity for capital, whether British or American. Ford, the dominant assembler, has continuously made very substantial profits in the UK, but has progressively switched production away from the UK despite increasing its share of sales in the UK market. Similarly, firms in the British motor components industry have occupied a dominant and profitable position in both the domestic and European markets. The British car industry is much less vertically integrated than in other countries, with 55 per cent of the cost of a British car going to component and materials suppliers. Five firms (Lucas, GKN, Dunlop, Automotive Products (AP) and Associated Engineering (AE)) dominate the industry, with individual firms dominating the market for specific products. For example, Lucas supplies 95 per cent of all starters and 80–85 per cent of lamps and horns, GKN 80 per cent of axle shafts, AP 90 per cent of clutches, and AE 75 per cent of pistons (see Bhaskar 1979). Recently these firms have been switching and increasing the proportion of their investment abroad, particularly within the EEC, due to the relative decline in the British car assembly sector.

Although it can be argued that entry to the EEC was one of the factors leading to the precipitous decline of the British motor industry it is necessary to identify gainers and losers. It is clear, in an era of monopoly or oligopoly capitalism, that the creation of a tariff-free area like the EEC need not imply an increase in international competition in the sense that prices are held below what they might have been. Imagine a reduction in tariffs between two countries, each with a tightly knit oligopoly group of similar size and efficiency dominating the car industry. Under such conditions potential rivalry will be seen more or less symmetrically by all participants, and this will serve to sustain the degree of collusion. Price cutting, and other attempts at market share expansion, will generally not take place because the response by rivals will be seen as substantial and immediate. The very closeness of rivalry will serve to sustain the oligopolistic structure. However, if the reduction in tariffs happens to coincide with an emerging asymmetry, then we would expect to observe a substantial change in market shares as the stronger oligopoly group expands at the expense of the weaker. The evolution of the EEC has witnessed both cases. While UK entry led to a rapid import penetration of the UK market, the same was not true of France and Germany where the reduction in tariffs led to a much slower interpenetration of markets. The symmetry of rivalry between the French and German motor industries led to the preservation of their domestic market shares. In contrast the UK motor industry entered the EEC in a position of grave weakness. It was no threat to the rest and therefore aggressive policies could be pursued in the UK by EEC importers. This process was made easier by the displacement of a large fraction of the distribution network within the UK by domestic firms. For instance, Bhaskar (1979) estimates that almost 7000 dealers of domestic cars were disenfranchised over the period of 1968–76 and a majority of those who remained in the industry established import franchises.

However, the story needs more differentiation. While BL had little to gain from entry into the EEC, this was not so for other important elements of the motor industry. The other major assemblers, Ford, Chrysler and General Motors (Vauxhall), were all seeking to integrate their European operations, and the British components industry was in a powerful position to gain from entry. Unimpeded intra-European trade meant that the American assemblers based in the UK were now free to source their UK sales from any production facility within the EEC. This implied that labour militancy within the UK would be met with the threat or reality of a switch in production or investment away from UK plants, and a reciprocal threat could be issued to labour forces in the other countries of the EEC. Similarly each nation state within the EEC would be more exposed to the threat of a switch in production and investment by capital with an actual or potential transnational production base within the EEC. As a result we would expect a growth in the subsidization of production and investment by the state. The Ford engine plant in South Wales was a case in point with the state providing more than 50 per cent of the investment expenditure, this outcome being the result of intense competition between the French and British governments.

What of the British components industry? The firms involved had secured a potentially powerful independent position because of the lack of vertical integration in the UK assembly industry and because of the early development of advanced engineering concepts in British cars. Given this favourable asymmetry they were anxious for easier access to the rapidly expanding European market for their products. Entry into the EEC initially led to a rapid expansion in the export of components, but subsequently there has been a switch from exports to direct investment within the EEC by the major British component firms. Gaffikin and Nickson (1984) detail the recent history of ten major transnationals with bases in the West Midlands and two of these, GKN and Lucas, have dominant positions in the motor components industry.

The outcome of all this is a British motor industry which is either simply part of the integrated European activities of American capital or which has an increasingly important EEC production base. De-industrialization within the UK has proceeded in this sector either because of the peripheral position of the UK economy in the European context or as a response to the power and militancy of workers in the UK. Production has been run down and investment shifted except where substantial State inducements are offered. Ford, for example, was producing 400 000 *fewer* cars in the UK in 1979 than it did ten years previously. Thus the crisis induced by entry into the EEC is a crisis of production, investment and employment in the UK rather than being directly a crisis for British or American capital with interests in the UK. The one exception to this is BL, which had neither the European production base of the American assemblers nor the relative strength of the British components industry.[4]

One consequence of these developments was that the British motor industry has proved very resistant to any suggestion that its problems may be alleviated by general import controls. Such controls would obviously impede trade and investment flows within its own sphere of influence. In contrast we would expect to observe a general inclination to recommend import controls where the trade flows were outside its sphere of influence. Japanese cars would be an obvious target, but so also would be imports from Eastern Europe, although they are, at least for the moment, much less threatening. The campaign by the British Society of Motor Manufacturers and Traders against Japanese imports goes back to 1975 when state intervention was obtained to secure 'voluntary' restraint by Japanese exporters. Since that time there has been a mounting crescendo of hysterical outbursts by the industry, which culminated in 1980–81, all aimed at this very selective target. More recently things have calmed down somewhat. This probably reflects the growth of accommodatory moves to the Japanese threat. Many European and American companies are engaged in talks with their Japanese rivals about various forms of joint venture.

While obviously a problem for 'British' capital, the reaction to Japanese expansionism has had an important diversionary role. The British motor industry (and increasingly other industries) has tried to allocate the blame for the de-industrialization of this sector on the

Japanese in order to cover up shifts in its own production and investment patterns which are largely responsible for the de-industrialization and resulting job loss which has been observed. The facts are clear. While the share of the British car market captured by imports rose dramatically from 33 per cent in 1975 to over 50 per cent today, the Japanese share of the market rose from 9 per cent to only 11 per cent, whereas the share of imports from the EEC rose from 20 per cent to 38 per cent, and a substantial fraction of this increase can be traced to the activities of the UK-based American assemblers, who have chosen to source an increasing proportion of their sales in the UK from their facilities on the continent. Ford dominates the UK car market with a share of around 30 per cent, more than half of which has, in recent years, been sourced from plants outside the UK. It is in fact the biggest car importer into the UK, followed by GM which also imports more than 50 per cent of its UK sales.

The question of the control of imports by elements of the domestic oligopoly groups also brings into focus the question of the impact of tariff reduction and currency appreciation on the price level. The myth of fierce price competition within the European car market has been exploded by well documented observations that the retail prices of the same car (before tax) showed enormous variation across countries within the EEC (Ashworth et al. 1982). It is clear that the European market is effectively cartelized – the major car companies are acting as discriminating oligopolists. The process of import penetration into the UK is not leading to lower prices but is leading to the loss of jobs. The process is being facilitated by the switching to the Continent of production and investment by the American assemblers and by the entry into the UK of an increasing array of imported models, with the associated stream of advertising expenditures. Market shares are being re-allocated by a process of non-price competition. Widening profit margins following from the dramatic appreciation in sterling between 1979 and 1981 gave an added inducement to such activity.

Despite a substantial drop in market share BL has survived with large scale government aid and a question which might reasonably be asked, given the monetarist stance of recent governments, is why has the State actively intervened to save a company like BL? Some might argue that the social consequences of its demise would have been too severe to contemplate. But why should the State draw the line at BL when it has revealed itself willing to allow the number of the unemployed to rise to 4 million? Or at least why did the State not eliminate the major loss-making division, Austin-Morris (i.e. volume cars), and either run or sell off the remaining profitable divisions? The answer would seem to lie in the crucial importance, at least in the short or medium term, of BL as an assembler of bought-in components produced by the then profitable segment of the British-owned motor industry. To shut down the volume car division of BL would have had a major impact on the profitability of companies like GKN, Lucas and Dunlop. In the long run they could look elsewhere for markets, and they have indeed been investing heavily in the EEC in order to capture an increasing share of a rapidly growing market (see Gaffikin and Nickson 1984), but in the short run they could easily have gone bankrupt. It was important that the State should manage BL in such a way as to give them a breathing space to reorganize their production and marketing. This is what the State obligingly arranged, under the direction of a chairman seconded from the components industry.

The 'British' part of the British motor industry therefore should be viewed as a small group of powerful and previously profitable components manufacturers being supplied with assembly services, at or below competitive rates, by an independent downstream assembler (BL), which, on becoming unprofitable, partly as a result of their own activities, was taken over by the State rather than being allowed to go bankrupt. Since that point, the components firms have progressively switched their production to a Continental EEC base, which has allowed BL gradually to be run down. One of the more recent developments in this realignment has been the introduction of the Metro, with, it is reported, 70 per cent of foreign components, but with 90 per cent, at least according to BL, supplied by British companies. Thus the circle is complete. BL's existing model range with a high fraction of British *made* components is phased out in orderly fashion to allow the British components industry time to adjust to its new European role, and at the same time new models are introduced using components supplied by the same British firms, but produced elsewhere. The British components monopolies maintain their dominance in the domestic market while jobs are being transferred out of the UK.

A negative sum global game

It is often argued that de-industrialization and industrialization are simply mirror images of each other. Industrial growth and decline are simply offsetting tendencies within the global system, representing part of a zero sum, or even positive sum, global game. Those who believe in a self-regulating market mechanism would see the transnational corporation as a suitably efficient and flexible capital-allocating device capable of securing an efficient allocation of resources at a global level. The shift of simple production processes from the advanced industrial countries to the developing countries would, at one and the same time, release an educated and skilled labour force for more sophisticated forms of production whilst allowing labour in the Third World to move from relatively unproductive employment in the agricultural sector to more highly productive employment in industry. Full employment, according to this view, is the norm and would be maintained as the world economic system adapted smoothly to the new opportunities. Some transitional or frictional unemployment may be observed but this would be of little significance compared with the enormous rewards attached to such a global reallocation of production.

Given the present global economic crisis this view will appear unrealistic to at least a segment of the prevailing orthodoxy and this segment will argue that the position can be restored by an international Keynesian intervention to secure a global expansion of demand which will allow the mechanism described above to operate without the frictions which have arisen as a result of the global dislocations following the OPEC crisis of the early 1970s. Thus a basically efficient process for the allocation of the world's material resources could be provided with a suitable international macro-economic environment in which to operate. While ignoring the problem of explaining how such a system could have degenerated into its present crisis, such a policy of reflation would be advocated on, what are claimed to be, pragmatic, non-ideological grounds. The Brandt report captures the flavour of this position.

In contrast to these alternative versions of the prevailing orthodoxy I wish to argue that the process of global industrialization and de-industrialization, which is being currently orchestrated by the transnationals, is a fundamentally inefficient and undemocratic process. Capital has become increasingly nomadic, leaving a trail of social disruption in its wake and imposing huge costs of growth on the industrializing nations. Although it will be privately efficient for each transnational corporation to adopt such an existence, reflecting as it does an appropriate response to rising labour costs, and the opportunities offered by improvements in communications and transportation and by a more flexible production technology and internal organizational structure, it nevertheless means that an international transmission mechanism for production, investment and jobs will have been largely adopted for distributional reasons. Wherever workers act to raise wages, or control the intensity or duration of work, they will lose their jobs to other groups of less well organized and less militant workers in other countries. Thus de-industrialization is a consequence of the struggle between labour and capital in such a world. We can expect to see long swings of development and decline being inversely related across economies with different industrial histories. The alternating long swings of international monopoly capital will follow the rise and fall of the power and militancy of the working class.

The process is basically inefficient because it is motivated by issues of control and distribution – the control of the work process by those who hire labour, and distribution in favour of those who control the location of production. Thus the allocation of production and investment is not guided primarily by questions of efficiency – that is getting more output from given resources – but by the question of profitability, where profitability is determined by the price of labour and the amount of work that can be extracted at that price. The process of de-industrialization can therefore be initiated by increases in wages or reductions in the input of effort in one country and may result in the industrialization of a country where the output resulting from any *given* amount of effort is lower. Two points arise from this: first the *direction* of movement need have nothing to do with social efficiency and second the *frequency* of movement will generally exceed the social optimum. Misdirection is possible because of distributional considerations – excessive frequency will occur because the transnationals are not faced with the full social costs of their locational decisions. Shifting production from country to country will not only mean that whole communities which have been built up to serve the interests of capital will simply be deserted, with all the social costs being absorbed by that society, but also the costs of social infrastructure required by the newly industrializing country will in turn be borne by that society. Thus the direction and frequency of locational change will tend to be inefficient in a world dominated by giant firms with a global reach. But the argument can be deepened. Not only are such giant firms flexible in their pursuit of profit on a global basis; they are also powerful. They are generally powerful enough to influence the terms under which they choose to operate. Not only do they react to the level of wages and the pace of work, they also act to determine them. Thus the distributional consequences are much more general, affecting those who remain in work as well as those who lose their jobs. The credible threat of the shift of production and investment will serve to hold down wages and raise the level of effort. By making investment conditional on the level of wage costs transnationals may also be able to gain the co-operation of the state in securing the appropriate environment in which wage costs will tend to be held down. By threatening to export investment, profits taxes can be held down and subsidies for investments can be raised. Such threats will stimulate competitive profits tax cutting and competitive subsidization of investment by national governments which must ultimately work in favour of a redistribution towards profits.

The increasingly nomadic nature of capital and its distributional implications are also likely to induce a general global tendency to stagnation. In part this is to do with the tendency toward the monopolization of product markets which is served by the growing dominance of giant global corporations and which leads to problems of maintaining a level of aggregate demand in the system as a whole sufficient to avoid a significant increase in unemployed resources (see, for example, Cowling 1982). But the more direct link to the processes of de-industrialization is via the inevitable frictions involved in such processes. For countries (and regions) where production and investment is moving out unemployment will inevitably rise and purchasing power will be lost. This will lead to a spiralling down in economic activity in general. The new nomadism will contribute to the quantitative significance of this effect and offsetting gains from expansion in the newly industrializing countries will be attenuated by the underlying redistributional tendencies. Forces leading to lower global wage shares are likely to contribute to stagnationist tendencies because of the reduction in aggregate demand which can be expected to result. Even though remedies are technically possible they are likely to be politically infeasible on the international plane within which these processes are operating and the very existence of transnationals makes the use of such remedies more difficult.

Thus we have a process, socially inefficient and eroding the gains made by working people in the older industrial countries in their recent history of struggle, but also contributing to the erosion of democracy itself. The process of the flexible international transmission of work within the transnational is encouraging the competitive, national bidding for jobs and competitive tendencies to the repression of labour. This whole process can be against the democratic wishes of not only the people whose countries are being de-industrialized, but also against the wishes of those whose countries are being industrialized. The terms in each country are being set by the transnationals and as a result the real democratic gains of universal suffrage are being undermined. The power to determine their own future is being taken away from the people at both ends of the process. The provision of investment and therefore jobs is being made conditional on the suppression of progressive forces which would allow the growth of economic and political self-determination.

Concluding remarks

Not only is rapid de-industrialization the outcome for many of the older industrialized economies in a world of industrial capital, but it is part of a negative sum global game. Flexible capital, rather than leading to an efficient allocation of the world's resources, leads in the opposite direction. It also contributes to increasing the share of potential, if not realized, profits; worsens the stagnationist tendency, which is a major feature of monopoly capitalism; and is fundamentally undemocratic. Clearly social control over the transnational corporations has to be established, but equally clearly this is an objective not easily realized. It is obvious that labour does not have the global organization and reach possessed by capital, and it is pretty obvious why this is the case. Realistic, but inevitably limited measures which can be taken in the near future must grow out of local, national and European initiatives. Thus enterprise boards at local level can seek to gain influence within transnationals based in Britain. Closely associated with this, trustees on pension fund boards can seek to establish some sort of control over the flow of funds, and can seek to ensure that enterprise board initiatives are funded and that overseas investment is subject to close social scrutiny. Much broader and longer term perspectives will be required to ensure that the pension funds contribute to the welfare of their members and beneficiaries. At the national level the regulation of capital and trade flows will be required to ensure the phased expansion of the British economy. While an international approach to the regulation of the transnationals is obviously desirable, it is important not to be pessimistic about what can be achieved at the national level. The nation state, if it chooses to use it, obviously has substantial leverage. For example, to return to the case of the 'British' car industry, it is clear that the British government could achieve much in terms of the expansion of production and investment in the UK by the American transnationals if it were willing to threaten them with progressive exclusion from the highly profitable UK market for cars. Clearly there are enormous political difficulties, but a determination to intervene decisively in a particularly crucial sector would provide a salutory lesson for the transnationals in general. However, as well as acting independently, the British government should be pressured to reverse its present stance regarding the international control of the transnationals. Irrespective of whether governments have been Conservative or Labour they have apparently held the same view of the national interest in voting within the UN agencies in favour of exempting the transnational from close regulation (see Cable 1980). It is clear that a voluntary code of conduct for the transnationals is insufficient. As Fine (1983) has argued, although such a code may appear under the guise of international control *over* the transnationals, it is better seen as a code of conduct *amongst* the transnationals themselves. While a more effective policy may be sought within the United Nations, perhaps a more immediately effective policy could be campaigned for within Europe, and specifically within the EEC.

General concern about de-industrialization could be used as a platform from which to advance a policy for effectively regulating the production and investment policies of the transnationals, at least within Europe, and hopefully growing into a more global strategy allowing the EEC to take a much more positive role in development issues.

Notes

1 While this term has been popularized by Fröbel *et al.* (1981), the basis of the analysis was laid by Adam (1975).
2 In some cases the production unit supplying the services will be large scale but still in some sense subordinate; examples are those of BL supplying assembly services to the dominant component monopolies (see p. 30) and the public utilities, under the prescription of marginal cost pricing.
3 This does not undermine the previous suggestion that the growth of the small business sector is being supported by the giants. That part of the small business sector which is seen as complementary by the giants we can expect to be financed. The current involvement of the State would support both views.
4 More recently, of course, the position of the British components industry has sharply deteriorated, along with most of British manufacturing.

References

Adam, G. 1975. Multinational corporations and worldwide sourcing. In *International firms and modern imperialism*, H. Radice (ed.): 89–103. London: Penguin.
Ashworth, M. H., J. A. Kay and J. A. E. Sharpe 1982. *Differentials between car prices in the United Kingdom and Belgium*. IFS Report Series no. 2. London: Institute of Fiscal Studies.

Bhaskar, K. 1979. *The future of the UK motor industry*. London: Kogan Page.

Cable, V. 1980. *British interests and Third World development*. London: Overseas Development Institute.
Cowling, K. 1982. *Monopoly capitalism*. London: Macmillan.

Dowrick, S. 1983. *Notes on transnationals*. Mimeo., Department of Economics, University of Warwick.

Fine, B. 1983. Multinational corporations, the British economy and the AES. *Economic Bulletin* No. 10, Spring/Summer, pp. 10–35.
Fröbel, F., J. Heinrichs and O. Kreye 1981. *The new international division of labour*. London: Cambridge University Press.

Gaffikin, F. and A. Nickson 1984. *Jobs crisis and the multinationals: deindustrialisation in the West Midlands*. Birmingham: Third World Books.

Krause, L. B. and J. S. Nye 1975. Reflections on the economics and politics of international economic organisations. In *World politics and international economics*, C. F. Bergsten and L. B. Krause (eds): 323–342. Washington, D.C.: Brookings Institution.

Rapoport, C. 1982. The FT European 500: Financial Times Survey. *Financial Times* 21 October 1982.

3 The internationalization of production and its implications for the UK

A. AMIN and I. SMITH

Introduction

As Ben Fine has noted, the international expansion of capital has a long history:

> 'The internationalisation of capital has developed from the beginnings of capitalism with the tendency to create a world market. But up to the Second World War, this was still restricted to competition between capitals on the basis of the imperialist division of the world into spheres of influence for the export of finance and commodities' (Fine 1979, p. 181).

The striking feature since the Second World War, however, has been the international expansion of productive and financial capital. This process represents something quite different from the previous phases of imperialism. It is a process which has fostered, through the activities of multinational corporations (MNCs) and transnational banks (TNBs), the creation and expansion of capital which operates at an *international* scale. An earlier imperialism based upon the intensive exploitation of empires and rivalries in trade between national capitals and nation states has given way to another in which transnational capital, bestraddling the nations, plays a more prominent role by laying down the terms for international trade and national economic development.

In industry a small number of MNCs now overwhelmingly dominate world output and trade and not just in the developing countries. In 1980, only 350 of the world's largest MNCs had sales equivalent to 28 per cent of the gross domestic product (GDP) of the developed and developing countries, and accounted for 25 per cent of the total manufacturing employment in the developed countries (UN 1983). In the ten EEC countries, the share of total manufacturing turnover accounted for by the 280 largest firms (all MNCs), was 31 per cent in 1972, rising to 36.6 per cent by 1981. These firms were also responsible for over 38 per cent of the EEC manufacturing workforce in 1981 (EEC 1984). The figures for MNC control over trade are even more startling. To begin with, MNCs are responsible for a very large proportion of visible trade; over 90 per cent of US trade in 1977, and about 80 per cent of UK exports in the same year (UN 1983). Furthermore, it is estimated that between 25 and 40 per cent of all world trade consists of purely internal transfers between subsidiaries of MNCs (Sutcliffe 1984); in 1977, 39 per cent of US imports and 36 per cent of exports of the USA were intra-firm transactions. Similarly, 29 per cent of the exports of the UK were intra-firm in 1976, rising to 31 per cent in 1980 (UN 1983).

The growth of the MNCs has been accompanied by a high degree of internationalization of their activities. In 1971, the foreign operations of 350 of the world's largest corporations accounted for about 30 per cent of their total sales and this proportion had risen to about 40 per cent by 1980 (UN 1983). International investments appear to have assumed greater significance than domestic investments. Foreign direct investment (FDI) increased substantially during the 1960s and early 1970s both in absolute terms and relative to domestic investment, visible trade and gross domestic production of all thirteen OECD countries. During the period 1960–73, the growth rate of FDI from the major advanced countries was equal to that of their international trade and one and a half times that of their GDP (OECD 1981). However, according to the OECD (1981), the current long recession has caused a fall in overseas investment. This view is misleading because it only considers data on capital flows from and into individual countries and therefore ignores important overseas or transnational sources of finance such as reinvested earnings, local borrowing or borrowings from transnational banks and other monetary funds. In contrast, studies (Altvater 1983, Andreff 1984, Coakley 1984) which take into consideration not only loans from the TNBs to Third World countries, but also the enormous increase in MNC borrowings from the TNBs during the 1970s, conclude that the internationalization of capital has intensified during the recession. In short, while domestic investments in manufacturing appear to have declined significantly in the majority of the industrialized countries, during the present long depression, the pattern for overseas investments has been the opposite.

We would not go far wrong in arguing that the capitalist world economy is now thoroughly integrated across national boundaries, and that capital in the individual countries is concentrated not only in fewer and fewer hands but in those with a global reach. In spite of this it is surprising how in the main the literature on national economic development, especially in the advanced countries, attributes only secondary importance to the nature and effects of internationalization and the transnational corporations. This chapter, which focuses on the current internationalization of productive capital, especially in manufacturing, seeks to redress this imbalance in the literature.

The integration of national productive structures into the international capitalist economy is no longer a problem which simply concerns the unequal relationship between two homogeneous blocks, namely the Third World and the advanced economies. It concerns growing inequalities within the Third World, between the lesser developed countries and the tax haven, OPEC and newly industrializing countries. It also concerns inequalities between the advanced countries and between the latter and some Third World countries (cf. Lall 1983) on the spread of MNCs from India, Hong Hong, Argentina and Brazil. The most notable aspect of the current international integration of capital is cross investments between the advanced countries and not investments from the latter to the Third World. In 1971, the USA, the UK and West Germany were responsible for over 70 per cent of global FDI, and the respective amounts of each country's manufacturing FDI directed towards the advanced countries were 82.3 per cent, 82.0 per cent and 72.2 per cent. By 1976, the latter shares fell only marginally to 81.3 per cent, 80.3 per cent and 73.1 per cent respectively.

The extensive interpenetration of capitals between *the advanced economies,* is, despite its importance, another phenomenon which has received little attention in the literature concerned with the impact of internationalization on economic development in the latter countries. This chapter attempts to explore some of the issues related to this phenomenon, especially in the context of the UK economy.

The chapter begins with a brief survey of the principal trends in global FDI in manufacturing since the mid-1960s. The new pattern of investment is then explained in terms of three historical developments: a shift in regulatory mechanisms, which has led to more direct investment; growing problems of over-capacity which have necessitated the restructuring of production on an international basis; and the intensification of inter-capitalist rivalries over markets.

The second half of the chapter explores the implications of internationalization for the UK economy. It surveys inward and outward investment in manufacturing over the past twenty years and suggests that the UK faces the dual problem of disinvestment and a growth which is increasingly dependent upon the ever-changing needs of organizations with international rather than national interests. An analysis of the type of investments which are entering and leaving Britain suggests that this country is emerging as a weak member in the international division of labour within the MNCs. This is included in a discussion of the implications of internationalization for the country's balance of payments, which is followed by a discussion of market power implications for revitalizing a national manufacturing base. The chapter concludes with a critical comment on views which explain the crisis in manufacturing in the United Kingdom in terms of the UK's inability to compete internationally – notably because of rising labour costs and declining productivity.

Trends in the internationalization of production since the mid-1960s

The interpenetration of capitals between the advanced economies has been one of the most significant developments in the world capitalist economy in the last two decades. In spite of the increasing value of capital flows both in current and real terms from the developed to the developing countries (OECD 1981), there has been a marked fall in the actual share of developed country assets in developing countries as a result of greatly increased foreign direct investment (FDI) within the developed countries themselves (Table 3.1). Currently, the leading host countries for foreign direct investments, in descending order of share, are the following: the UK, the USA, West Germany, France, Switzerland, Belgium, Holland, Australia, Brazil, South Africa, Singapore, Canada, Mexico, Hong Kong, Italy, Japan, Lebanon, South Korea and Indonesia. Eleven of

Table 3.1 Changes in the share of outward capital flows from major OECD sources to major developed regions and the developing countries during the 1970s.

	Destination regions			
	Western Europe (%)	United States (%)	Other OECD countries (%)	Developing countries (%)
France*	−1.0‖	2.3	11.6	−12.9
West Germany†	−2.1‖	8.9	−0.4	−6.4
Japan†	−27.2	7.6	0.0	19.6
Netherlands‡	−15.0‖	12.0	0.5	2.5
United Kingdom§	9.1	7.7	−10.3	−6.5
United States§	8.8	N.a.	−8.2	−0.6
Canada*	−2.6‖	−9.3	4.2	7.7

Sources: OECD (1981); UK Census of Overseas Assets (1978).
* 1973–78.
† 1970–79.
‡ Change in three-year cumulative totals from 1968–70 to 1977–9.
§ Book value data (UK 1971–78, USA 1970–79).
‖ EEC countries only (other European investment in column 3).

these countries are also the principal overseas investors, accounting for well over 90 per cent of global foreign direct investments. The countries, in decreasing order of importance, are the following: the USA, the UK, West Germany, Japan, Switzerland, France, Canada, the Netherlands, Sweden, Belgium and Italy (UN 1978).

In 1960, the USA and the UK were still responsible for 65.4 per cent of the world's stock of FDI. By 1980, their aggregate share had dropped to 56.7 per cent, as enterprises from the majority of OECD countries increasingly internationalized their operations (Stopford and Dunning 1983). While the sources of FDI have become more diversified, inward flows, as demonstrated above, have become more concentrated geographically. Interestingly, within the developed countries, there has been a major redirection of FDI towards the advanced economies such as the USA and West Germany (UN 1978, 1983). In the developing world, the main recipients of FDI have been that small group of higher income countries mentioned above. Between 1978 and 1980, an annual average of 50 per cent of OECD FDI and 85 per cent of bank loans destined for the developing countries were concentrated in this handful of countries, predominantly in Latin American and South East Asia, with a per capita GNP of over $1000 (UN 1983). In other words, as Andreff concludes:

'Most foreign direct investment, *industrial or financial* takes place *between the same countries*: principally among the developed capitalist economies and, by extension, in the newly industrialising countries (NICs). Over 90 per cent of the overseas activities of MNCs and TNBs is concentrated in these two groups of countries' (Andreff 1984, p. 61).

In terms of the distribution of the accumulated stock of MNC activity, almost 57 per cent of a total of about 98 000 affiliates were, in 1980, in the advanced countries of Europe, a further 9 per cent in North America and about 25 per cent in the developing countries (UN 1983).

The geographical convergence in FDI has been matched by a sectoral convergence (Table 3.2). First, there has been a global increase in FDI in the 'service', most notably the financial sectors (UN 1983). Historically, in contrast to MNCs from the UK and the USA, West German MNCs have tended to avoid the service sector and Japanese MNC investments in manufacturing have been relatively low. These differences have narrowed considerably in recent years. Between 1971 and 1976, West German service sector investments in the developed and the developing countries rose at an average annual rate of 32 per cent and 40 per cent respectively. In the case of Japan, the increase in the same sector was even more dramatic: 58 per cent in the developed countries and 70 per cent in the

Table 3.2 Changes in the industrial structure of foreign-owned assets of four major overseas investors in developed and developing nations, 1971–76.

Investment source	United States A (%)	United States B (%)	United Kingdom A (%)	United Kingdom B (%)	West Germany A (%)	West Germany B (%)	Japan A (%)	Japan B (%)
developed countries	68.7	15.5	72.1	15.4	71.9	18.4	50.9	61.1
extractive	19.3	15.3	6.4	10.0	5.4	10.8	10.7	60.0
manufacturing	34.1	15.1	47.5	13.1	55.3	16.2	9.1	73.3
services	15.1	16.8	18.2	21.7	11.2	31.9	31.2	58.2
developing countries	25.3	7.7	27.9	8.4	28.0	32.4	49.1	70.0
extractive	11.5	6.4	2.0	0.0	1.5	40.0	20.7	51.4
manufacturing	7.2	18.0	11.5	12.5	20.4	15.5	17.7	64.0
services	6.5	26.3	14.4	6.0	6.2	40.0	10.7	70.0
Total	100.0	13.1	100.0	13.4	100.0	19.5	100.0	68.3

Source: OECD (1981).

Columns labelled A show the share of investment in sector in 1971; columns labelled B show the average annual increase 1971–76 (billions of US dollars).

Notes: Amounts referring to industrialized and developing countries do not always add to the total as investments per business establishment are not disaggregated on a regular basis. United Kingdom figures are for 1971–75 and exclude petroleum.

Table 3.3 Percentage of US entries through acquisition in the manufacturing (M) and non-manufacturing (NM) sectors of selected OECD and developing countries.

	1951–66		1967–69		1970–72		1973–75	
	M	NM	M	NM	M	NM	M	NM
United Kingdom	68.0	49.0	74.3	65.7	84.5	65.2	78.6	55.4
West Germany	60.0	41.6	70.9	52.3	67.4	34.9	72.1	46.0
Japan	28.8	23.2	37.0	45.5	20.3	7.5	22.7	20.0
Australia	54.0	42.5	71.4	42.5	69.8	45.3	81.3	48.0
East Asia	28.2	18.8	23.5	18.2	25.7	26.4	20.0	9.8
Brazil	48.0	20.6	58.0	37.0	60.8	35.0	66.2	30.0
world	51.6	34.8	62.1	42.8	63.9	38.1	54.6	29.6

Source: Harvard multinational data bank (Curhan *et al.* 1977).

developing countries. Similarly, Japanese FDI in manufacturing rose by 78 per cent in the developed countries and by 64 per cent in the developing countries during the same period (OECD 1981). This convergence is not simply intersectoral. Traditionally, manufacturing investments by the British, Japanese and French MNCs have been in the so-called 'low value added' industries such as wood, metal and food processing, and textiles and clothing. In contrast, US overseas investments have also been significant in the high value added industries such as motor vehicles, pharmaceuticals, chemicals, plastics, electrical and precision engineering. This distinction is breaking down as a result of the major increase, in the 1970s, of outward investment in the latter industries by the British, French, Japanese and German MNCs (Quiers-Valette 1979, Dicken 1982, Olle & Shoeller 1982, Panic 1982).

Thus, the new trend in the internationalization of productive capital is the erosion of national differences in the activities of MNCs. There has also been a growth in the overseas activities of capital from the majority of the OECD countries to reduce the overwhelmingly international dominance of British and American MNCs. More importantly, the investment behaviour of the different MNCs seems to be converging: MNCs from the advanced countries investing in each other's markets and sectors.

Another notable feature of FDI during the recession concerns the increasing tendency for MNCs to expand externally through acquisition in preference to new investment. It is not surprising therefore that the bulk of FDI has been between the advanced countries which possess a large industrial stock. The only substantial time-series data relating to method of overseas entry is that compiled by the Harvard Business School for the period up to 1975 (Table 3.3). As the data apply to the largest 180 US manufacturing corporations, there may be a tendency to exaggerate the significance of acquisition entry given a well established positive relationship between size and external growth. On the other hand, as the firms concerned were responsible for approximately 71 per cent of the total overseas sales of US majority-owned affiliates in 1975, it is safe to infer that acquisition has accounted for the lion's share of US manufacturing investment in the majority of developed and some of the newly industrializing countries since the late 1960s. The data does, however, show a decline in the contribution of take-overs in the period immediately following the international merger wave, although this was not the case in the majority of developed host nations such as West Germany and Australia and some of the NICs such as Brazil.

Unfortunately, data on the method of entry during the late 1970s and early 1980s are extremely restricted, although it is probable that acquisition entry has assumed increasing importance as the recession has intensified. For example, the recent escalation to record levels of the *value* of take-overs in the UK suggests the growing involvement of MNCs, a significant proportion of which are of foreign origin. It is not possible, however, to assess accurately the contribution of FDI because official statistics do not classify acquisitions through the medium of existing foreign affiliates as being of foreign origin (Smith 1982). A similar tendency toward large scale transactions and entry through take-over is shown by US Department of Commerce data in the case of FDI in the USA during the late 1970s. Although a high proportion of the entries were effected by firms engaged predominantly in financial and service activities, many of the interests acquired were in the manufacturing sector. Excluding Canada, in 1979, acquisition entry accounted for 65 per cent of all FDI transactions by the six largest investing nations in the USA with MNCs from the UK (76 per cent) and France (81 per cent) showing a particularly marked preference for inward investment mergers (Hood and Young 1982a).

Explaining the recent FDI trends in manufacturing

The forms and the reasons for the internationalization of production are numerous and vary in time between economies, industries and firms. For instance, Dunning (1979a) in his 'eclectic theory' identifies no less than 40 factors related to the monopolistic advantages of giant firms alone which promote international production. Our purpose in this section is not to look for more factors or to apportion importance between them; nor is it to integrate the various factors into a general theory of FDI. Instead our aim is to explain the emergence of the pattern of investment described in the preceding section. The explanation, however, does attempt to generalize by emphasizing causes with a wider applicability rather than those which are industry or firm specific.

It is argued below that the current internationalization of production in manufacturing is, as it has always been, an attempt by the multinationals to maintain or raise their rates of profit, but is underpinned in particular by three historical developments. The first refers to a series of external or regulatory conditions favouring, or in some cases necessitating, the internationalization of production on a wider scale. Among the most significant are the following conditions: the collapse of the Bretton Woods Agreement and the emergence of excess liquidity in the advanced countries; the growth of protectionism on imports during the 1960s and 1970s coupled with rising government incentives for inward investment as domestic growth rates declined during the current world recession. The second historical development is the massive build up of capacity during the boom years, notably in the mass production industries. The recession, by exaggerating the problem of excess capacity, has prompted MNCs to internationalize production even further in order to restructure (by reducing production costs and reorganizing the division of labour) and also to purchase assets in new or high growth markets. The final development, related to the second one, is the intensification of oligopolistic rivalries, especially during the recession, in the most concentrated industries. This has led to greater cross investments between the advanced countries so that the MNCs can protect their markets and ward off competitors.

The new external conditions

The Bretton Woods international monetary system which fixed currency exchange rates to the dollar standard had been an effective means of regulating world trade, and to the advantage of the USA (Aglietta 1982). The introduction of flexible exchange rates after the collapse of the Bretton Woods Agreement in 1972 broke down US trade hegemony and disrupted world trade, affecting FDI in two distinct ways. Firstly, the dollar crisis and the ability to trade in individual currencies stimulated a dramatic increase in investments into the USA (German, Japanese and British MNCs) and elsewhere, as it became possible to speculate on individual currencies *and* finance investments abroad. Secondly, it fostered the dislocation between real and financial accumulation and also the expansion of money through the emergence of a private international credit market no longer subject to US regulation (Altvater 1983, De Vroey 1983). This internationalization of finance capital signified not only the creation of excess liquidity to finance investments globally, but also the availability of finance from international sources, freeing debtors from financing investments from internally accumulated or national resources. Interestingly, although loans to some Third World countries from the private TNBs did increase as a result of the internationalization of bank capital, the principal beneficiaries appear to have been the MNCs, with the geographical trajectory of TNB investments being astonishingly similar to that of the MNCs (Michalet 1979, Andreff 1984), namely principally towards the advanced countries. In other words, while it is true that the international private banks redirected surplus finance from the advanced countries (as domestic investment rates dropped) towards the newly industrializing countries (Altvater 1983), they also financed cross investments between the advanced countries.

The internationalization of production especially as a replacement for exports has also been influenced by the growth of protectionism against the import of finished goods, and by the liberalization of government controls on capital flows during the 1970s. The industrialization programmes pursued by the NICs (with the exception of the Free Trade Zone countries) for a decade after the mid-1960s relied upon import substitution strategies consisting of a variety of tariff and non-tariff restrictions on imports. The trade barriers had the impact of promoting inward investment, which has been reinforced even further during the current recession owing to a reversal of earlier restrictions on foreign investment. Severe balance of payments problems, stagnant economic growth, deterioration in the terms of trade, and the sharp escalation of external debt servicing burdens, aggravated by the recession and protectionism in the advanced countries, have forced many developing countries to turn to the MNCs for industrial investment (UN 1983).

The combination of restrictions on imports and open-door policies towards the MNCs, with its positive impact on inward investment, has also become a characteristic of the advanced countries in their efforts to cope with chronic unemployment in the depression. For instance, tariffs, quotas, orderly marketing arrangements and anti-dumping measures have contributed significantly to the growth of Japanese investments in the USA and the EEC. The import controls pose no real threat to the MNCs, especially when we consider that some OECD countries are reported to offer them incentives equal to 25–50 per cent of the total value of new investment (UN 1983). In any case this threat applies mainly to finished products and does not interfere greatly with the free flow of components on an intra-firm basis (Helleiner 1981). In fact, it could be argued that this kind of selective tariff policy encourages FDI by promoting international intra-firm transactions.

It should not be assumed from the above that protectionism is unimportant, but as a general cause of FDI its explanatory power is weak because other factors such as international variations in factor endowments, oligopolistic rivalries and various ownership-specific advantages can actually make FDI a more desirable alternative to exports. Nonetheless, the timing and flow of FDI seems undoubtedly to have been influenced by a shift in regulatory policies in favour of direct investment.

Over-accumulation and the international reorganization of production

The recent internationalization of production in manufacturing should not be interpreted so much as the expansion of output and capacity overseas than as an attempt by the MNCs to reorganize their global operation in order to maintain or raise profitability. New openings have been accompanied by rationalization and closures, mergers and acquisitions and diversifications into new branches of production. For instance, while the number of foreign manufacturing subsidiaries of 187 major US MNCs grew by 6879 between 1951 and 1975, 2204 subsidiaries (amounting to 32 per cent of the new entries) were sold off or liquidated in the same period (Curhan et al. 1977). The divestment of subsidiaries was much higher in the period between 1966 and 1975 when subsidiaries were divested at the rate of 3.0 per cent per annum, as opposed to 1.3 per cent per annum in the years between 1951 and 1965 (Smith 1985). Also interesting is that while the majority (78 per cent) of the new investments by these MNCs (1951–75) were made in Canada, Europe and Latin America, the bulk of divestment took place in the same areas (87 per cent.).

Thus, while the growing globalization and integration of production undoubtedly continues to express the expansion of 'monopoly capital' – through the ability of giant corporations to exploit, on an international scale, their advantages over other firms in production and in exchange, and also national differences in economic policy and factor endowments – it also represents an attempt by such corporations to extend and modify their international division of labour in response, as argued below, to the excessive build-up of global capacity during the boom years.

The writings of Itoh (1980, 1983) on the current international depression, and those by some French Marxists (Aglietta 1979, 1982, Boyer 1979, Lipietz 1982, 1984, Mistral 1982, De Vroey 1983) on the conditions responsible for the postwar growth in the advanced economies, offer explanations which are pertinent to the present international reorganization of production. According to the French, the rapid and enormous growth in world trade and output during the boom years was underpinned by the international expansion of the US model of growth, or the regime of 'intensive accumulation and monopoly regulation'. Intensive accumulation refers to the extraction of relative surplus value on the basis of mass production in the advanced countries which allowed simultaneous increases in productivity and real wages. This latter phenomenon, by enabling the growth of mass consumption, allowed the parallel growth of production in the means of production and means of consumption industries. The balance between production and exhange nevertheless required the regulation of commodity and financial markets which was achieved partly through the domination of markets by large corporations and partly by the State through a variety of Keynesian regulatory mechanisms.

The balance in the system began to break down primarily because of disruptions caused by the excessive *global* development of the productive forces (Itoh 1983) brought about by this regime of accumulation, especially during the boom years after World War II. The innovative long-wave matured to limit further growths in the technical productivity of capital; and Fordism reached its own limits, to slow down growths in productivity (Aglietta 1979). In turn, the massive build-up of world productive capacity through over-investment began to generate excess fixed capital which, in being difficult to dismantle, also generated disproportional exchange between the production goods and the consumer goods industries. This over-accumulation of capital also exacerbated the twin problem of over-production and under-consumption of commodities as consumption fell more rapidly than capacity: 'excess idle capacity forms a vicious circle with increasing unemployment and a stagnant or declining real income of workers' (Itoh 1983, p. 51). The pressure on profits was further exacerbated in some industries and countries by wages rising at a faster rate than productivity (De Vroey 1983).

Given the fact that postwar capitalism has progressively operated on an international scale, not only through trade but also through the activities of transnational corporations, Itoh is correct in maintaining, in contrast to the French 'school', that the problem of over accumulation and disproportional exchange originates from capital operating collectively on a world scale. It is a common problem, affecting different firms and industries unequally, rather than one originating in and being restricted to specific countries. This problem, exacerbated by the MNCs' contribution to the chronic build-up of capacity and by their monopolistic control of markets, has threatened capitalist profitability with rising production costs and insufficient demand. The weaker firms, unable to compete under such conditions, have simply gone to the wall, whereas the response of the MNCs has been quite different: one involving a search for new economies in production and greater control over markets, with internationalization lying at the heart of both strategies. As the issue of the relationship between internationalization and markets is taken up later in this chapter, the argument below is restricted to the question of the international reorganization of capacity.

Clearly the forms of international restructuring pursued by the MNCs in order to establish a new basis for production have varied from one branch to another in relation to variations in the build-up of capacity, and to differences in the social and technical relations of production and the level of competition. For instance, the MNCs in the Fordist industries (e.g. motor vehicles and electronics) have established new economies in production on the basis of the following methods: the replacement of separate but fully integrated factories and workforces in the large industrial cities of the advanced countries, by smaller and highly automated factories specializing in particular tasks which are dispersed globally but productively integrated in order to achieve new scale economies, eliminate pressures on productivity due to the demands of organized labour, raise technical productivity and reap the benefits of lower costs in new locations; the relocation of deskilled operations into cheap and non-militant labour reserve areas; and the 'putting-out', both locally and internationally, of production tasks which involve high costs or low volumes of output.

The MNCs in other industries (e.g. chemicals, electrical and mechanical engineering, food, drink and tobacco) have gone the other way by diversifying into product areas related to their main line of business, in order to benefit from the economies of interdependent activities and from other cost savings accruing from internalizing the flow of goods. This form of productive integration now, however, is an international process involving the flow of raw materials from Third World sites to factories in the advanced countries producing the intermediate goods which are then transferred to other Third World or advanced country sites for completion and then re-exported (at least in part) to other countries for sale. For instance, in 1972, the Brazilian and Mexican affiliates of US companies imported respectively 50 and 58 per cent of their total material import requirements from the parent organization, and exported respectively 73 and 82 per cent of their output to other subsidiaries of the organization (UNCTAD 1978). Nevertheless, the international integration of MNC activity concerns above all the advanced countries; in 1970, 91 per cent of intra-firm trade of US MNCs in manufacturing originated in or was directed to the advanced countries (UNCTAD 1978). This suggests that one important reason behind the MNCs' strategy to rely upon acquisition as a dominant mode of cross investment between the advanced countries (between 1967 and 1965, the top 187 US MNCs established 77 per cent of their new manufacturing subsidiaries in Canada and 67 per cent in Europe through acquisition) is to purchase existing capacity and diversify without raising overall capacity in the industry. This option has become even more attractive in the depths of the depression when companies can be acquired at share prices well below the real value of the assets purchased (Anon. 1985).

The third type of response to the growth of excess capital has been large scale divestment from unprofitable product areas and reinvestment (notably through acquisitions in the advanced countries) into the high-profit new product sectors. The evidence suggests that this form of international restructuring has gained considerable importance in recent years (Hood & Young 1981, Muchielli & Thuillier 1982).

The international reorganization and integration of production has been an important but not the only MNC response to the threat of idle capacity. The extension of MNC domination over world production has been accompanied by an equally aggressive drive to control market outlets in order to sustain demand.

FDI and market control

The upsurge in cross investments between the advanced countries, principally through merger and acquisition, and the concentration of investments in the Third World among those countries offering large domestic markets or easy market access to neighbouring countries, suggests that FDI is also a means by which the MNCs can maintain or extend their market shares. The threat of over-production at a time when global demand is depressed, and growing competition in international markets due to the rise of MNCs from Japan, Germany and the NICs, has served to intensify market-oriented FDI. The essence of this strategy is to keep demand consonant with output by changing the terms of competition between firms through a variety of monopoly practices (Michalet 1983). Market concentration on an ever-increasing international scale has become a means of raising MNC profits despite the pressure on profits resulting from the over-accumulation of capital.

Direct investment, facilitated by the various economic advantages which MNCs have over their weaker competitors, offers a number of ways in which market power can be increased. To begin with, it is a means of penetrating tariff and non-tariff barriers on imports, giving the MNCs not only free access to the markets of host countries, but also direct contact with local distribution networks. Secondly, acquisition as the dominant form of FDI allows not only the ready purchase of the market share and the marketing skills of the company which is bought, but also reduced competition when the acquired firm is a rival in the market. Furthermore, the establishment of a major stake in the market has the effect of warding off competitors, especially when accompanied, as is normal, by the use of restrictive marketing practices (e.g. exclusive arrangements with dealers, the exploitation of brand names, patent agreements, advanced advertising methods and monopoly pricing practices). Thirdly, the considerable forward integration by the major manufacturers (notably in clothing, food, cosmetics, pharmaceuticals) into retailing (Hood & Young 1981, Muchielli & Thuillier 1982) has given them direct market outlets for their products. Finally, the purchase of companies specializing in new products has provided the MNCs with a ready mechanism for monopolizing nascent markets through the appropriation of the material and mental technologies developed by the purchased company (Negandhi & Baliga 1981).

Direct investment into countries with large or growing markets, in combination with the utilization of various monopoly practices, has been an MNC strategy to avoid a realization crisis by controlling and protecting demand, i.e. by tempering the anarchy of the market. The MNCs' response to the threat posed by the global over-accumulation of capital has been to maintain profitability by reorganizing the capacity and extending their control over markets increasingly on an international scale through the mechanism of FDI.

Another important reason for the internationalization of production concerns the perpetuation of oligopolistic rivalries in various product markets. The internationalized industries are also those which are highly concentrated (Hymer 1960, Kindleberger 1969), with markets shared out between a handful of giant corporations and rivalries operating at a scale where any change in the balance of power could involve huge gains or equally huge losses for each corporation. Furthermore, in being industries subjected to monopoly forces and therefore also to reduced competitive pressure continually to scrap fixed capital, they are the very industries in which the threat of excess capacity and under-consumption has loomed largest during the recession. Oligopolistic conditions would appear, therefore, to have promoted a further internationalization of production as the process of cross investment in respective product and national markets ('follow the leader' behaviour) has widened and gathered pace in an attempt by the MNCs to maintain the balance of power. The relationship of FDI to oligopoly is developed more fully in the section later in this chapter on the market power implications of internationalization.

Whatever the reasons for FDI, the MNCs, in keeping with the Darwinian principle of the strong getting stronger, have remained profitable and perhaps even gained from the recession, while profit rates in the advanced and developing countries have fallen. The overall profit rate (ratio of net profits to net assets) of 373 MNCs from the eleven major investing countries dropped from an average of 5.6 per cent between 1967 and 1970 to 4.9 per cent in the period between 1971 and 1976, but rose again to an average of 5.5 per cent, as the recession deepened, between 1977 and 1980 (Andreff 1984). The internationalization of production has undoubtedly helped in the restoration of profit rates.

Internationalization and the UK manufacturing sector

The distinctive feature of the current phase of internationalization is the large scale global expansion of all three circuits of capital (financial, commodity and productive) and also the growing international integration of production. This enables, more than ever before, the accumulation of capital on a transnational scale, alongside or perhaps even at the expense of accumulation within national boundaries (Radice 1984). In other words, the postwar period capitalist order, which was characterized by rivalries between nation states or national capitals, and the exploitation of the Third World by the advanced countries, is giving way to a different order. This new order is characterized by rivalries between capitals operating and reproducing themselves on a transnational scale on the basis of an uneven division of labour among *both* the advanced and the developing countries. In short, national economies are becoming either locked into, in more or less dominant positions, or left out of the accumulation process of transnational capital.

The preceding discussion has suggested that internationalization implies 'de-industrialization' and 're-industrialization' at one and the same time in the same country. The real significance of these two processes on national economic development is not so much the quantitative balance between them, but more the fact that they are both an expression of the growing international integration of national economies. It has also been emphasized that the relative positions of individual countries within the international division of labour are subject to historical transformation. That the status of the UK within the international economy is at present undergoing such a transformation, as a result of changes in the level and nature of inward and outward manufacturing investment flows, is the major thesis of the remaining section of this chapter. In particular, it is argued that there is an association between declining domestic manufacturing investment and a marked deterioration in the UK's net direct investment position. Whereas UK-based MNC's have increasingly preferred to invest in Europe and the USA, manufacturing investment from Europe has remained at a low level while US manufacturing FDI has increasingly been diverted towards other EEC countries. In general, the analysis of FDI stocks and flows which follows supports the idea that the recession has accelerated a tendency for MNCs to focus manufacturing investment in high income, high buying-power markets, so that both developing and slower growing developed countries like the UK are receiving a declining share of internationally mobile investment. More recent data relating to the structure of manufacturing FDI also provides support for the view that a low wage, low buying-power market such as the UK will increasingly attract low value added, labour-intensive investment while MNCs already operating in the UK will increasingly invest in high value added, research-intensive activities overseas.

In making these assertions, one is, however, conscious of the inherent deficiencies of official FDI data which is collected on a balance of payments basis through the banking system and cannot be directly equated with fixed capital formation. Both the net capital flow data, published anually, and the net capital asset data, published triennially, are independently influenced, for example by relative movements in prices and exchange rates and, in the case of the capital flow data, by changes in the capital sourcing policies of MNCs. Thus, for example, it is difficult to gauge the contribution of accelerating inflation and the weakening of sterling to the meteoric rise in the value of outward manufacturing FDI during the 1970s, although both have undoubtedly contributed. On the other hand, an increased tendency by UK MNCs to source their overseas invest-ment from abroad suggests that capital flow data will increasingly understate the level of overseas investment over time because of the exclusion of local borrowing from unrelated concerns or borrowing in third countries. For this reason, the stock value data, although published only triennially, are preferred in the analysis which fol-lows.

Recent trends in manufacturing FDI and disinvestment in the UK

Even allowing for a faster rate of inflation, there seems little doubt that the rate of growth of UK-owned overseas assets accelerated markedly during the 1970s, and that investment in the manufactur-ing sector made a major contribution. Although 'non-manufactur-ing' investment grew at a slightly faster rate than manufacturing, the average annual growth rate of overseas manufacturing assets be-tween 1971 and 1981 was over double that of the late 1960s. There was also an acceleration in the rate of growth of foreign-owned assets in the UK during the 1970s, but in this case, 'non-manufacturing' investment made a proportionately greater contribution than manu-facturing, so that the ratio of outward to inward manufacturing investment gradually increased as the decade progressed. Figure 3.1 shows clearly, in terms of both the capital flow and stock value data, the growing gap between outward and inward manufacturing investment which is likely to have made an important contribution to the UK's 'de-industrialization' problem.

By averaging the net capital flow data over three-year periods, it is possible to smooth some of the extreme annual variations (shown in Fig. 3.1). This has been done in Table 3.4, which shows ratios of outward to inward net investment flows both in total and for manufacturing for each three-year period since 1965. It can be seen that the two series closely parallel one another with major increases

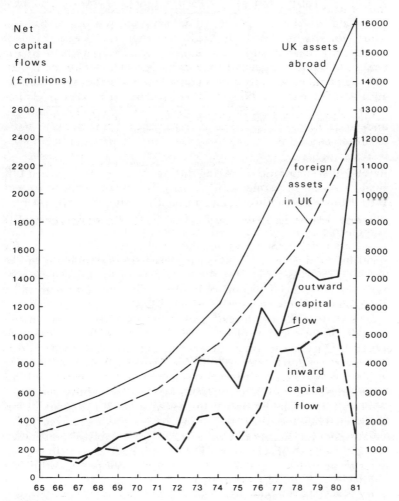

Figure 3.1 UK inward and outward FDI in manufacturing, 1965–81 (information taken from DTI 1984a,b).

Table 3.4 Ratios of UK outward to inward net investment flows,* 1965–82, by major source and host regions.

Years	All areas		Western Europe		North America	
	Total	Manufac-turing	Total	Manufac-turing	Total	Manufac-turing
1965–67	1.54†	1.05	1.32	0.77	0.45	0.27
1968–70	1.59	1.14	1.96	1.56	0.58	0.37
1971–73	2.01	1.62	3.60	4.10	0.84	0.53
1974–76	2.30	2.05	2.37	2.40	1.19	0.93
1977–79	1.78	1.38	1.28	1.38	1.35	0.91
1980–82	2.38	2.79	1.36	2.65	2.61	2.31

Source: *Business Monitor MA4: overseas transactions*, various years.
* Excluding oil and insurance company transactions.
† Three-year averages.

in the investment ratio occurring during the early 1970s, when UK manufacturing investment in Western Europe outstripped invest- ment from Western Europe, and during the early 1980s, when a large net manufacturing deficit with North America was primarily responsible. It must be stressed, however, that these ratios are based upon *net* investment flows and hence also reflect changes in the incidence of divestment. This is particularly important in the case of the high ratios recorded for the early part of the present decade, which are influenced by a major upturn in the rate of divestment by foreign manufacturing enterprises in the UK.

The second major feature of manufacturing FDI has been a major shift in the orientation of outward capital flows from Common- wealth (Canada and other developed nations) and Third World developing countries towards the higher growth economies of the more developed nations (the USA and the EEC countries). Table 3.5 shows the share of UK manufacturing assets in each of the major regions for which the data is provided in 1965, 1974 and 1981. Between 1965 and 1974, the most rapid growth occurred in the countries of the European Community, presumably in preparation for, or as a result of, UK entry. During this period less than average rates of increase occurred in Canada, other developed countries and the developing countries. After 1974, there was a major shift towards the USA, which more than doubled its share of total UK assets abroad so that the individual share of all other regions declined, in some cases markedly so. The average annual growth rate of UK manufacturing assets in the countries of the European Community and the European Free Trade Area, and in other developed nations, decreased markedly after 1974, although there was a slight increase

Table 3.5 Changes in the share of UK manufacturing assets* abroad and foreign manufacturing assets in the UK, 1965–81, by major host and source regions.

	UK manufacturing assets abroad			Foreign manufacturing assets in UK		
	1965 (%)	1974 (%)	1981 (%)	1965 (%)	1974 (%)	1981 (%)
European Community†	12.6	25.3	20.2	7.3	13.4	11.9
rest of Western Europe‡	2.7	3.8	3.1	10.9	11.7	11.5
Canada	14.0	7.6	7.1	12.2	6.9	6.3
United States	12.1	14.5	32.2	68.0	65.7	66.9
other developed nations	35.7	32.0	21.0	0.3	1.7	2.8
developing nations	23.1	19.3	16.4	n.a.	n.a.	n.a.

Source: DTI (1981).

* Book values of net assets.
† Denmark, Greece and Irish Republic included in all periods.
‡ The columns do not sum to 100 per cent because some parts of Western Europe are also classified as developing nations.

in the growth rate of UK manufacturing assets in the developing countries. Nevertheless, as Table 3.5 shows, the *share* of UK manufacturing assets located in the less developed parts of the world continued to fall throughout the whole period, which lends little support to FDI theories based upon the premise of a new international division of labour.

Because of confidentiality restrictions, time series asset data for individual host countries are rarely complete. Nevertheless, it is clear from the statistics which are available that UK manufacturing investment during the 1970s has been heavily concentrated in some nations in both the developed and less developed parts of the world. Data are more complete for the period after 1974, and, in the case of the advanced countries, suggest an increasing preference for market-oriented investment as the world economic recession has deepened. Panic (1982) has suggested that much of the *internal* flow of capital within the OECD countries represents movement from slower to faster growing economies as MNCs attempt to weather the recession by investing in markets with the best growth prospects. To some degree, evidence from the *Census of overseas assets* (DTI 1981, 1984a) supports this view, particularly for the period after 1974, when the United States, Switzerland and Japan amongst the OECD countries experienced the fastest rates of growth of UK manufacturing assets, In all three countries also, the asset growth rate markedly accelerated compared to the period between 1965 and 1974. On the other hand, the high rate of asset growth which occurred in some of the more peripheral European markets, such as the Irish Republic and Portugal, between 1965 and 1974, fell away markedly after 1974. Although the Netherlands and West Germany also appear to have become less attractive to UK manufacturing investment after 1974, the value of UK manufacturing assets in both countries continued to increase at a rate well above the OECD average.

As with the advanced countries, UK manufacturing investment in the developing countries has been heavily concentrated in relatively few host nations with either sizeable local markets (Brazil, India) and/or factors enabling reductions in production costs (Malaysia, Nigeria, Spain). Since 1974, there has been a tendency for the rate of net asset growth to slacken in the first group, probably as a result of the development of over-capacity behind tariff walls. With the development of integrated world-wide production systems, MNCs have focused attention on newly industrializing countries (NICs) with specific advantages for low cost production and exporting. In this respect, MNCs from the United Kingdom appear to have been no exception; some of the most rapid rates of manufacturing net asset growth since 1974 have been in host nations with free production zones (Singapore, Malaysia, Mexico) or in tax havens (Bermuda).

Fear of asset expropriation or potential political instability has, however, kept investment at a relatively low level in some NICs such as Ghana and Hong Kong with similar factor endowment advantages. Elsewhere, restrictions on inward investments through acquisition, local component sourcing requirements, or minimal inward investment incentives, all of which could be expected to assume increasing importance as the international recession deepened, have contributed towards a diminished rate of net asset growth. It is also important to stress that although some NICs display relatively high rates of net asset growth, it is often because of the low level of investment before the mid-1960s; compared to the advanced countries, investment in Third World economies is still small in absolute terms.

Turning now to sources of inward manufacturing investment, Table 3.5 shows that, with the exception of Canada, there has been remarkably little change in the share of manufacturing assets owned by enterprises from each of the major source regions. The share of EEC-based enterprises, after increasing in the period immediately before the entry of the UK, fell away again after 1974, whereas the US share remained fairly constant at approximately two-thirds of all foreign manufacturing assets in the UK. Dunning (1979b) has noted the imbalance in manufacturing FDI flows between the UK and EEC. Between 1972 and 1978, UK manufacturing investment in the Community was more than twice as large as EEC investment in the UK, suggesting that while UK firms have continued to set up production units within the EEC, EEC-based firms have preferred to service the UK market through exports. Alternatively, given the development of internationally integrated productive structures, which suggests that the same MNCs may be responsible for trade and investment flows in *both* directions, expansion in Europe and external servicing of the UK market through intra-firm trade obviates the need for an explanation which looks for national differences between the investment strategies of MNCs.

It is important to emphasize that although the US share of manufacturing assets in the UK has not shown much tendency to decline, the UK's share of US manufacturing investment in Europe has decreased dramatically since the formation of the Community in 1957 (Dicken, 1982). In 1978 the UK had little more than a quarter of US manufacturing assets in Europe, whereas in 1956 well over half of US assets were in the UK. Membership of the Community in 1973 does appear to have reduced this trend somewhat, by increasing the importance of the UK as an initial point of entry into the enlarged EEC market. There is some evidence, however, that with the onset of the current recession and the development of EEC-wide integrated production systems, some US MNCs have shifted investment away from the depressed UK market to take advantage of the scale economies to be derived from centralized production systems in Europe (Hood & Young, 1982b). This and the previous example would imply both an increasing tendency to service the UK market through imports and an increase in the disinvestment rate of UK and non-UK MNCs *alike* in the UK, and it is to a consideration of the evidence on this latter issue which we now turn.

Existing data on disinvestment by MNCs in the UK is for the most part limited to specific regional economies or to the 1960s and early 1970s. The absence of an up-to-date *national* time series is a particular handicap given the stated aims of this paper; nevertheless, the fragmentary evidence available does suggest that some MNCs have rationalized production in the UK in preference to elsewhere in Europe and that this trend may have become more pronounced towards the end of the 1970s. Firstly, the Harvard data show that the largest US manufacturing MNCs had a relatively high rate of disinvestment through closures and sell-offs in the UK during the period between 1951 and 1975. During this period 41 per cent of US-owned affiliates established in the UK were subsequently divested by the parent company compared to an average for Europe of 33 per cent. Secondly, the Department of Trade and Industry's *Record of openings and closures,* reveals that the closure rate of establishments moving between regions (long distance movers) increased more markedly after 1972 than that of establishments relocating within regions (short distance movers), particularly in the UK development areas. Assuming that the long distance movers were predominantly large branches of MNCs, this is an early indication that such enterprises were becoming increasingly involved in divestment decisions in the UK and in an important way corroborates the trends shown by the Harvard data.

For the period since 1975, reliance must be placed on evidence supplied by the few existing analyses which show the employment impact of the largest 'prime mover' firms on particular regional economies. For example, Lloyd and Shutt (1983) show that the 54 largest manufacturing employers in the North West shed more than one-fifth of their manual employment between 1975 and 1980 so that their share of total manual employment in the region declined by 5 per cent. Similarly, Gaffikin and Nickson (1984) found that the ten largest manufacturing employers in the West Midlands reduced their UK employment by 25 per cent between 1978 and 1981 while at the same time increasing their overseas workforce by 9 per cent. Finally, unpublished evidence from the North East of England shows that externally-owned establishments accounted for 75 per cent of employment in 1978, but 82 per cent of job losses through closure between 1978 and 1981.

Market power implications

The significance of relatively high levels of aggregate and market concentration in the process of internationalization has been recently emphasized by Panic (1982), who maintains that the absolute number and size of a country's multinationals will be an important influence on the level of outward and inward investment. The existence in the UK of a relatively large number of enterprises with the requisite resources for overseas investment is suggested by the prevalence of concentrated market structures across a wide range of industries. The association of concentrated industries with high levels of internationalization stems from the ability of firms in such sectors to exploit ownership-specific advantages overseas under the protection of high entry barriers (Hymer 1960). This provides the basis for a link between relatively high levels of market concentration in the UK and relatively high levels of outward direct investment. Further, in so far as oligopolistic behaviour is more likely to occur in concentrated industries, there may also be a tendency for highly concentrated markets to result in a reduced level of *inward* FDI. For example, evidence is emerging that enterprises investing overseas commonly avoid industries which are already highly oligopolized (Lall & Siddarthan, 1982). If, as seems to be the case, a wider range of industries in the UK is more highly oligopolized than in other industrialized countries, the *opportunities* for inward investment may be correspondingly less. This may have contributed to the UK's growing net FDI deficit in manufacturing throughout the 1970s.

It has commonly been assumed that FDI will normally increase the level of competition prevailing in host countries, because foreign multinationals have the resources to override barriers to entry. It is obvious that this assumption overlooks the possibility that entry may be deterred because of fear of retaliation by host country firms in the home market of the prospective entrant (Cowling 1982). It also, however, ignores the fact that by far the largest proportion of manufacturing FDI in industrialized countries is carried out through take-overs. In contrast to entry through new investment, the competitive effects of entry through takeover are by no means clear cut. For example, Hood *et al.* (1981) consider that foreign-sourced acquisitions may be beneficial if smaller or ailing host country firms become more competitive through the injection of a foreign acquirer's superior financial, technological or managerial resources. However, evidence relating to the type of company commonly involved in inward mergers does not suggest that either of these characteristics are particularly prevalent; the majority of overseas-acquired UK firms appear to have been large or medium-sized public companies headquartered in the faster growing regions of the UK, in particular the South East (Smith 1982). The absorption of such enterprises may not only reduce the self-generating growth potential of the UK economy (which is notably weak in medium-sized firms), but also may actually reduce competition in *international* markets. The recent take-over of the Scottish mining machinery manufacturer, Anderson Strathclyde, by Charter Consolidated is a case in point (Monopolies & Mergers Commission 1982). Although Charter itself has limited interests in the mining industry, its ownership links with the leading world producer of mining machinery, the South African-owned Anglo-American Incorporated, has clear implications for the international level of competition in the industry. Unfortunately, the remit of the Monopolies & Mergers Commission does not require them to consider such implications as their terms of reference are limited to a consideration of competitive effects *within* the UK.

Although relatively few industries have as yet reached the stage of tight international oligopolies, it is obvious that FDI through acquisition is likely to raise the level of international concentration across a wider range of industries. The danger, as Hymer and Rowthorn (1970) pointed out, is that once a certain level of market concentration is achieved, dominant enterprises will abandon rivalistic behaviour and resort to collusion. Collusive pricing behaviour is already commonplace in sectors oriented towards local, regional or even national markets, but particularly where some kind of product differentiation exists for national markets recent evidence suggests that even industries oriented towards international markets are not immune.

The relatively high cost of automobiles in the UK compared to other EEC countries has recently been the subject of an investigation by the competition authority (EEC 1982). The investigation found that prices for the same model were generally higher in member countries with dominant manufacturers; elsewhere competition between importers resulted in lower retail prices. Thus the price differential between the UK and Belgium for the same model rose from 14 per cent in 1976 to 40 per cent in 1982. The ability of the major manufacturers to maintain high prices in the UK arises from their monopolization of the market for right-hand drive cars and their refusal to sell to continental dealers for re-importation into the UK. It also arises from their control over imports into the UK, an increasing proportion of which are intra-company. Between 1974 and 1979, for example, related (intra-firm) imports of automobiles increased from negligible proportions to account for over one-fifth of the total UK market, while the share of competitive imports hardly increased at all. The manufacturers thus appear to be capitalizing on a situation in which they have the double advantage of low production costs in Europe and high returns in the UK. In so far as high prices have reduced demand for cars in the UK the existence of the international car oligopoly may thus have contributed to increased over-capacity and reduced output and employment.

Balance of payments implications

The increase in related imports in the automobile industry raises the question of whether FDI has played a part in the UK's deteriorating balance of payments situation in manufactured goods.In 1983, for the first time since the Industrial Revolution, the value of UK finished manufactured imports exceeded that of exports and it was only the contribution of North Sea oil which prevented a serious deterioration in the UK's visible trade balance. Unfortunately, data on related imports are not generally available, so that it is difficult to assess how much of the increased import penetration is attributable to increased overseas production by multinationals already manufacturing in the UK. Certainly, during the last few years, the UK has had a substantial and growing visible trade deficit with Western Europe from which a high proportion of 'non-competitive' imports are likely to have originated. On the other hand, the fact that Japanese import penetration has also been increasing suggests that 'competitive' imports have also made some contribution. However, it is important to bear in mind that, even in 1983, when Japanese imports were at a maximum, they still only accounted for less than 10 per cent of imported manufactured goods.

A number of recent studies have in fact provided indirect evidence on this issue by showing that industries with high or rapidly increasing levels of concentration (Pickering & Sheldon 1984), or with high levels of MNC participation (Panic & Joyce 1980, Utton & Morgan 1983) have been characterized by an above average deterioration in their international trade performance during the 1970s. For example, Pickering and Sheldon found that product groups (MLHs) with the greatest increases in concentration during the 1960s or with high five firm concentration ratios at the beginning of the 1970s had the weakest international trade performances during the 1970s. The authors consider that market dominance, apart from discouraging MNCs actively to seek out export markets, also increases import penetration as customer firms turn to alternative overseas sources of supply in the face of higher domestic prices. As argued previously, increased international integration of production activities may also be at the root of the problem, particularly since the UK's entry into the EEC, which may have encouraged some MNCs to service the market externally from production sites in Europe (Hood & Young 1982b).

The extent to which these developments will exacerbate differences in the relative economic performance of the major industrialized countries, however, depends largely on the extent to which FDI flows represent *diversion* of investment from the source to the host nation. As a high proportion of UK outward investment to the USA is through acquisition, it is unlikely to represent diverted investment if the objective is to secure a market foothold in the USA. Nevertheless, there is still the possibility of supplying the UK market from acquired plants abroad. Cowling (1983), for example, has argued that, faced with declining demand, multinationals will prefer to rationalize production in lower income, slower growing markets which they will then service externally from higher income, faster growing markets. Although there has been a big increase in import penetration across a wide range of manufactured goods in the UK, information on the origin of these imports is extremely scanty.

In considering the relationship between FDI and de-industrialization in the UK therefore, account must also be taken of the links between FDI and import penetration. Another important link to be taken into account is that between FDI and export replacement. For example Holland (1979) has argued that as FDI normally follows exports, there will be a marked tendency for substitution to occur. He quotes evidence produced by the Labour Research Department that larger UK multinationals have a very low share of exports in national production compared to their smaller counterparts; if the latter have gone abroad more recently, as seems likely, increasing experience abroad should lead to export replacement.

Recent evidence provided by Gaffikin and Nickson (1984) for the West Midlands also tends to support the view that FDI does not have a beneficial effect upon exports. Earlier it was stated that the ten 'prime mover' firms in this region have been responsible for a high proportion of the job losses since 1978. That this represents a shift in the productive base of these companies abroad, and not merely the introduction of more capital-intensive processes in the UK, is suggested by a corresponding decline in the UK share of world-wide turnover; the value of overseas sales of these ten firms increased at five times the UK rate and in all cases there was a decrease in the British share of global turnover (Table 3.6). The authors consider that the productive shift abroad is probably understated because of the ability of multinationals to conceal the value of overseas production through transfer pricing and the exclusion of the production of associated companies overseas. Finally, they provide evidence that FDI by these companies did not have a beneficial effect upon UK exports, as is often claimed; in fact the contribution of UK exports to

Table 3.6 Ten major West Midlands companies: changes in distribution of global workforce and turnover and contribution of UK exports to overseas sales.

	UK share of employment		UK share of turnover (£m)		Share of UK exports in overseas sales (£m)	
	1978 (%)	1982 (%)	1978 (%)	1982 (%)	1978 (%)	1982 (%)
GEC	85	76	79	66	54	39
GKN	67	52	69	52	26	16
Cadbury	62	60	63	54	12	10
Dunlop	48	42	40	33	15	11
Lucas	81	73	69	65	25	30
TI	86	82	83	71	51	34
IMI	80	75	81	70	50	35
Delta	80	71	78	71	42	29
Glynwed	80	66	89	67	26	13
BSR	95	44	81	33	73	10
weighted average	75	67	70	59	35	26

Source: Gaffikin and Nickson (1984), Tables 4.6, 4.7 and 4.9.

overseas sales fell by 9 per cent during this period, as a higher proportion of overseas sales was accounted for by overseas production.

(It should be noted, however, that intra-firm imports also make a contribution to UK sales figures. In the absence of import data, Gaffikin and Nickson have been forced to assume that imports have not accounted for a higher or lower share of UK sales in 1982 than in 1978. If intra-firm import penetration increased during this period, the share of turnover accounted for by UK production will have declined even more dramatically. Conversely if intra-firm import penetration decreased the decline will be less pronounced than is shown in Table 3.6.)

In considering the balance of payments effects of FDI, it is important also to consider the *type* as well as the quantity of investment flowing into and out of the UK. Dunning (1979b) suggests that the UK has benefited from a high proportion of inward investment in high technology sectors compared to a high proportion of outward investment in low technology sectors. Both Dicken (1982) and Panic (1982) have provided evidence that this difference may have been disappearing during the 1970s and in fact more recent evidence from the 1981 *Census of overseas assets* (DTI 1984a) suggests that the industrial structure of inward and outward capital flows has tended to converge. Between 1978 and 1981, for example, as Table 3.7 shows, the greatest relative increase in the book value of UK assets overseas occurred in the five industrial sectors classified by Dunning (1979b) as being 'more technology intensive'. In contrast, three of the five sectors in which book values of foreign assets in the UK increased most rapidly during this period – food, drink and tobacco, metal manufacture, and paper, printing and publishing – were classified as 'less technology intensive'. This is the first clear evidence of a reversal in the traditional structure of outward and inward FDI flows and supports the contention that high value added investment is now leaving the UK, which in turn is increasingly attracting low value added investment. The long run effect of this change may be to exacerbate balance of payments problems through an increase in high value added imports and a decrease in high value added exports.

It has also been suggested that relatively low unit labour costs, and low incomes, will increasingly attract low value added production to the UK, while UK multinationals produce a higher proportion of their sophisticated products overseas in higher income markets. Hood and Young (1982a) also provide indirect support for this view by pointing out that the share of R&D employment of US foreign affiliates in the UK fell between 1975 and 1978 whereas their share of total employment continued to rise. The same authors have noted

Table 3.7 Relative changes in the book value of UK assets overseas and foreign assets in the UK by industrial sector, 1978–81.

		1978–81		
Industrial sector	1978 A/B ratio	A UK assets overseas (% change)	B Foreign assets in UK (% change)	1981 A/B ratio
food, drink and tobacco (L)	2.91	31.7	75.6	2.18
chemicals and allied industries (M)	2.27	53.0	83.7	1.89
metal manufacture	1.44	−40.8	74.6	0.49
mechanical and instrument engineering (M)	0.40	44.5	22.6	0.47
electrical engineering (M)	0.97	35.0	50.5	0.92
vehicles and components (M)	0.25	143.7	48.7	0.41
textiles, leather, clothing and footwear (L)	6.74	12.3	31.2	5.77
paper, printing and publishing (L)	2.06	4.7	62.2	1.33
rubber (M)	0.89	82.7	3.1	1.58
other manufacturing including shipbuilding (L)	2.21	14.1	19.2	2.11
total	1.50	33.1	50.1	1.33

Source: DTI (1981, 1984a).

(L), Less technology intensive sector; (M) more technology intensive sector (Dunning, 1979).

the high propensity for UK multinationals to invest through acquisition in the USA between 1974 and 1978 and suggest that access to high technology was a major motive (Young & Hood 1980). In this case, the possibility of supplying the UK market with high technology products seems very real. In fact, several recent reports by the Monopolies and Mergers Commission bewail the increasing level of imports of high technology goods into the UK, and the inability of domestic producers to compete with these imports (e.g. Monopolies & Mergers Commission 1980), The similarity to the situation of external technological dependence which has given rise to increasing concern in Australia and Canada is striking; in so far as the competitiveness of domestic manufacturing is reduced, FDI in high technology industries is thus likely to reinforce the growth differences between industrialized nations.

Conclusion

This chapter has emphasized the significance of the growth of the net manufacturing FDI deficit in the UK as the rate of outward investment has gradually outpaced the rate of inward investment. It has often been suggested that the investment deficit has arisen because the UK is no longer a favourable production site for MNCs in view of higher production costs (notably due to labour) and lower productivity. These same factors have also been held to be responsible for the contraction of UK MNC and nationally based firms alike to the extent that goods produced in the UK are relatively expensive.

An alternative view raised by the present authors places emphasis on the significance of relatively high levels of industrial concentration and international integration in the UK economy. As far as the 'de-industrialization' issue is concerned, this view has the following implications:

(a) The development of internationally integrated production makes it almost impossible to assess the extent of the damage caused by high production costs and low productivity in one country: when profits obtained through oligopolistic practices reduce the need to lower production costs; when MNCs have increased opportunities for transfer pricing; when they are much less reliant upon local (national) linkages; and when the profitability of individual sites assumes less importance than the net profit margin of the corporation as a whole.

(b) The net manufacturing FDI gap may well have a lot more to do with Britain being less attractive not so much because of poor returns on investment but because the level of market concentration and monopoly control acts as a disincentive for inward investment and promotes outward investment irrespective of location costs. Further, the investment gap may be connected with the problem of excess capacity, in so far as market saturation in the UK has discouraged market-oriented inward investment and fostered the need for MNCs in the UK to reorganize capacity internationally in the search for new economies. This has perhaps been reflected in very severe rationalization of capacity by the largest UK-based MNCs during the current recession (Lloyd & Shutt 1983, Stopford & Dunning 1983, Gaffikin & Nickson 1984).

(c) It should be realized that the collapse of small and medium-sized firms in the UK has more to do with unfavourable terms of competition against the MNCs which dominate their product markets than with their inability to compete in a 'free market'. It should be recalled that a good proportion of UK imports are intra-company and not from Third World countries, Japan or America. Evidence from the Monopolies and Mergers Commission on unfair pricing practices by MNCs in several industrial sectors also suggests that the real threat to the SMEs has come from these corporations, rather than from foreign sources.

In conclusion, the effect of the internationalization process on the UK, already a heavily concentrated economy, has been particularly dramatic, representing de-industrialization on a massive scale, which is being aggravated by the present government's suicidal vogue for liberalization. Further, in the light of the recent shift in the structure of FDI, the growth prospects which remain are not very encouraging; on this evidence the UK may shortly become a semi-peripheral economy within the international capitalist hierarchy, increasingly dependent upon imported technology and with increasingly severe balance of payments problems.

References

Aglietta, M. 1979. *A theory of capitalist regulation*. London: New Left Books.
Aglietta, M. 1982. World capitalism in the eighties. *New Left Review* **136**, 5–41.
Altvater, E. 1983. *The insolvency of highly indebted Third World countries*. Mimeo., The Free University of Berlin.
Andreff, W. 1984. The international centralization of capital and the re-ordering of world capitalism. *Capital and Class* **22**, 58–79.
Anon. 1985. Big business: takeover mania. *Labour Research* January, 19–21.

Boyer, R. 1979. La crise actuelle: une mise en perspective historique, *Critiques de l'Economie Politique*, 7–8.

Coakley, J. 1984. The internationalization of bank capital. *Capital and Class* **23**, 107–120.
Cowling, K. 1982. *Monopoly capitalism*. London: Macmillan.
Cowling, K. 1983. Excess capacity and the degree of collusion: oligopoly behaviour in the slump. *The Manchester School* **4**, 341–59.
Curhan, J., W. Davidson and R. Suri 1977. *Tracing the multinationals: a source book on US-based enterprises*. Cambridge, Mass.: MIT Press.

DTI 1981. *Census of overseas assets 1978*. London: HMSO.
DTI 1984a. *Census of overseas assets 1981*. London: HMSO.
DTI 1984b. *Business Monitor MA4: Overseas Transactions*. London: HMSO.
De Vroey, M. 1983. La crise actuelle: diagnostique et enjeux strategiques. *Working Paper 8304*, Catholic University of Louvain.
Dicken, P. 1982. Recent trends in international direct investment with particular reference to the United States and the United Kingdom. In

Geographical agenda for a changing world, B. T. Robson and J. Rees (eds). SSRC, London.

Dunning, J. H. 1979a. Explaining changing patterns of international production: in defence of the eclectic theory. *Oxford Bulletin of Economics and Statistics* **41**, 269–95.

Dunning, J. H. 1979b. The UK's international direct investment position in the mid-1970s. *Lloyds Bank Review* **132** (2), 1–21.

EEC 1982. *12th report on competition policy*. Brussels: European Commission.

EEC 1984. *13th report on competition policy*. Brussels: European Commission.

Fine, B. 1979. World economic crisis and inflation: what bourgeois economics says and why it is wrong. In *Issues in political economy*, F. Green and P. Nore (eds): 174–207. London: Macmillan.

Gaffikin, F. and A. Nickson 1984. *Job crisis and the multinationals: deindustrialisation in the West Midlands*. Birmingham: Third World Books.

Helleiner, G. 1981. Intra-firm trade and the developing countries: an assessment of the data. In *Multinationals beyond the market*, R. Murray (ed.): 31–67. Brighton: Harvester Press.

Holland, S. 1979. Comment on Morgan, A. D.: 'Foreign manufacturing by UK firms. In *Deindustrialisation*, F. Blackaby (ed.): London: Heinemann.

Hood, N. and S. Young 1981. Recent strategic expansions by British Corporations in the United States. *Working Paper 8109*, University of Strathclyde Business School.

Hood, N. and S. Young 1982a. US multinationals R & D: corporate strategies and policy implications for the UK. *Multinational Business* **2**, 10–23.

Hood, N. and S. Young 1982b. *Multinationals in retreat: the Scottish experience*. Edinburgh: Edinburgh University Press.

Hood, N., A. Reeves and S. Young 1981. Foreign direct investment in Scotland: the European dimension. *Scottish Journal of Political Economy* **28**, 165–84.

Hymer, S. 1960. *The international operations of national firms: a study of direct foreign investment*. Cambridge, Mass.: MIT Press.

Hymer, S. and R. Rowthorn 1970. Multinational corporations and international oligopoly: the non-American challenge. In *The international corporation*, C. P. Kindleberger (ed.). Cambridge, Mass.: MIT Press.

Itoh, M. 1980. *Value and crisis*. New York: Monthly Review Press.

Itoh, M. 1983. The great world depression and Japanese capitalism. *Capital and Class* **21**, 49–60.

Kindleberger, C. 1969. *American business abroad*. New Haven, Conn.: Yale University Press.

Lall, S. (ed.) 1983. *The new multinationals: the spread of Third World enterprises*. New York: Wiley.

Lall, S. and N. S. Siddarthan 1982. The monopolistic advantages of multinationals: lessons from foreign investment in the US. *The Economic Journal* **92**, 668–83.

Lipietz, A. 1982. Towards global Fordism? *New Left Review* **132**, 33–47.

Lipietz, A. 1984. Imperialism or the Beast of the Apocalypse. *Capital and Class* **22**, 81–109.

Lloyd, P. and J. Shutt 1983. *Recession and restructuring in the North West Region: the policy implications of recent events.* Discussion Paper 13. North West Industry Research Unit, Manchester University.

Michalet, C. A. 1979. Les BMN: nouvelle vague des multinationales. *Les Cahiers francais* **190**, 47–54.

Michalet, C. A. 1983. Multinationals: change of strategy in the face of crisis. *Multinational Business* **1**, 1–10.

Mistral, J. 1982. La diffusion internationale de l'accumulation intensive et sa crise. In *Economie et finance internationales,* J. L. Reiffers (ed.). Paris: Dunod.

Monopolies and Mergers Commission 1980. *Domestic gas appliances: a report on the supply of certain domestic gas appliances in the United Kingdom.* London: HMSO.

Monopolies and Mergers Commission 1982. *Charter Consolidated PLC and Anderson Strathclyde PLC: a report on the proposed merger,* Cmnd 8771. London, HMSO.

Mucchielli, J. L. and J. P. Thuillier 1982. *Multinationales européennes et investissements croises.* Paris: Economica.

Negandhi, A. and B. Baliga 1981. *Tables are turning: German and Japanese multinational companies in the United States.* Cambridge, Mass.: Oelgeschlager, Gunn and Hain.

OECD 1981. *International investment and multinational enterprises: recent international direct investment trends.* Paris: OECD.

Olle, W. and W. Shoeller 1982. Direct investment and monopoly theories of imperialism. *Capital and Class* **16**, 41–60.

Panic, M. 1982. International direct investment in conditions of structural disequilibrium: UK experience since the 1960s. In *International capital movements*, J. Black and J. H. Dunning (eds). London: Macmillan.

Panic, M. and P. L. Joyce 1980. UK manufacturing industry: international integration and trade performance. *Bank of England Quarterly Bulletin* March 1980.

Pickering, J. F. and I. M. Sheldon 1984. International trade performance and concentration in British industry. *Applied Economics* **16**, 421–42.

Quiers-Valette, S. 1979. L'investissement mondial des FMN: les nouveaux challengers face an geant americain. *Les Cahiers francais* **190**, 18–22.

Radice, H. 1984. The national economy – a Keynesian myth? *Capital and Class* **22**, 111–140.

Smith, I. J. 1982. The role of acquisition in the spatial distribution of the foreign manufacturing sector in the United Kingdom. In *The geography of multinationals*, M. Taylor and N. J. Thrift (eds). London: Croom Helm.

Smith, I. J. 1985. Foreign direct investment and divestment trends in industrialised countries since the mid-1960s. In *Progress in industrial geography*, M. Pacione (ed.). London: Croom Helm.

Stopford, I. M. and J. H. Dunning 1983. *Multinationals: company performances and global trends.* London: Macmillan.

Sutcliffe, B. 1984. *Hard Times*. London: Pluto.

UN 1978. *Transnational corporations in world development: a re-examination*, New York, United Nations.

UN 1983. *Transnational corporations in world development*. New York: United Nations.

UNCTAD 1978. *Dominant positions of market power of transnational corporations*. New York: United Nations.

Utton, M. A. and A. D. Morgan 1983. *Concentration and foreign trade*. National Institute of Economic and Social Research, Occasional Paper 35. Cambridge University Press, Cambridge.

Young, S. and N. Hood 1980. Recent patterns of foreign direct investment by British multinational enterprises in the United States. *National Westminster Bank Review* **2**, 20–32.

4 The regional implications of inward direct investment

S. YOUNG and D. STEWART

The effects of inward direct investment in the UK

Interest in issues relating to the effects of foreign multinationals (MNEs) in the UK as a whole has been spasmodic. Beginning with the optimistic findings of the Steuer Report (1973) and supported by the generally favourable economic indicators relating to multinational versus indigenous company performance, a positive attitude emerged toward foreign direct investment (FDI). In this same vein, a recent review by Stopford (1979), as part of wider ILO work (ILO 1981) on the employment effects of MNEs, argued that measured against competitors in the same industry MNEs have had substantially higher rates of per capita output, recorded growth in employment in all but one sector, and paid equal or marginally higher wages. It was argued that even allowing for the possibilities of distortion due to growth from the acquisition of UK firms, this record was an 'impressive testimony of the beneficial effects on the UK economy of the foreign presence' (Stopford 1979, p. 44).

With the reduced flows of mobile international direct investment, increased competition for this investment and high unemployment domestically, the assessment of impact in terms of jobs and job-related issues is inevitable. Nevertheless, as Table 4.1 indicates, a complete evaluation of the effects of multinational enterprises would require a more in-depth and a wider study. While broadly accepting the positive effects of FDI, the narrowness of the debate in the UK has meant that important issues are only now beginning to be given some attention. These include, for example, questions relating to input sourcing and local content, sparked off by the strategies of the Japanese consumer electronics companies and the production and sourcing policies of the American motor manufacturers.

What has been largely absent in the UK, furthermore, has been much discussion of the alternative means of obtaining the benefits

Table 4.1 Some criteria for evaluating the effects of multinational enterprises. *

Employment and related	Technology transfer and innovation	Output, productivity, value added, profitability	Economic structure and competition	Trade and linkage effects	Decision-making and control
level (and cost) of job creation (gross and net, including role of acquisitions, displacement of domestic employment)	introduction of new products and processes (and lags compared with introduction elsewhere)	previous factors, plus managerial organization and control, planning, etc.	number and size of firms	destination of sales	location of headquarters' functions
			product and process structure	control of sales destinations	decision-making authority of head-quarters functions
	terms of technology transfers	production technology	economic power and control	sourcing of inputs (and local content issue)	
employment stability		degree of in-house manufacture		control of input sources	
sectoral mix and penetration	forms of technology transfers (packaged/unpackaged, embodied/disembodied)	specialization of output		intra-MNE exports and imports	
nationality of ownership mix		financial performance		service and financial linkages	
concentration by size of enterprises	existence of and nature of local R&D (relation to corporate R&D)			relationship with local suppliers	

locational
concentration

skill breakdown

qualification
breakdown

sex breakdown

wage and salary
levels

training of manage-
ment and labour
force

employment of local
versus expatriate
personnel

labour relations
practices and
performance

organization and
mechanisms for
incorporating
R&D into
production)

technological
concentration and
dependence

* Most of these factors are significant for both regional and national economies, but in the latter instance other variables would need to be included, such as those relating to the balance of payments – dividend remittances, licence and management fees, capital inflows, etc. No attempt has been made to derive first or second order consequences of these criteria. For a general classification of the first and second order consequences see Biersteker (1978), and on the market structure and competition question specifically see Dunning (1974). Many of the criteria could be either positive or negative in terms of their impact on the regional economy depending on circumstances, objectives, etc. Foreign MNEs would, moreover, need to be compared with British MNEs, multi-location national firms and single location national firms. There is also the cost of attaining a particular position to be considered, in relation to the alternatives.

accruing from multinationals and the relative cost. The question of 'debundling' the foreign direct investment package and 'rebundling' through joint ventures, licensing arrangements, management contracts and collaboration agreements have been in the forefront of the minds of policymakers in other countries for a good many years. Aside from these points, dynamic questions relating to the way in which multinational corporate strategy may change the balance between benefit and cost over time have only begun to be considered (Hood & Young 1980, 1982).

Given the prevailing views about inward investment, UK policy has emphasized the attraction of multinationals. A number of recent pieces of work have begun to question the 'value for money' of this policy (Brech & Sharp 1984), and the awareness of the government itself has been shown in its recent White Paper on regional policy (Secretary of State for Trade and Industry 1983). Other work has attempted to suggest policy possibilities for improving the contribution of existing MNE subsidiaries in some of the areas noted in Table 4.1, while maintaining the competitiveness of the UK attraction effort (Hood & Young 1983). It should be added, as a final point in this introductory section, that from a policy perspective greater attention has attached recently not to the effects of inward investing MNEs *per se* but rather to outward/inward balance questions and the behaviour of British multinationals; the latter theme is taken up elsewhere in this volume.

Inward direct investment in the UK regions

At the regional level, there has been a much more continuing interest in the multinational phenomenon, a consequence of the general concern over external control (of which MNEs represent the extreme example) and the regional aid focus of policy in the UK. Much of the interest has again stressed job issues: employment creation and the role of regional policy (see Department of Trade and Industry 1983 for a recent summary of the evidence); the relative responsiveness of multinational and indigenous firms to regional policy instruments in terms of employment and firm moves (in the latter case, see Ashcroft and Ingham 1982); acquisition versus greenfield entry methods (Smith 1980); the contribution of multinationals to regional equilibrium or disequilibrium (Dunning 1981).

While the conclusions on these topics are not wholly consistent, a number of points can be made. During the 1960s, FDI made a substantial contribution towards a reduction in regional employment inequalities, but this trend stopped in the late 1970s with a slightly greater increase in foreign-owned employment in the non-

Table 4.2   Large plant closures in the UK, 1978–82.

| | Closures of plants employing more than 500 people in 1978 | | | | |
	England	Wales	Scotland	Northern Ireland	UK
total manufacturing (no. of plants)	243	10	24	9	286
foreign-owned manufacturing (no. of plants)	32	3	8	5	48
foreign-owned as a percentage of total	13.2%	30.0%	33.3%	55.5%	16.8%

Source: Hansard, 29 February–7 March 1984.

assisted areas. On the other hand, the pattern in the second half of the 1970s seems to have been due chiefly to a high level of acquisition activity by foreign-owned firms in the non-assisted areas, for the assisted regions have continued to attract a very high proportion of greenfield investments (Killick 1983). Related to the above, the stability of multinational employment has been an issue of concern, especially in the recession conditions from the late 1970s. Recent Department of Trade and Industry work (Killick 1982) has shown little difference between foreign-owned and indigenous firms in terms of expansion and contraction. Yet there is still cause for concern, particularly as regards large foreign-owned enterprises, as Table 4.2 shows. The issue of concentration implied by this table also emerges in the context of sector, nationality of ownership and location on a regional basis. Once again, however, the contribution of foreign firms to short term job creation has been regarded as paramount, with fairly little consideration being given to the implications of high concentration and penetration levels.

Discussions on closure rates have been linked to wider questions concerning the nature and characteristics of branch plants in regional economies in the UK. Low proportions of managerial occupations and low levels of research and development activity in the assisted areas are now well established. The conclusion derived from such observations is that the capacity for self-generating growth in the regions will be reduced. On the questions of technology and innovation, it is a fact, however, that there is still an inadequate understanding of technology transfer within the multinational enterprise, the role of local R&D in technology creation and transfer, the linkage between R&D location and manufacturing location, etc. (Malecki 1980, Haug *et al*. 1983, Howells 1984). There is evidence for American MNEs of a shortening in the time lag between product introduction in the USA and introduction abroad (Vernon & Davidson 1979); for some technologies the shortening of product life cycles necessitates almost simultaneous worldwide production and marketing. Both the level of technology and pace of technological advance may therefore be higher in foreign-owned than in indigenous plants in the same region. Of course, plants at the leading edge of technology are likely to be very sensitive with regard to the diffusion of technology. This fact, plus the job mix in foreign-owned facilities and limited linkages with the local economy, may restrict the birth of new independent firms. But this brings in much broader issues relating to whether or not the region itself has a favourable environment for new firm formation, a tradition of entrepreneurial activity and so forth (Watts 1981). On a related theme, there have been allegations that FDI has contributed to the creation of a dual economy in the assisted areas, with the locally oriented indigenous sector being contrasted with an externally controlled sector which maintains its existing backward linkages, meaning supply, administrative and financial ties outside the region.

In comparison with the favourable conclusions relating to the effects of MNEs at national level in the UK, therefore, the view from the assisted areas has been both more cautious and rather more critical. Stress has been placed on the characteristics of the FDI obtained and on longer term and dynamic implications for regional economies. Despite this, the fact remains that it is difficult to deny a substantially positive impact overall; the cost of achieving this is a different matter.

The inter-regional inward direct investment position

Inevitably the most detailed work relating to the implications of FDI has been undertaken at the level of the individual region. Considered in terms of the employment contribution within the assisted areas, MNEs are most important to the economies of Northern Ireland, Wales and then Scotland. Thus the foreign-owned share of all manufacturing employment ranged between 17 and 21½ per cent in these areas in 1981, compared with the figure for the assisted areas in total, of 15.9 per cent, and the UK penetration level of 14.9 per cent (*Business Monitor*, PA1002, 1981). The North is the one region which is truly under-represented in terms of employment contribution.

Looking at the position during the recent recessionary period, it has been concluded that there were no marked differences in most regions in the employment behaviour of foreign-owned and all manufacturing industry (Killick 1982). The two main exceptions to the overall pattern on a regional basis were Wales and Scotland. In Wales surviving foreign-owned plants declined much less than average whereas in Scotland the reverse was true. The position in Scotland is an interesting one. Attention has been centred on the 'retreat of the big multinationals' (Hood & Young 1982), but painstaking work by the Industry Department for Scotland (1983) found that both in terms of closure rates and overall employment performance, branch plants performed better than all other units opened during the same period. In Northern Ireland too, Harrison (1982) noted that employment in foreign-owned projects did not fall as rapidly as overall manufacturing employment in the 1974–79 period. By contrast, in the Northern Region, Smith (1979) established that externally controlled plants were much more vulnerable to closure than those controlled within the region. The high closure rate of (previously independent) plants acquired by companies with their headquarters outside the region was especially important in this pattern.

Traditionally, foreign direct investment has been concentrated in a fairly narrow range of industry sectors, with chemicals, mechanical, instrument and electrical engineering, and vehicles dominating in the UK as in other host developed countries. The mix within regions does differ and the SIC Orders in which the foreign employment share is at least double the share of employment in manufacturing overall are as follows: South East – chemicals, vehicles; Wales – chemicals, electrical engineering; Scotland – mechanical, instrument and electrical engineering; North West – vehicles; North – instrument engineering; Northern Ireland – electrical engineering, other manufacturing industries. These patterns correlate reasonably in some areas with patterns of manufacturing industry as a whole, and suggest that the regions possess certain locational characteristics which are attractive to particular types of industry irrespective of ownership.

Descriptive data are also available on the output and productivity performance of MNEs in the regions. In terms of net output per employee there was generally a small but consistent balance in favour of foreign-owned enterprises in the assisted areas throughout the period 1971–81. Among the assisted areas themselves quite wide differences exist both in terms of net output per employee in the foreign sector and in comparisons of foreign-owned and all manufacturing performance. Net output per employee among foreign firms was highest in Scotland in 1981 (*Business Monitor*, PA1002, 1981); this represented a marked improvement in comparison with earlier years and was presumably related to the closures of large, low productivity plants and growth in the electronics sector.

Table 4.3 Some dimensions of the electronics industry (with special reference to foreign direct investment) in Scotland.

(a) Growth of employment in the Scottish electronics industry

	1959	1983
electronics employment	7400	42500
electronics as a percentage of total manufacturing employment	1.1%	9.9%

(b) Offers of selective financial assistance to the electronics industry (Scotland and Great Britain)

	Great Britain	Scotland*	Scotland share of Great Britain (%)
1972–83			
no. of offers	615	174	28.3
offer value (£m)	179	89	49.7
new jobs	74000	31000	41.9
safeguarded jobs	39500	12500	31.6
1979–83			
no. of offers	345	104	30.1
offer value (£m)	127	69	54.3
new jobs	39000	17500	44.9
safeguarded jobs	17000	4500	26.5

(c) Share of employment and units in foreign-owned companies in Scotland (1981)

	Employment	Units
all manufacturing industry	17.0	n.a.
electronics industry	47.9†	30.0
of which:		
(MLH 354) scientific and industrial instruments and systems	51.2	21.4
(MLH 363) telegraph and telephone apparatus and equipment	38.2	40.0
(MLH 364) radio and electronic components	78.1	43.6
(MLH 365) broadcast, recording and sound reproduction equipment	n.a.	14.3
(MLH 366) electronic computers	94.0	50.0
(MLH 367) radio, radar and electronic capital goods	3.1	16.7

(d) Share of female employment in the electronics industry in Scotland (1978)

	MLH						Total
	354	363	364	365	366	367	
female share (%)	39.8	59.5	63.4	52.8	28.7	26.9	44.9

(e) Market destination for Scottish electronics industry production (1978)

	Percentage of production	
Destination	USA-owned firms	All firms
Scotland	7	7
rest of UK	31	55
exports	62	38

(f) Purchase of components and subcontract services by Scottish electronics OEMs (1979)

Origin	Percentage of purchases
Scotland	19
rest of UK	49
imports	32

Sources: Original sources are the Scottish Manufacturing Establishments Register (SCOMER); Booz, Allen & Hamilton; Makrotest; Scottish Development Agency; Scottish Council (Development and Industry), but mostly reproduced from Young and Reeves (1984) and Firn and Roberts (1984). Item (b) was provided by the Industry Department for Scotland in private correspondence and item (d) is from SCOMER.

Note: Electronics industry taken to encompass MLHs 354 and 363–367, but slightly different definitions may have been used in consultants' studies. The one additional figure which is interesting covers net output per head in Scotland in relation to that for the UK electronics industry as a whole. In 1979 the figure was 114.8 (Scotland as a percentage of UK).

* Data relate to indigenous and foreign firms, but, as an example, in the 1979–82 period 88 per cent of offers by value were to foreign companies.

† More up-to-date figures (based on a June 1983 survey by the Scottish Development Agency) indicate that of the employment in non-overseas owned companies, 16.5 per cent was accounted for by Scottish-owned enterprises.

Equal interest attaches to recent and likely future trends across these dimensions. In terms of nationality of ownership, the position of Japanese FDI is interesting (Dicken 1983). While still very small, the locational concentration of this in Wales and Scotland may be of major significance because of the strong likelihood of new entrants and the evidence on clustering among Japanese companies. On a sectoral basis, the electronics industry is especially important for the future. The data in Table 4.3 indicate that Scotland has been the most favoured assisted area, and together with the South East of England accounts for the bulk of electronics industry employment. The Scottish share of new jobs associated with 'selective financial assistance' (SFA) offers in Great Britain was 45 per cent for the 1979–83 period and was set to rise substantially above that for 1984.

Besides showing the way in which the regional employment impact differs in the fastest growing sector of foreign direct investment, the items in Table 4.3 also indicate some of the problems which arise when trying to evaluate the effects of multinational enterprises on a regional or national basis in host countries. Thus the foreign-owned component of the industry is very high and rising (as the figures on SFA offers show). About 45 per cent of the workforce are women, rising to nearly two-thirds in some segments (especially the rapidly growing semiconductor sector). It is also true that many of the MNE subsidiaries in electronics employ a high proportion of graduates. For a company like IBM in Scotland, about 30 per cent of employees are graduates (Young 1984). Yet even this has been interpreted differently by observers. On the one hand, a high graduate employment may be seen as improving the status of multinational subsidiaries; on the other hand, it could be seen as a form of brain drain, depriving indigenous companies of skilled labour. The ambiguity of the conclusions to be drawn could be seen again in relation to the very low level of unionization in multinational plants in Scotland. On the trade side, the impressive export record of the companies (especially US-owned firms) has to be set against the low linkages with the regional economy in Scotland.

The issues which emerge in this electronics case are in many respects no different from those identified elsewhere in the multinational sector. Where electronics does stand out is in terms of its growth rate, the dominance of the USA and Japan in the relevant technologies and the globally integrated nature of companies within the industry. To a greater extent than in the past, therefore, the policy option of trying to stimulate indigenous growth as opposed to relying on multinationals may not exist (but see Oakey 1983).

Overall, the implications of foreign direct investment are rather different as between regions when consideration is taken of the industry breakdown of multinational activity and differential employment performance in the recent past. Prevailing trends in the ownership and industry mix of FDI, when taken together with other factors such as the conflict in Northern Ireland, may well widen the gulf between the assisted areas in terms of foreign ownership. What has yet to be established is whether or not there are differences in the characteristics and behaviour of multinationals inter-regionally. This is best handled on an industry basis to eliminate inter-sectoral variations, and is dealt with in the next section.

Inward direct investment in the UK regions and the Republic of Ireland in the chemical, mechanical and electrical engineering industries.

A fairly large scale survey study has been published recently (Hood & Young 1983), based on a sample of 140 foreign multinational affiliates operating within various assisted areas in the UK as well as in the South East of England and the Irish Republic. The sample was equally divided between American and Continental European MNEs and focused on three industry sectors: chemicals, mechanical engineering and electrical engineering. It thus facilitates some direct comparisons between similar multinationals operating in different regions. The information obtained from the sample companies by personal interviews ranged quite widely, considering locational determinants and entry methods, patterns of multinationality in the UK and Europe, the influence of regional incentives on investment and reinvestment, plant characteristics, product characteristics and markets, workforce characteristics, management functions and plant performance.

In the published report, various differences were identified in the nature of multinational activity in the regions studied. For the assisted areas, these major differences are highlighted in Table 4.4. It seemed, however, that the subsidiaries operating in the South East and in the Irish Republic were rather more distinctive than those operating in the various assisted areas. In comparison with the assisted area establishments, the South East sample was characterized by higher acquisition propensity; lower capital intensity and some-what higher skill intensity; greater sales orientation towards the UK market; and a higher degree of integration into parent company distribution systems; a much higher representation of sales offices; and, more generally, in management, and especially in marketing and finance terms the South East establishments were of higher status. Lower unionization levels, and a much smaller decline in employment between the year of peak employment and 1980 were

Table 4.4 Some differences* in multinational activity within the assisted areas.

	Above average	Below average
Background and affiliate characteristics		
size of plants (employment)	Scotland	Wales, North, Northern Ireland
sales value per employee	North West, North	Wales, Scotland
incidence of greenfield entry	Scotland, North, Northern Ireland	Wales, North West
incidence of administrative functions at plant	Scotland, North West	Wales, North, Northern Ireland
number of other group plants in Europe	Wales, North West	Northern Ireland
Locational determinants		
importance of UK market access	North West, North	—
importance of government financial assistance	North, Northern Ireland	Wales
importance of available acquisitions	Wales, North West	Northern Ireland
Plant characteristics		
capital employed per employee	Northern Ireland	Scotland, North
decline in costs with larger plant size	North, Northern Ireland	Scotland
material costs as a percentage of total costs	—	Scotland
direct labour costs as a percentage of total costs	Northern Ireland	Wales
Product characteristics and markets		
incidence of single source activity	Scotland	North, Northern Ireland
UK orientation of 1980 output	North West	Wales, Northern Ireland
percentage of inputs from within region	Scotland, North West, North	Wales, Northern Ireland
net exports	Scotland, Wales, Northern Ireland	North West, North
Workforce characteristics		
ratio of 1980 to peak employment	Wales, North West, North	Northern Ireland
percentage of managerial and professional personnel	Northern Ireland	Wales, North
percentage of labourers and other manual workers	North, Northern Ireland	Wales, North West
percentage of male employment	North West	Scotland
incidence of non-unionization	Scotland, North West	Wales, North, Northern Ireland
absence of strikes and stoppages	Scotland	North, Northern Ireland

Source: Hood and Young (1983), Table 3.17.
* There is no implication of statistical significance in the observed differences recorded here.

further characteristics of the manufacturing facilities in the South East. These results run broadly in line with expectations.

The multinational subsidiaries operating within the three industries in the Republic of Ireland were also rather distinctive. Characteristics of the Irish affiliates included relatively small plant size, which could not be satisfactorily explained by recent entry dates; somewhat lower plant status; lower capital employed per head and a higher proportion of blue collar workers in Irish than in assisted area establishments; a higher level of unionization and a rather poorer performance in terms of strikes. In addition, government incentives seemed to be a good deal more important as a locational determinant than was the case in other areas. In this regard both the Irish tax structure and government financial assistance were given substantial weight.

Given these observed differences, it is clearly important to establish the statistical significance of the results, and to identify whether any particular groupings of variables are helpful in distinguishing between areas. To this end, a discriminant analysis was undertaken on the seven regions studied, incorporating most of the variables contained in Table 4.4. The results of this analysis are contained in the appendix to this chapter.

Three discriminant functions accounted for 82 per cent of the variation in the data and were statistically significant at or below the 4 per cent level. The first two functions are represented graphically in Figure 4.1 and the seven regions are positioned on the graph. What is immediately apparent from this is the clustering of the British assisted areas, in contrast with the more distinctly positioned South East, Northern Ireland and Eire. Testing the predictive power of the discriminant functions, the data show that classification was most successful for the latter two regions and especially the Irish Republic, and therefore provides strong support for the differences observed previously.

In an attempt to establish whether clearer differences could be identified between the UK assisted areas only, a further discriminant analysis was undertaken based on the sample of 100 MNE affiliates (Fig. 4.2 & Table 4.7). Within these five regions, Northern Ireland is distinctive (and the predictive success of the discriminant analysis was highest for this area). While the other regions do show differences along the lines of those identified in Table 4.4, predictive success is not improved, thus confirming that regional similarities are more in evidence than regional differences. On a variable by variable analysis (and confirmed by the discriminant functions), there are still, of course, some statistically significant differences between the British assisted areas. These relate, for example, to the incidence of R&D (highest in Scotland, lowest in the North), the

level of net exports per employee (which ranged from £4000 and
£4500 in the North and North West to £8400 and £9100 in Scotland
and Wales), workforce characteristics, trade union recognition, etc.
It should also be added that some of the regional differences are
probably disguised by sectoral variations which swamp inter-
regional variability: this applies to the capital intensity of plant
facilities.

What explanations can be suggested for the patterns of results
observed? The level and nature of regional policy instruments
together with the peripherality of the areas would seem to be
important in explaining the distinctiveness of Northern Ireland and
Eire. The fact that assistance levels are higher in these two regions
than elsewhere in the British Isles shows up in the weight given to
financial aid as a locational determinant; but the different character of
the incentive packages would also be expected to influence the nature
of the FDI. It might be presumed *inter alia* that peripherality would
encourage the establishment of large, capital-intensive facilities,
where economies of scale were important and/or where transport
costs for finished outputs were low. The facilities located in such
peripheral regions might also have wider market area respon-
sibilities. In the case of Northern Ireland, the regional aid package
would reinforce any such tendency, whereas in the Irish Republic
export profits tax relief (of major significance for the companies in
this sample, although now dropped) might have a different impact.

Higher capital intensity of operations and the importance of scale
economies is suggested by the evidence for Northern Ireland; the
high percentage of general labourers and other manual workers in
the labour force (a very important factor distinguishing Northern
Ireland in the discriminant analysis) might also support the general
proposition. Excluding the small number of chemical companies in
the Irish Republic, the operations were markedly less capital intensive than the equivalent plants in the United Kingdom. At the same
time, the proportion of total costs represented by material costs in
Eire was much higher than elsewhere (a point again emerging in the
discriminant analysis), although this is more difficult to encompass
within the simple model outlined here. Finally, the proportion of
sales from plants in Eire to destinations outside the British Isles was
much greater than for any of the other regions studied, and plants in
Northern Ireland too were above average by this measure.

Turning to the South East, the results of the discriminant analysis
are less clear cut statistically, but, as earlier comments have revealed,
the observed differences in comparison with the assisted areas were
mostly in line with expectations and confirm other evidence. For the
British assisted regions, the relative similarity of the overall characteristics of MNE subsidiaries does suggest that peripherality and

regional policy have fostered a particular type of enterprise. Differences do exist in regard to individual dimensions of multinationality: the North seems to occupy a fairly unique position, the discriminant analysis emphasizing the low incidence of R&D, the substantial reduction in costs which could be achieved with increasing plant size (and related to this, facilities were rather small in employment terms and in terms of capital employed), and the high proportion of labourers and other manual occupations in the total workforce. Scotland is positioned at the other extreme on these same characteristics, and it is tempting to argue that the strong policy emphasis placed on inward investment in that region is a factor.

Before concluding these remarks on the factors influencing the nature of multinational operations in the British Isles, it should be noted that some of the observed differences accrue from the entry methods used by MNEs, as between greenfield and acquisition ventures. The nationality of ownership issue is also relevant. Generalizing, it can be concluded that the 'characteristics package' (representing the results across a range of variables) is much more obviously positive for greenfield facilities and US-owned enterprises.

Various implications seem to emerge from the above. In the first place, and relevant to recent discussions on the nature of regional policy, it appears that the character of FDI (as regards capital/skill intensity, etc.) can be changed through government aid schemes. Secondly, the evidence does not seem to offer many pointers to or much hope for raising the status of multinational plants in the regions. If some success has been achieved, as perhaps in Scotland, this is a reflection of fairly intensive activity over a long period. Thirdly, there are obvious implications for the direction of attraction efforts (USA) and for the proposed types of operations (greenfield).

It is interesting to consider these points in relation to the requirements and characteristics of high technology industries, the major growth area in FDI. A recent study of the location of high technology firms and regional economic development in the USA (US Congress 1982) highlighted the labour-intensive nature of production operations, with the companies employing a high percentage of technicians, engineers and scientists. In considering the factors that are important in both the choice of region in the USA for location and the choice within the chosen region, labour skills and labour availability dominated company rankings. However, other factors such as property costs, space for expansion, good transport facilities for people, etc., ranked above market access and vicinity, and proximity to raw material and component supplies. Such facts might seem to offer opportunities for the assisted areas, since the companies are much more footloose than traditional manufacturing firms. The importance of universities and colleges in the provision of workers with the necessary skills (especially at technician level) is also implied. But, in addition, questions have to be asked about the relevance of incentives on capital to such companies.

The issue of raising the status of branch plants is much more problematic. Suggestions have been made regarding the possibility of upgrading MNE affiliates, through the 'additionality' concept in selective financial assistance offers. Whether this offers real possibilities is dubious, in the light of the poor supply of sophisticated business services at local level, and limited demand as the headquarters functions of indigenous companies also move closer to the market centre. In a multinational context, indeed, it may be that as much attention should be given to promoting London and the South East as UK and European headquarters' locations for MNEs, against competition from Brussels, Paris and elsewhere. (On the factors influencing MNE office location, see Dunning & Norman 1979.) It is possible that a greater policy focus on the service sector may encourage multinational service firms to set up branch offices in the assisted areas; but set against this is the low or non-existent autonomy which MNE manufacturing branches have in their purchase of services.

Concluding remarks

This paper has been rather wide ranging but hopefully also forward looking. The main points that seem to emerge are as follows:

(a)   For the UK as a whole, the benefits associated with the foreign manufacturing presence are very real.

(b)   The contribution of multinationals may change considerably during the subsidiaries' life cycles, suggesting that closer attention should be paid to the evolution of corporate strategies internationally.

(c)   At the assisted area level, the same general conclusions apply but there are genuine fears that multinational branch plants may reinforce problems of dependent development.

(d)   The high proportion of greenfield MNE operations in the assisted areas is important, and over time there has been some reduction in inter-regional disparities in the employment contribution of MNEs. The latter may change again for the future with the growth of Japanese FDI and the expansion of electronics investment.

(e)   Inter-regionally within the British Isles, peripherality and regional policy appear to have had some influence on the nature of multinational subsidiaries. Traditional policies may be less relevant to the attraction of skill-intensive, high technology industries. Raising the status and decision-making authority of MNE subsidiaries remains the major but intractable problem at regional level.

(f) Accepting the characteristics of MNEs, it may be that other modes of technological and managerial transfer need to be considered (e.g. support for technology acquisition, management contracting); more innovative approaches taken towards FDI itself (e.g. purchase of equity stakes in foreign enterprises); and more encouragement given to managerial spin-offs from existing MNEs in the UK. In relation to the former two issues, however, existing promotional agencies in the UK are not set up to consider internationalization as a total process, encompassing a range of forms of international involvement.

Appendix: Discriminant analysis of corporate data on multinationals in the British Isles

Discriminant analysis is a statistical technique which enables an observation to be classified into one of a number of pre-selected groups dependent on the number of groups chosen, in this case seven – five UK assisted areas plus the South East of England and the Republic of Ireland. Multiple discriminant analysis derives a linear combination of the characteristics which determine the grouping of the variables. The variables incorporated into the analysis included locational determinants, entry methods, plant characteristics, product characteristics and markets, workforce characteristics and management functions.

Discriminant analysis of the seven regions yielded six discriminant functions. Table 4.5 illustrates the percentage variation explained by each.

Table 4.5 Variation explained by discriminant functions.

Function	Percentage of variation explained	
1	52.5	
2	18.7	82.2
3	11.0	
4	9.4	
5	7.0	
6	1.4	

The first three of these were significant at or below the 4 per cent level and cumulatively accounted for 82.2 per cent of total variation; consequently, the last three can be ignored. To ease graphical interpretation and because the first two functions account for a substantial proportion of the variation (71.2 per cent), these latter were used to highlight important distinctions between affiliates operating in the seven regions.

Examination of the first and most important discriminant function indicates that differences amongst regional affiliates can be explained principally in terms of the following factors:

Function 1	Variable
positive coefficients	importance of government financial assistance as a locational determinant
	percentage of sales within region
	percentage of sales within rest of UK
	incidence of R&D activity
	percentage of sales to rest of world (excluding Europe and the USA)
negative coefficients	days lost in strikes and stoppages
	importance of access to UK market as a locational determinant
	material costs as a percentage of total costs
	percentage of general labourers and other manual occupations in total workforce

Note: Only variables with the highest discriminant coefficients are included.

The above function thus appears to be a contrast between *output* (marketing) factors (positive coefficients) and *input*-related factors (negative coefficients).

The second dimension of discrimination can also be regarded as a contrast but here the interpretation is not clear. The factors that discriminate between the regions are presented below:

Function 2	Variable
positive coefficients	percentage of sales within region
	incidence of headquarters at plant level
	importance of scale economies
	material costs as a percentage of total costs
	incidence of sales offices at plant level

negative coefficients	percentage of sales within rest of UK
	percentage of male workers in labour force
	availability of acquisition as a locational determinant
	percentage of general labourers and other manual occupations in total workforce

Examination of this reveals that the positive factors are essentially affiliate plant characteristics but the negative factors are too broadly dispersed to describe or classify in any meaningful general way.

Figure 4.1 illustrates a mapping of the regions on the above two discriminant functions, and Table 4.6 presents 'hits and misses' results for the regions: the latter indicates that the discriminant analysis has a reasonable level of internal validity although the predictive success varies a good deal between regions. Classification was most successful for the Republic of Ireland (95 per cent) and to a lesser extent Northern Ireland (70 per cent). In the former case, the importance of government financial assistance as a locational determinant, the orientation of output towards Continental Europe and the USA, the high level of material costs in total costs and the greater number of days lost in strikes and stoppages were distinguishing

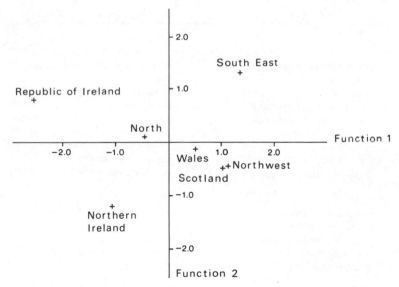

Figure 4.1 Positioning of regions on two major discriminant functions. The values on axes are canonical discriminant functions evaluated at group means.

Table 4.6 'Hits and misses' results.*

	Predicted group (%)				
Actual group	Correct region	South East	British assisted areas	Northern Ireland	Republic of Ireland
South East	65	—	35	—	—
Wales	60	—	25	5	10
Scotland	60	10	25	5	—
North West	65	5	15	15	—
North	55	5	25	15	—
Northern Ireland	70	—	20	—	10
Republic of Ireland	95	—	5	—	—

* Overall percentage of cases correctly classified = 67.1 per cent.

Table 4.7   Variables included in the assisted area discriminant functions.

Positive coefficients	Negative coefficients
function 1	
incidence of R&D activity	percentage of labourers and other
percentage of sales within	manual occupations in total
region	workforce
importance of government	material costs as a percentage of
financial assistance as a	total costs
locational determinant	availability of acquisitions as a
importance of scale	locational determinant
economies	importance of access to UK
percentage of sales within	market as a locational
rest of UK	determinant
function 2	
percentage of managerial	importance of economies of scale
and professional	ratio of 1980 to peak
employees in total	employment
workforce	material costs as a percentage of
sales per employee	total costs
incidence of R&D activity	days lost in strikes and stoppages
availability of acquisitions	
as a locational	
determinant	

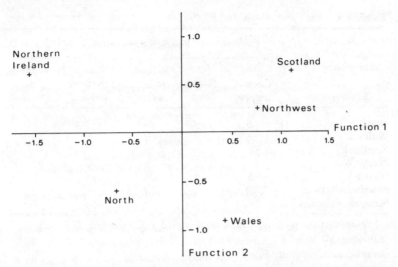

Figure 4.2   Positioning of assisted areas on two major discriminant
functions

factors; in Northern Ireland, government assistance was again significant, as was the proportion of sales made to the UK and Continental Europe, but the most important distinguishing variable was
the high proportion of general labourers and manual workers in the
labour force. What is equally interesting in the results is that despite
the modest predictive success of the discriminant analysis for the
British assisted areas, incorrect prediction resulted in most cases in a
particular region being classified into another British assisted region;
this indicates a good deal of similarity between the areas in terms of
the characteristics analysed.

In an attempt to differentiate more clearly between the UK
assisted areas, a second analysis was undertaken incorporating only
five regions. The discriminant functions emerging were, however,
less clear cut in terms of variable groupings. The overall percentage
of hits was 65 per cent, rising to 80 per cent for Northern Ireland. In
this latter case, to the variables identified above were added a low
incidence of R&D at plant level and a variable proxying the importance of economies of scale (see Figure 4.2 and Table 4.7).

References

Ashcroft, B. K. and K. P. D. Ingham 1982. The comparative impact of UK
regional policy on foreign and indigenous firm movement. *Applied
Economics* **14**, 81–100.

Biersteker, T. J. 1978. *Distortion or development? Contending perspectives on the multinational corporation*. Cambridge, Mass.: MIT Press.

Brech, M. and M. Sharp 1984. *Inward investment*. London: Routledge and Kegan Paul.

Business Statistics Office, *Business Monitor* series, PA1002, London: CSO.

Department of Trade and Industry 1983. *Regional industrial policy: some economic issues*. London: DTI.

Dicken, P. 1983. Japanese manufacturing investment in the UK: a flood or a mere trickle? *Area* **15**, 273–84.

Dunning, J. H. 1974. Multinational enterprises, market structure, economic power and industrial power. *Journal of World Trade Law* **8**, 575–613.

Dunning, J. H. 1981. *International production and the multinational enterprise*. London: Allen & Unwin.

Dunning, J. H. and G. Norman 1979. *Factors influencing the location of offices of multinational enterprises*. London: Location of Offices Bureau.

Firn, J. R. and D. Roberts 1984. High technology industries. In *Industry, policy and the Scottish economy*, N. Hood and S. Young (eds). Edinburgh: Edinburgh University Press.

Harrison, R. T. 1982. Assisted industry, employment stability and industrial decline: some evidence from Northern Ireland. *Regional Studies* **16**, 267–85.

Haug, P., N. Hood and S. Young 1983. R&D intensity in the affiliates of US owned electronics companies manufacturing in Scotland. *Regional Studies* **17**, 383–92.

Hood, N. and S. Young 1980. *European development strategies of US-owned manufacturing companies located in Scotland*. Edinburgh: HMSO.

Hood, N. and S. Young 1982. *Multinationals in retreat: the Scottish experience*. Edinburgh: Edinburgh University Press.

Hood, N. and S. Young 1983. *Multinational investment strategies in the British Isles: a study of MNEs in the assisted areas and in the Republic of Ireland*. London: HMSO.

Howells, J. R. L. 1984. The location of research and development: some observations and evidence from Britain. *Regional Studies* **18**, 13–29.

Industry Department for Scotland 1983. Employment performance of overseas-owned manufacturing units opening in Scotland 1954–77. *Statistical Bulletin* no. A1.1.

International Labour Office 1981. *Employment effects of multinational enterprises in industrialized countries*. Geneva: ILO.

Killick, T. 1982. Employment in foreign-owned manufacturing plants. *British Business* 26 November 1982.

Killick, T. 1983. Manufacturing plant openings, 1976–80: analysis of transfer and branches. *British Business* 17 June 1983.

Malecki, E. J. 1980. Corporate organization of R&D and the location of technological activities. *Regional Studies* **14**, 219–34.

Oakey, R. P. 1983. *Research and development cycles: investment cycles and regional growth in British and American small high technology firms*. Discussion Paper No. 48. CURDS, University of Newcastle.

Secretary of State for Trade and Industry 1983. *Regional industrial development*, Cmnd 9111. London: HMSO.
Smith, I. J. 1979. The effect of external takeovers on manufacturing employment change in the Northern region. *Regional Studies* **13**, 421–38.
Smith, I. J. 1980. *Some aspects of direct inward investment in the United Kingdom with particular reference to the Northern Region*. Discussion Paper No. 31. CURDS, University of Newcastle upon Tyne.
Steuer, M. D., P. Abell, J. Gennard, M. Perlman, R. Rees, B. Scott and K. Wallis 1973. *The impact of foreign direct investment on the United Kingdom*. London: HMSO.
Stopford, J. M. 1979. *Employment effects of multinational enterprises in the United Kingdom*. Working Paper No. 5. Multinational Enterprises Programme. Geneva: ILO.

US Congress, Joint Economic Committee 1982. *Location of high technology firms and regional economic development*. Washington, D.C.: US Government Printing Office.

Vernon, R. and W. H. Davidson 1979. *Foreign production of technology-intensive products by US-based multinational enterprises: report on a study funded by the National Science Foundation*. Mimeo., Boston, Mass.

Watts, H. D. 1981. *The branch plant economy: a study of external control*. London: Longman.

Young, S. 1984. The foreign-owned manufacturing sector. In *Industry, Policy and the Scottish Economy*, N. Hood and S. Young (eds). Edinburgh: Edinburgh University Press.
Young, S. and A. Reeves 1984. The engineering and metals sector. In *Industry, policy and the Scottish economy*, N. Hood and S. Young (eds). Edinburgh: Edinburgh University Press.

5 The role of technical change in national economic development[1]

C. FREEMAN

This chapter discusses the problems of structural change associated with the introduction of major new technologies. It first describes the theoretical framework of the Technical Change and Employment Opportunities Programme (TEMPO) at the Science Policy Research Unit, and seeks to explain the persistence of unemployment in terms of long cycles of economic development. It then briefly summarizes the empirical work which has attempted to relate technical change to the main trends of investment, employment and output in the major sectors of the UK economy since 1948. Finally it discusses the future direction of technical change and some of the policy implications.

Technical change, structural change and long cycles of economic growth

The theoretical framework for the TEMPO project has been set out in a recent book (Freeman *et al.* 1982). This section provides only an outline of the main ideas and then goes on to indicate their relevance for the empirical analysis which formed the main substance of the research programme.

Any satisfactory theory of long term trends in employment and unemployment must take account of the fact that there have been long periods of high growth when the creation of new employment opportunities through technical change and demand expansion far outstripped the displacement of labour in declining occupations and industries. However, it must also take account of the periodic deep crises of structural change experienced in the UK and other countries in the 1880s, the 1930s and the 1980s.

A dynamic economy will always simultaneously experience a process of job loss 'compensated' to some degree by growth of new employment. However, no economist of any stature ever suggested that this 'compensation' mechanism operated without time-lags or in a simple, painless or automatic manner. Surveys of the theory of technical change and employment from Gourvitch (1940) and Neisser (1942) to Heertje (1977), and Cooper and Clark (1982) all confirm this point.

The problem of the time-lags involved in the adjustment of the capital stock and the skills of the labour force to the emergence of radically new technologies and the growth of new branches of industry is generally recognized as one of the most important problems of structural adaptation. Our TEMPO project has been primarily concerned with this problem and we have attempted to tackle it within the framework of Schumpeter's theory of long waves.

During the course of the 20th century we have had two long swings in the conventional wisdom about unemployment: from a relatively optimistic view at the beginning of the century to deep pessimism during the 1930s; then once more to over-optimism in the 1950s and again to deep pessimism in the 1980s. It seems therefore that the beliefs of economists, and of the governments which they advised, were heavily influenced by the experience of the previous decade, and that their notions of the feasibility and desirability of full employment or of low levels of unemployment varied accordingly. Those involved in the business of long term forecasting will recognize this as a familiar syndrome.

Some eminent economists have explicitly assumed that growth rates will remain depressed for a long time. They frequently also did this in the 1930s and 1940s: 'It is my considered guess', said Paul Samuelson (1981), 'that the final quarter of the 20th century will fall far short of the third quarter in its achieved rate of economic progress. The dark horoscope of my old teacher Joseph Schumpeter may have particular relevance here.'

Samuelson's reference to Schumpeter serves to remind us that, rather than simply extrapolate the experience of recent years, it may make more sense to try and understand the long term fluctuations in the behaviour of the economic system. Indeed, this may help to explain the long term changes in the opinions and theories of the economists themselves.

During the 1980s there has been a series of international seminars and conferences on long waves and economic development. Indeed it would be astonishing if the experience of the 1970s and 1980s had not given rise to a revival of interest in such theories. Economists generally refer to these long-cycle theories as 'Kondratiev cycles' or 'Kondratiev long waves' after the Russian economist who directed the Institute of Applied Economic Research in Moscow in the 1920s. Before his premature death, Kondratiev did a great deal to analyse and popularize the idea of long cycles. However, it is true that he was not the originator of the idea. There were many others who, even before World War I, pointed to an apparent tendency for long term series of prices, interest rates and trade to follow a cyclical half-century pattern. Among them were Pareto, Parvus, and the Dutch Marxist, van Gelderen (Barr, 1979).

It was Joseph Schumpeter (1939), who more than any other 20th century economist attempted to explain the cyclical pattern of growth largely in terms of technical and organizational innovation. He suggested that the long cycles of economic development were based on the diffusion of major new technologies, such as the railways and electric power.

In Schumpeter's theory, the ability and initiative of entrepreneurs, drawing upon the discoveries of scientists and inventors, create entirely new opportunities for investment, growth and employment. The profits made from these innovations are then the decisive impulse for new surges of growth, acting as a signal to swarms of imitators. The fact that one or a few innovators can make exceptionally large profits, which they sometimes do, does not of course mean that all the imitators necessarily do so. When the bandwagon starts rolling some people fall off, profits are gradually 'competed away' until recession sets in, and the whole process may be followed by depression before growth starts again with a new wave of technical innovation and organizational and social change.

Whereas in the Keynesian framework the emphasis is on the management of demand, with Schumpeter it is on autonomous investment, embodying new technical innovation which is the basis of economic development. In such a framework economic growth must be viewed primarily as a process of reallocation of resources between industries. That process necessarily leads to structural changes and disequilibrium if only because of the uneven rate of technical change between different industries. Economic growth is not merely *accompanied* by fast growing new industries and the expansion of such industries; it primarily *depends* on that expansion. However, it is not just a question of the rapid expansion of *new* branches of industry but also of the transformation of methods of production in the older branches too.

Schumpeter justified on three grounds his view that technical innovation was more like a series of explosions than a gentle and incessant transformation. First, he argues that innovations are not at any time distributed randomly over the whole economic system, but tend to be concentrated in certain key sectors and their surroundings, and that consequently they are by nature lopsided and disharmonious. Secondly, he argued that the diffusion process is also inherently an uneven one because first a few and then many firms follow in the wake of successful pioneers. Kuznets (1930) had already emphasized the cyclical pattern underlying the growth of new industries. Product life-cycle theory and international trade theory have since confirmed these insights: a hesitant start, fast growth and subsequent saturation followed by decline or stagnation constitute the main phases in the cycle. Finally, as we have seen, Schumpeter stressed that changing profit expectations during the growth of an industry are a major determinant of this sigmoid pattern of growth. As new capacity is expanded, at some point (varying with the product in question) growth will begin to slow down. Market saturation and the tendency for technical advance to approach limits, as well as the competitive effects of swarming and changing costs of inputs, all tend to reduce the level of profitability and with it the attractions of further investment. Exceptionally this process of maturation may take only a few years, but more typically it will take several decades and sometimes even longer. Schumpeter maintained that these characteristics of innovation imply that the disturbances engendered could be sufficient to disrupt the existing system and enforce a cyclical pattern of growth.

As Kuznets (1940) pointed out, whether or not the very rapid growth of new leading sectors of the economy and new technologies offers a plausible explanation of long term cycles in economic development depends crucially on whether some of these innovations are so large in their impact as to cause major perturbations in the entire system – as, for example, can plausibly be argued in the case of railways – or on whether such innovations are bunched together systematically in such a way as to generate exceptional booms and spurts of growth alternating with periods of recession.

Such a Schumpeterian approach to the role of technical innovation implies a distinction between various types of innovation. We may distinguish between the following:

(a) *Incremental innovation*. This is a relatively smooth continuous process leading to steady improvement in the array of existing products and services and the ways in which they are produced. It is reflected in the official measurements of economic growth simply by changes in the input–output coefficients within the framework of an established matrix. The rate of incremental change may of course vary greatly between different industries.

(b) *Radical innovations*. These are discontinuous events and may lead to serious dislocations, economic perturbations and adjustments for the firms in a particular sector. An example would be the introduction of an entirely new material in the textile industry. Although Mensch (1979) has maintained that the occurrence of such radical innovations is concentrated in deep depression periods, our own work suggests that their first introduction is more randomly distributed over long cycles of growth. The *diffusion* of such innovations, however, may often take a cyclical form and may be associated with long cycles of the economy as a whole. As new products and services are diffused, they would ultimately lead to the requirement for the reclassification of an established input–output matrix by the introduction of new rows and columns.

(c)   *Technological revolutions.* These are the 'creative gales of destruction' which are at the heart of Schumpeter's long wave theory. The introduction of the steam engine or electric power are examples of such transformations. For a change to justify the description of a 'technological revolution' it must not only lead to the emergence of new leading branches of the economy and a whole range of new product groups, it must also have deep effects on many other branches of the economy by transforming their methods of production and their input cost structure. Thus a technological revolution virtually requires a new input–output matrix for a satisfactory re-classification of economic activities. Only this third category could satisfy Kuznets' requirement for major perturbations in the system. A transformation of this kind would of course carry with it many clusters of innovations of the first and second category as described above; but it would have much more far-reaching effects on the behaviour of the system as a whole.

Within such a framework great importance attaches to the identification and specification of the major technological transformations. For example, does nuclear technology constitute such a transformation, as some authors have suggested? Or biotechnology?

In this context the work of Carlota Perez (1983) is of particular interest. She describes the Schumpeterian revolutions as shifts in the prevailing 'techno–economic paradigm' accompanying each successive wave of development. Dosi (1983) has also used the expression 'technological paradigm' and made comparisons with the analogous approach of Kuhn (1962) to 'scientific revolutions' and paradigm changes in basic science. In these terms 'incremental innovation' along established technological trajectories may be compared with Kuhn's 'normal science'. I and my colleagues (Freeman *et al.* 1982) have used the expression 'new technological systems' to describe the main Schumpeterian revolutions. While there are close similarities in all these definitions, the approach of Carlota Perez is the most systematic and has some important distinguishing features in relation to structural crises of adaptation.

Perez has suggested that the big boom periods of expansion occur when there is a 'good match' between the new technological 'paradigm' or 'style' of a long wave and the socio-institutional climate. Depressions, in her view, represent periods of mis-match between the emerging new technological paradigms (already quite well advanced during the previous long wave) and the institutional framework. The widespread generalization of the new technological paradigms, not only in the 'carrier' branches of the upswing but also in many other branches of the economy, is possible only after a period of change and adaptation of many social institutions to the requirements of the new technology.

Thus, for example, during the 1970s and 1980s labour productivity growth has slowed down markedly, especially in the USA. Yet almost every engineer and scientist would agree that the *technological* potential for productivity increase has never been greater. Labour productivity has continued to increase very rapidly in the electronics industry itself and the potential applications of microelectronics, computerization, robots and communication technology are innumerable, extending to every tertiary service sector, as well as all branches of manufacturing. Productivity slow-down therefore cannot be explained by the slow-down of technology, but must on the contrary be explained by some degree of incompatibility or 'mis-match' between the new technological paradigm and the institutional and social framework. The recent labour productivity gains in the UK during a period of depression are due not so much to the 'Verdoorn' effect as to the 'Verdun' effect – the closure or scrapping of the less efficient older vintages of capital equipment, which exist in every industry. They are not yet due to the widespread adoption of new technological paradigms outside the electronics industry:

Perez (1983) points out that Schumpeter did not develop any real theory of depression or of the government policies which might overcome depression. He did rather belatedly acknowledge the need for such policies in very general terms, but he adopted a generally hostile stance towards Keynesian economics. Despite his acceptance of the importance of organizational and managerial innovations and the breadth of his approach to the development of social systems, his theory of depression is narrowly economic. But it is the 'mis-match' between the institutional framework with its high degree of inertia, and the outstanding revealed cost and productivity advantages of the new technological paradigms, which, according to Perez, provides the impulse to search for social and political solutions to the crisis:

> 'The structural crisis thus brought about is then, not only a process of "creative destruction" or "abnormal liquidation" in the economic sphere, but also in the social-institutional. In fact, the crisis forces the re-structuring of the socio-institutional framework with innovations along lines that are complementary to the newly attained technological

style or best practice frontier. The final turn the structure will take, from the wide range of the possible, and the time span within which the transformation is effected to permit a new expansionary phase will, however, ultimately depend upon the interests, actions, lucidity and relative strength of the social forces at play' (Perez 1983).

Such institutional changes include the education and training system, the industrial relations systems, managerial and corporate structures, the prevailing management styles, the capital markets and financial systems, the pattern of public, private and hybrid investments, the legal and political framework at both regional and national level and the international framework within which trade and investment flow and technologies diffuse on a world-wide scale.

Perez stresses in particular the role of *costs* in relation to successive techno-economic paradigms. Thus, for example, the big boom after World War II was based on the rapid growth of the leading sectors, such as vehicles, organic chemicals, plastics, and consumer durables, taking advantage of the general easy availability of very low cost energy and energy-intensive materials. This meant that it made managerial and engineering 'common sense' in this period to base investment decisions and design philosophies on large scale mass production or flow production of energy-intensive standardized products and systems. Similarly, in an earlier period (the great Victorian boom of the 1850s and 1860s) the railways were not only the leading sector of investment and employment generation in their own right and in their direct effects on the iron and steel and engineering industries, but they also changed the 'least-cost' combination of factors of production for every other industry and service by drastically reducing transport and distribution costs.

In the present period of structural change, when energy costs have risen and the growth potential of the old leading sectors has been partially exhausted, a new techno-paradigm has emerged based on the extraordinarily low costs of storing, processing and communicating information. The structural crisis of the 1980s is in this perspective a prolonged period of social adaptation to this new paradigm.

The SPRU programme of research on technical change and employment opportunities (TEMPO)

In our programme of research on technical change and employment at the Science Policy Research Unit (SPRU), we have attempted to take some account of these long term effects of technical change. This involves both an analysis of the pattern of technical innovations in the previous decades and the identification of the major new technological systems, which might plausibly be supposed to be the engines of any new upswing in the British and in the world economy over the next 10–20 years.

In the empirical research for the TEMPO project we have examined the process of technical change in relation to each major sector of manufacturing and service employment in the UK since World War II. Basing ourselves on the forty-sector disaggregation of the Cambridge growth model we have attempted in particular to identify the ways in which successive vintages of capital investment have embodied changes in technology and in the employment profile associated with 'best practice' productivity.

For each of the main sectors we first produced a working paper, which included an analysis of the postwar trends of employment in the sector, as well as some speculative questions about probable future trends. These formed the basis for a series of industry workshops in which a representative group of industrialists, technologists, economists and government experts was invited to discuss the relevant working paper with the SPRU research team. Subsequently each working paper was revised to take account of criticisms, comments and additional information from industry and elsewhere. The sector studies are being published in a set of volumes by the Gower Publishing Company (Clark 1984, Guy 1984, Soete 1984, Freeman 1985).

Although I shall make reference to some of the results of the electronics study, it is not possible in a short paper to describe any of the sectors in detail. What I will attempt to do is rather to indicate some of the *general* trends which we identified in many industries. For manufacturing the general picture which emerges is rather similar to that for the EEC as a whole (Fig. 5.1). It can be described in a very over-simplified way in terms of three distinct phases:

(1) During the 1950s growth in output was associated with some growth of employment in most sectors. New investment was directed to the expansion of capacity often on new sites.

(2) During the 1960s, while investment and output continued to grow at a moderately high rate, the expansion of employment slowed down or ceased in many sectors. Labour productivity grew more rapidly associated with the exploitation of production economies of scale, but capital productivity showed a continuous tendency to decline in almost all sectors.

(3) During the 1970s investment and output growth slowed down while employment declined rather sharply. In the early 1980s these tendencies became even more marked with the deep recession in the economy. Capital productivity continued to decline while labour productivity grew more slowly.

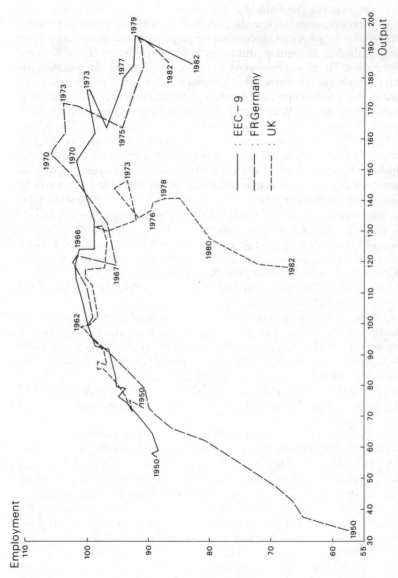

Figure 5.1 Industrial output and employment, EEC (1962 = 100) (OECD and SPRU estimates).

This picture is in general quite consistent with the theoretical framework which has been postulated. The first phase of growth in the early postwar period was based on Schumpeterian investment and 'swarming' in the energy and materials intensive mass production leading sectors of the economy: oil, chemicals (especially plastics), vehicles, consumer durables, paper, and the associated capital equipment and component suppliers. The techno-economic paradigm associated with this growth was already established in the 1920s and 1930s (especially in the USA), but social and institutional changes in World War II and immediately afterwards made for a particularly good 'match' between institutions and technology – hire purchase and other consumer credit facilities; Keynesian tax, expenditure and investment policies; the rapid expansion of secondary and higher education; and so forth. Technical innovation in many sectors involved the use of new materials and energy sources, e.g. synthetic fibres and synthetic rubber.

The second phase in the 1960s was a period in which technical economies of scale in the new large plants in industries such as chemicals, vehicles and consumer durables, as well as in the energy industries themselves, yielded substantial labour productivity gains. As the new technologies became standardized in large scale production facilities, however, capital intensity increased rapidly in many industries, and the increment of employment associated with each new vintage of investment diminished. Profitability began to decline markedly in the 1960s, as the Schumpeterian model had predicted. Profit margins were eroded through a combination of competitive pressure (including of course increasingly intense international competition), growing pressures on input costs (especially energy and labour), market saturation factors in some sectors and the exhaustion of technical economies of scale with mature technologies.

In the third phase in the 1970s the symptoms of a major structural crisis of adjustment became increasingly evident. As profit margins fell, investment was increasingly directed *either* towards labour-saving and energy-saving rationalization of existing production facilities *or* into the new high growth leading sectors of the emerging new techno-economic paradigm.

In common with most other researchers, our findings point to the overwhelming importance of microelectronics and the associated information technologies as the basis of the emerging new paradigm. There is a cluster of new industries which in the 1970s and 1980s have been among the fastest growing in all the leading industrial countries, such as computers, electronic components and telecommunications. But even more important is the fact that this new technological system affects every other branch of the economy, both in terms of its present and future employment and skill requirements, and its future market prospects.

This cluster of innovations has resulted in a drastic fall in costs and a counter-inflationary trend in prices, as well as vastly improved technical performance both within the electronic industry and in many other areas. This combination is relatively rare in the history of technology but it means that this new technological system satisfies all the requirements for a Schumpeterian revolution in the economic system.

By contrast, the newer biotechnologies, although they certainly also have enormous future potential, have not yet reached the point where their macro-economic impact could be great enough to carry the entire economy forward in the next decade or two. This illustrates the importance of the Mensch debate. It is the *diffusion* of the innovations of the 1950s, 1960s and 1970s rather than the first innovations of the 1980s, which must provide the main impetus for a new economic upswing. The new biotechnologies will provide very important auxiliary growth areas and they will ultimately revolutionize agriculture, the food industry and the chemical industry; but the main elements of the new technological paradigm for the fifth Kondratiev upswing cannot come from this source.

Still less can nuclear technology play this role. Its applications are extremely limited. Its capital cost is astronomical, so that any large programme would severely aggravate any capital shortage problems. Its cost advantages are even now dubious and there are strong environmental, social and political arguments for limiting its diffusion, especially in the case of the fast breeder reactor.

There are of course innumerable other types of technical change, which affect particular processes and products, many of them important for individual industries. But our research, like that of similar work elsewhere, points unambiguously to the conclusion that the dominant new technological paradigm is associated with the combination of microelectronics, computers, telecommunications and information technologies. This new paradigm may be loosely described as the 'information revolution'.

Although our sector studies have identified a very large number of innovations associated with the computerization of production systems, offices and services, they also indicate a relatively slow rate of diffusion of these innovations outside a few leading edge industries. Moreover the pattern of diffusion is often of a type which cannot yield the full productivity gains which are potentially available from the new technology. For example, often only *one* new piece of equipment is installed in an office or machine shop which is otherwise still geared to an older technological style, or the maintenance system for the new equipment may not be capable of coping with the new technology, or the management may not understand how to exploit the technology for capital–saving gains in inventories and work in progress.

All of these indications suggest a rather prolonged period of social adjustment before training systems, management practices, industrial relations, government policies and other social institutions and practices are geared to match the emerging technological paradigm.

In the past experience of long waves, the tendency to diminishing marginal productivity of capital has been overcome on the one hand by structural change, i.e. a shift in the pattern of demand towards more labour–intensive sectors, with lower than average investment needs per unit of output, and on the other hand by major technical changes in various sectors of the economy, which brought about a rise in capital productivity, reversing the previous trend of the downswing of the long wave.

I certainly would not underestimate the importance of the remaining labour–intensive areas of employment in advanced economies. On the contrary I would stress that there are certain types of service which are in principle rather labour–intensive, in the sense that direct human contact is the very essence of the service or activity. These include many types of caring and personal service, such as child care, psychiatric care, counselling services, many types of health care, and (I would say) much education and training. They also include many types of creative work, including artistic, scientific and craft activities.

The provision of these services has depended historically on a combination of growing public provision (usually on a non–profit basis) and voluntary part–time provision. The growth of such services is, I would maintain, one of the hallmarks of a civilized society, but for that growth to be sustained, and employment growth to continue in this area, then it is essential to sustain high rates of productivity increase in the rest of the economy. This points to the great importance of reversing the downward trend in the marginal productivity of capital in the market sector of the economy.

The reversal of the trend and the impetus to a major upswing of the economy could come in principle, as it has come in the past, from a major new technological paradigm. I stress the particular significance of *capital* costs, because of the importance of generating new employment quickly with relatively small increments of new investment. Where this is not possible, and/or when the scale of investment is very large and of an infrastructural type (as was the case, for example, with electric power and motorways in the past), then there is a very strong case for big programmes of public investment. This is particularly important when there is a 'technological multiplier', i.e. when the secondary effects are not simply of the conventional type of Keynesian public works, but promote the widespread adoption of new technology. This obviously applies in the case of the new information revolution to many types of communication systems as well as to education and training. There is also a major role for public investment in the 'cabling' infrastructure necessary for the full development of many types of information service.

However, the stimulus from such neo–Keynesian public investment will only be adequate to generate widespread secondary investment and employment effects in other sectors of the economy, if there are substantial capital-saving gains to be made from such investment. Consequently, one of the most important findings of our empirical research is that of Soete and Dosi (1983) that there are very big increases of *capital productivity*, as well as labour productivity, in some sectors of the electronics industry. Whereas most manufacturing sectors show persistent declining marginal capital productivity over the past ten or twenty years, the computer industry and (to a lesser extent) the electronic component industry show major gains in capital productivity. Since the computer is at the heart of most applications of the information revolution, this is extremely important, especially as there are potentially also very large gains in capital productivity in the communication sector, through the use of optical fibres and fully electronic exchanges.

For such gains in capital productivity to generate widespread effects throughout the economy, it will be necessary to make big advances in the design and development of other types of capital goods, such as robots, sensors, process control instrumentation, and so forth. There is some evidence of parallel gains in these areas too, but for the potential benefits to be realized, an enormous wave of technical change will be needed in sectors far removed from the electronic and communication industries.

Whether or not such capital and labour productivity gains can be realized throughout the economy depends upon whether the type of problems identified by Perez can be resolved. If changes in the institutional framework can lead to a good 'match' with the characteristics of the new technological paradigm, then the potential gains could be realised and a new wave of economic expansion would be feasible.

However, it is essential not to underestimate the vast scope of institutional change which is needed. It will involve enormous changes in the pattern of skills of the workforce and therefore in the education and training systems; in management and labour attitudes; the pattern of industrial relations and worker participation; in working arrangements; in the pattern of consumer demand; in the conceptual framework of economists, accountants and governments, and in social, political and legislative priorities.

Perhaps the most important point is that 'intangible' capital investment must now be recognized in its own right as *more* important than the transitory physical capital investment, which is today the main focus of attention for·most managements, accountants and economists. For a long time already firms in the computer industry (and other R&D intensive industries) have devoted greater resources to R&D, education and training, information services, design and software development, than to physical capital investment. This balance will now be tilted even more towards intangible investment as the information system available to firms, government departments and other institutions is becoming its most critical resource. There is of course a very close link between the 'intangible' software and the 'tangible' hardware in an information system. But it is increasingly necessary for the 'intangible' resources to be recognized fully as the main focus for strategic long term development.

Note

1   We are grateful to the ESRC for their support of the TEMPO research programme.

References

Barr, K. 1979. Long waves: a selected annotated bibliography. *Review* **11**, 675–718.

Blattner, N. 1979. Some well-known theoretical propositions on the employment effects of technical change. *Informations Bulletin der Programmleitung, No. 2.* Berne: Nationalfonds, Nationales Forschungsprogramm "Regional problems".

Clark, J. (ed.) 1984. *Technological trends and employment; 2: Basic process industries.* London: Gower.

Cooper, C. M. and J. Clark 1982. *Employment, economics and technology: the impact of technical change on the labour market.* Brighton: Wheatsheaf.

Dosi, G. 1983. Technological paradigms and technological trajectories. *Research Policy* **11**, 147–64.

Freeman, C. (ed.) 1985. *Technological trends and employment; 4: Engineering and vehicles.* London: Gower.

Freeman, C., J. Clark and L. L. G. Soete 1982. *Unemployment and technical innovation: a study of long waves and economic development.* London: Frances Pinter.

Gourvitch, A. 1940. *Survey of the economic theory on technical change and employment.* New York: A. M. Kelley.

Guy, K. (ed.) 1984. *Technological trends and employment; 1: Basic Consumer Goods.* London: Gower.

Heertje, A. (1977). *Economics of technical change*. London: Weidenfeld and Nicholson.

Kuhn, T. 1962. *The structure of scientific revolutions*. Chicago: Chicago University Press.

Kuznets, S. 1930. *Secular movements in production and prices*. Boston: Houghton Mifflin.

Kuznets, S. 1940. Schumpeter's Business Cycles, *American Economic Review*, **30**, 257–71.

Mensch, G. 1979. *Stalemate in technology: innovations overcome the depression*. New York: Balinger.

Neisser, H. P. 1942. Permanent technological unemployment. *American Economic Review* **32**, 50–71.

Perez, C. 1983. Structural change and the assimilation of new technologies in the economic and social system. *Futures* **15**, 357–75.

Samuelson, P. A. 1981. The world's economy at century's end. *Japan Economic Journal* 10 March 1981, p. 20.

Schumpeter, J. A. 1939. *Business cycles: a theoretical, historical and statistical analysis of the capitalist process*, 2 vols. New York: McGraw-Hill.

Soete, L. (ed.) 1984. *Technological trends and employment, 3: electronics and communication*. London: Gower.

Soete, L. L. G. and G. Dosi 1983. *Technology and employment in the electronics industry*. London: Frances Pinter.

6 Growth and structural change: the role of technical innovation

M. D. THOMAS

This chapter provides a brief examination of the nature and significance of a number of relationships between technical change and innovation and the processes of economic growth and structural change. The intent is to seek a greater understanding of the explanatory mechanisms underlying these relationships as perceived within an advanced economic system such as that of contemporary USA. For this purpose I intend to draw selectively from relevant literature some of the important theorizing and conceptualizing concerning these relationships which have taken place during the past 30 years.

The state of theorizing concerning economic growth and structural change in the 1950s

In the early 1950s there was a significant interest in the USA in the development of economic growth theory. At that time, Simon Kuznets (1952, p. 180) suggested that the contemporary interest in explaining the growth process in an economy over a long period of time stemmed from three major events associated with the pattern of the world economy between 1920 and 1950.

First, accumulated evidence persuaded many economists that the industrialized countries in Western Europe and North America had reached a level of maturity such that unemployment could be expected to be a chronic rather than a transitory problem. Secondly, there was a general recognition that most of the world's population lived under conditions of extreme poverty. Thirdly, the emergence of the Soviet Union as a world power and the growing rift between it and the Western countries after World War II led, among other things, to a growing interest in the long term growth rates of national economies and especially those of the strategic sectors in these economies.

115

At this time it is pertinent to ask whether or not, under the stimulus of the three major events described above, there emerged by the close of the 1950s a body of thought or set of principles that could confidently be called the 'modern theory of economic growth'. Henry J. Bruton (1960), an authority on the subject, stated categorically that there was no such theory and his assessment was that:

> 'Current and recent literature abound with seminal ideas, revealing insights, penetrating bits and pieces of analysis, loose ends, and unrealistic assumptions. There are elegant and rigorous models, concerned with explaining a very narrowly conceived phenomenon; there are general discussions, which introduce in an ambiguous, imprecise fashion, all the factors that may conceivably be related to the economic process; and there are contributions at every point between these extremes' (Bruton 1960, p. 239).

Twenty-five years later, Bruton's assessment still holds. There is still considerable merit, however, in examining briefly and selectively some of these 'seminal ideas', 'revealing insights' and 'penetrating bits and pieces of analysis' which are still important and helpful in attaining greater understanding of both the process of economic growth and structural change and the role of innovation and technical change in this process.

Macro–economic growth theories: selected aspects

Capital stock adjustment theories

In the USA formal theorizing on the process of economic growth has been primarily carried out within the general framework of an assumed stable, equilibrium-seeking economy. These conditions were initially specified by Keynes (1936) in his short-run growth theory. In the Keynesian model the effect on the equilibrium level of income of once-and-for-all changes in exogenous variables such as technology or capital stock could be examined by a comparative cost technique. Keynesian equilibrium, however, required equality between desired savings and desired investment, while the long-run growth form of the model required for equilibrium the continued maintenance of the desired ratio between capital stock and the rate of output. In the early formulations, this ratio seemed to be determined solely by technological considerations, i.e. by a technological constant (Bruton 1960, pp. 243–4). This kind of theory, known as the capital stock adjustment theory, clearly underscored the perceived great strategic significance of capital in the growth process (Hahn & Mathews 1965, Harcourt & Laing 1971, Jones 1976).

The Keynesian setting of growth modelling changed to neoclassical after the mid-1950s largely as a result of Robert Solow's (1956) contribution to the theory of economic growth. The resetting by Solow was largely achieved by the introduction of strategic new assumptions.

These assumptions were that:

'(a) at each instant of time all existing capital stock and all labor are thrown on the market; and

'(b) quasi-rents and wage rates adjust immediately to clear the market. With such a flexible productive system, the perfectly adjusting input prices would assure – under a wide range of conditions – that the capital output ratio, which did in fact obtain, was the desired one. The system could then always adjust to a given labour supply in such a manner that the full employment of labor and the satisfying of entrepreneurs are achieved at the same time, not accidentally, but by a substitution of inputs responding to changed factor prices' (Bruton 1960, p. 252).

Disaggregation

Initially the capital stock adjustment theory viewed the economy as one large firm producing a single product for a single giant consumer. Such aggregation simplified analysis but at the same time it concealed many problems. To deal with a number of these problems and thereby increase realism, many theorists reduced the level of aggregation. Disaggregation facilitated investigation of the intersectoral conditions which would have to be satisfied if relatively smooth growth were to continue. With minor modifications Leontief's multisectoral model proved to be useful for this purpose (Bruton 1960, p. 254).

Several writers viewing the economy in a disaggregated form in the 1950s noted that economic growth could be dominated by one or a small number of industries whose rates of growth exceeded that of the economy as a whole (Rostow 1952, Chenery & Watanabe 1958, Hirschman 1958, Bruton 1960). It became clear to some of these writers that a theory of behaviour of individual sectors was an essential component of a general theory of economic growth.

Francois Perroux's growth pole theory published in 1955 was later a much discussed example of such a theory (Perroux 1955). His theory explained the growth process associated with the rapid growth of a large, technically advanced oligopolistic industry. Related policy-oriented, unbalanced growth theories, utilizing a disaggregated perspective, attracted considerable attention in the late 1950s and early 1960s (Hirschman 1958).

Over the past four decades most theorizing about economic growth has concentrated on explaining how and why per capita income grows over a long period of time. Attention has focused mainly on the per capita income time path of an economy already experiencing 'institutional' growth. Little theorizing has taken place in the USA, however, on the problem facing societies seeking to extract themselves from the quicksand of poverty in the 'lesser developed' countries of the Third World.

Capital stock adjustment theory – additional features

One may be very critical of the capital stock adjustment theory both for the deficiencies in underlying concepts as well as in various basic relationships. However, some of its features have been useful in many ways. In particular it has helped to focus attention on some important requirements which must be satisfied if an economy is to enjoy smooth and continuing growth.

Early, rigid forms of aggregative and disaggregative models stemming from the capital stock theory, with fixed production coefficients, were clearly unsuited for explaining long run growth. Strategic factors such as population, the social and cultural environment, market structure, capital stock, saving habits, technology, etc., do not remain unchanged in the long run. Yet, in the growth models these factors were held to be constant. A viable long run growth theory, however, must incorporate these strategic growth factors into the explanatory growth mechanism as endogenous factors.

The relaxation of the fixed capital stock assumption revealed many important relationships. For example, net positive saving provides net positive investment and net positive investment leads to a changing capital stock. This formal modelling also 'pointed up the fact that investment is capacity-creating as well as income-generating' (Bruton 1960, p. 261).

Among the important ideas generated by the theoretical writings on macro-economic growth from the mid-1930s to the 1950s was the establishment of a formal explanatory relationship between technical advance and innovation and the process of economic growth (Abramovitz 1952, Solow 1957, Denison 1962). Of particular interest was the identification of relationships between innovations and the time paths for income, capacity and structural change. It was shown that 'where growth is taking place, innovations are necessary to maintain the profit rate at the equilibrium level' (Bruton 1960, p. 261). It thus became clear that technical advance and innovations were both necessary and most important in the long run growth mechanism. In the long run, innovations could be expected to change the nature of the economy's inputs, outputs and its capital output coefficients. In other words, innovations could be expected to contribute profoundly to change in the structure of the economic system.

Major deficiencies in the contemporary state of knowledge concerning the nature and significance of the long run innovation time path itself were also recognized. Similar deficiencies, however, existed with respect to the long run time-paths of other strategic growth factors whose influence on the process of growth was thought to be insignificant in the short run. It became clear that the effects of long run changes in the economy influenced by factors such as population, social and cultural environment, market structure, institutions, etc., as well as innovation could no longer be effectively ignored. Consequently, much subsequent research has been devoted to the study of the time-paths for these variables in the long run. There has also been some modest attempt to articulate, within primarily a neoclassical framework, how these variables must behave to bring about long run economic growth.

Empirical foundations for theorizing

By the latter part of the 1950s, theoretical discussions concerning structural change were more frequently based on a wealth of data on economic growth patterns for many countries, broad sectors and individual industries over a considerable period of time. The data provided by Kuznets (1930), Fisher (1933), Burns (1934), Clark (1940), Hoffman (1958), and others showed clearly the differential growth rates among national economies and among individual industries within each national economy.

The empirical studies suggest important questions such as the following: Why are there differential growth rates among individual industries in an economy? Why do industries exhibit differential expansion (positive or negative) time-paths? If industries embark on careers of decadence once they cease to grow, how are their contributions replaced so that the economy may continue to receive regenerative impulses? Answers to these questions should throw a great deal of light on the process of economic growth and structural change.

Macro-economic theory in the 1950s suggested that an array of factors affect differentially the prospective outputs of individual products and their industries. Among those explanatory factors discussed were changing income elasticities of demand and changing patterns of consumer demand with the passage of time. Attention was focused on the effects of these factors on the structure of the economy, especially on the tendencies towards greater industrialization with rising per capita incomes (Thomas 1964).

This body of theory also showed that growth in demand for an industry's product, when associated with increased population, permitted scale economies to accrue which in turn tended to lower production costs and output prices. Autonomous productivity increases, when associated with higher real incomes and appropriate price elasticities, tended to increase the demand for the outputs of industries which lowered both production costs and the price of their products. These impacts were discussed in the context of the expansion of current markets, and in terms of the creation of new markets through geographical extensions as well as by the development of new uses for the individual products of the industries.

Technical change in neoclassical macro-economic theory

The dominant neoclassical macro-economic literature, in the late 1950s as well as in contemporary times, portrayed 'technical change as a predominantly mechanical process, independent of human will and behaviour' (Heertje 1977, p. 207). Exogenous and autonomous technical changes were associated with the passage of time without further explanation. They were associated with increases in output in various sectors and with increases in the economic efficiency of producing the enlarged outputs.

Induced technical change or the expansion of technical possibilities, however, was explained by one or some combination of such factors as '(a) long-term changes in the ratio between prices of the factors of production, (b) learning processes concerning production, and (c) investment in education and research' (Heertje 1977, p. 176).

The winds of change

By the end of the 1950s theorizing on the role of technical change in processes of growth and structural change came under the dynamic influence of new major events associated with the rapidly changing pattern of the world economy. The major events identified by Kuznets in 1952 also continued to influence our theorizing, in modified forms, up to the present.

In the early 1950s, in the industrialized parts of the world, recovery from the ravages of war was slow in some countries. Others recovered more quickly. As the decade passed the tempo of growth, especially with respect to manufacturing production, grew rapidly in the USA, Western Germany and Japan.

The multinational era of the high technology firms was ushered in first by an increasing volume of US exports to Canada and Western

Europe. This was rapidly followed by a significant rate of expansion of direct investment in the same regions by the US multinationals. By the 1960s offshore direct investment in developing countries was at a significant level (Vernon 1971).

By the mid-1970s the pace of growth of the manufacturing sector had begun to decline appreciably in most industrialized countries. The rate of growth of US multinationals declined relative to Japanese and West German multinationals. Newly industrialized countries such as Brazil, Taiwan, Korea, Singapore, Hong Kong and Mexico began to attract growing attention by their significant, or in some cases spectacular, structural transformation and growth rates.

At the global level these events registered profound impacts on patterns of world trade and industrial growth and development. The perceived results included the creation of a 'new international division of labour' and movement on the part of developing countries to establish a 'new international economic order'. In North America and Western Europe there was growing concern with respect to over-urbanization and pollution and their impact on the quality of growth. By the 1980s, economically depressed conditions at national and subnational scale were attracting increased attention from governments at various levels as well as the interest of academics.

During the past two decades these major events have generated considerable theoretical and empirical research on the role of technology in the process of growth and structural change. At the global level technical change is widely perceived as the new basis of hope for a better material future (Pavitt 1979, p. 458). At the subnational level we hear the plea for the development of 'innovation-oriented regional policy' if economically depressed conditions are to be eradicated or their effects ameliorated (Ewers & Wettmann 1980, p. 161).

The current literature suggests that the strengthening of macroeconomic growth theory will come about largely through a better understanding of the micro-foundations of growth (Rosenberg 1982, Schelling 1982, Elster 1983).

The remainder of this paper examines some of the micro-foundations for innovation and technical change, primarily at the level of the firm, as important components in the mechanism which explains the process of economic growth in the long run.

'The *search for micro-foundations*, . . ., is in reality a pervasive and omnipresent feature of science. It corresponds to William Blake's insistence that "Art and Science cannot exist but in minutely organized Particulars." To explain is to provide a mechanism, to open up the black box and show the nuts and bolts, the cogs, the wheels of the internal machinery. (Here the term "mechanism" should be understood broadly, to cover intentional chains from a goal to an action as well as causal chains from an event to its effect.)' (Elster 1983, p. 23–4).

Micro-foundations for theorizing about technical change and innovation

Behavioural competition in innovative firms

A useful organizing framework for the discussion of technical change and innovation in innovative firms is provided by Schumpeter's notion of behavioural competition:

> 'It is not . . . price . . . competition which counts but the competition from the new commodity, the new technology, . . . the new type of organization . . . competition which commands a decisive cost or quality advantage and which strikes not at the margin of the profits and the outputs of the existing firms but at their foundations and their very lives' (Schumpeter 1950, p. 84–5).

Thus innovations in the form of a new commodity or product; a new kind of process; a new form of organization; and new management practices, provide innovators or entrepreneurs and innovative firms with attributes which enhance their effectiveness in various forms of 'behavioural competition'. Innovations are assumed to provide the firm with a 'competitive edge' or 'comparative advantage' over firms in the same industry and same market.

One may also infer that the viability and growth of a firm will decisively depend on its innovative capabilities. Furthermore, to the extent that innovative behaviour and capability is unequally distributed among firms in an industry, one may hypothesize that innovation contributes to differential growth rates among the firms. One may further hypothesize that where innovation-based behavioural competition is strong in an industry, there will tend to be an oligopolistic market structure which involves large, successful, innovative firms with substantial economic influence. A measure of support for these hypotheses has been provided in recent studies (Kohn & Scott 1982, Kamien & Schwartz 1982, Nelson & Winter 1982a).

The innovative firm and the innovation process

Let us now structure some of the qualitative notions about the nature of the innovative firm and its activities, focusing attention on its behaviour during the innovation cycle for a traditionally new, science-based product. The time-path of a specific new product innovation represented by this cycle may be conceptualized as extending through two stages. The main focus in this paper is on the first stage, which begins when the attributes of the embryonic new product may be recognized and defined as an invention and it ends with the act of innovation – the first commercial production of the new product. The second stage concerns the period of commercial production when the new product may be modified by subsequent product innovations and when additional process innovations may affect the economic efficiency of the new product's production technology (Thomas 1981, Rosenberg 1982). Not all firms in the new product industry will necessarily carry out innovative activities throughout the innovation cycle for the new product. In addition the innovator firm for the new product need not be, and usually is not, the innovator firm for all subsequent product and/or process innovations in the new product industry during the second stage of the innovation cycle.

The innovation time-path for a radically new product

This conceptualization of stage I of the innovation cycle for a radically new product may conveniently begin with a brief discussion of how and why the innovation cycle begins. For this purpose Usher's conceptualization of the process of 'primary invention' is useful. On the basis of the general principles of Gestalt analysis (Usher 1971, p. 48), he identified three distinct steps in this process, namely (1) perception of an unsatisfactory pattern; (2) setting of the stage (to react to the perception); (3) the primary act of insight or invention.

Usher believed that the study of technical change had been hindered by a tendency to place overwhelming emphasis on the acts of insight in the process of invention and on the role of invention in technical change. This perspective, he felt, failed to deal effectively with the nature and significance of the kinds of novelty that are a normal and continuous consequence of the skilled activities of engineers and technicians (Usher 1971, p. 42). In practice, it may be difficult to deal with the boundary between novelties which result from acts of skill and those which result from acts of insight by superior persons under special constellations of circumstance (Usher 1971, p. 44).

Usher also believed that primary inventions, in practice, usually represent a substantial cumulative synthesis of old knowledge with new acts of insight (Usher 1971, p. 50). He underscores the lengthy period usually involved for the cumulative synthesis of individual primary inventions to occur, particularly in the case of major inventions (Usher, 1954, 1971).

Usher's theory of invention is perceptive but it does not enable one to predict when the act of insight will occur or to predict precisely the solution to a perceived 'unsatisfactory pattern'. There is, of course, no guarantee that the identification of an unsatisfactory pattern will inevitably result in an invention.

Invention and the firm

The processes involved in the creative endeavours associated with invention manifest the uncertainties and other characteristics of basic research. In the USA activities which result in significant technical inventions are primarily carried out by universities, public and private sector research institutes and major firms in the private sector. The roles of these different kinds of centres for the discovery of inventions tend to vary from country to country (OECD 1971).

In the USA many of the larger firms with significant levels of expenditure on R&D carry out basic research, in house or by contract with universities and/or private research organizations (Hoffman 1976, Freeman 1977, Baker & Sweeny 1978). Such research often results in inventions. Most inventions are patented but it is widely believed that many technical discoveries are kept secret. A large number of the patented inventions are not developed further, immediately or even later, by the inventor firm (Freeman 1977). Many patents are, however, sold or leased by the inventor firm. In addition, it seems that the level of a firm's basic research is, among other things, positively associated with product diversification (Link & Long 1981), innovative output and firm size (Mansfield 1981).

Many firms attempt to screen basic scientific and technical knowledge relevant to the firm's mission. The intent is to convert, if possible, the conditions of uncertainty with respect to the utility of a particular body of knowledge to conditions of risk for the firm (Dasgupta & Stiglitz 1980). In other words, the firm attempts to convert a particular body of knowledge into a particular body of information; the firm then places a measure of probability on the information having a specific kind of utility for the firm.

The identification by Usher of distinctive steps in the process of invention is useful in evaluating the behaviour of innovative firms which carry out basic research 'directed toward the creation of new and improved practical products and processes' (Nelson 1959, p. 151–2). Such firms hope to discover inventions which will enhance the firm's future. Many inventions do result from directed basic research but many inventions 'are a by-product of activity directed in a quite different direction' (Nelson 1959, p. 151).

The innovation process

Once the invention process culminates in a primary invention of a potential new product, those individuals and/or firms that have access to the invention are in a position to assess, to a considerable degree, its technical characteristics. The act of invention, in a sense, signals the technical viability of the potential new product. However, the economic potential of the primary invention as a commercial product is still highly uncertain when the act of insight is made.

When the firm decides to attempt to transform the primary invention into an innovation it takes what Usher (1971, p. 48) calls the 'critical revision and development' fourth step. The successful completion of this step is generally referred to as the act of innovation. Usher, however, refers to it as secondary invention.

Non-routine decisions

Usher's four distinctive steps in the processes of invention and innovation represent, for innovative firms taking these steps, four sets of non-routine decisions that will profoundly affect the firm's life cycle. It would appear that for the firm, each of the four distinctive steps involves novel situations and conditions which reflect high levels of uncertainty. Clear-cut procedures for the firm indicating how to deal appropriately with such situations and conditions would therefore not be expected. Decisions such as whether or not the firm should 'set the stage' and move towards the 'primary invention' phase or move to the 'critical revision and development' phase are major decisions and normally one would not expect them to be made in a routine fashion using only routine procedures. It is, therefore, important to understand the behaviour of the firm when it needs to make non-routine decisions.

Do all innovative firms faced with the same kind of decision behave in the same manner when, for example, firms decide whether or not they should move into the 'critical revision and development' phase? Do all innovative firms carry out similar routine and non-routine information searches before making specific kinds of decisions? Are assessments of information for the same specific kinds of decisions carried out in the same way? Clearly one would expect considerable interfirm variations in behaviour on the basis of critical differences that are generated internal and external to each firm.

Trying to understand and explain correctly how and why a firm behaves in the way it does at various major steps or decision points along a radically new product innovation time-path is seemingly an impossible task. Attempts are, however, being made to develop a useful way of looking at this problem (Mansfield *et al.* 1977, Nelson and Winter 1982b).

Work activities and decision points

From a study of the literature, it seems plausible to conclude that (a) the innovation process involves non-routine creative decisions and activities or entrepreneurial behaviour within the firm, and (b) the commercial future of the innovation is influenced, in some cases to a considerable extent, by how well these non-routine decisions are made and the associated activities are carried out. Unfortunately, we do not have much information on entrepreneurial behaviour within the firm as it relates to the innovation process for a broad range of innovations in a variety of industries.

Under these circumstances there is merit in examining surrogate information for entrepreneurial behaviour by the firm during the innovation process. For example, the work activities (non-routine and routine) leading up to the act of innovation in a few industries have been classified into a number of stages (Stead 1976, Horesh & Kamin 1983). One may surmise that at each stage certain kinds of critical decisions are made. The classification scheme hopefully facilitates the search for non-routine decision points in the innovation process. Studies may then be carried out to explain the nature and significance of the firm's behaviour at these points.

Table 6.1 provides results obtained from four studies which classified the different kinds of work leading up to the act of innovation. These studies use similar categorizations for innovation activities for product and process innovations in broad industry groups such as chemicals, wood, machinery, transportation equipment and electronics. There are, however, many problems associated with these data. For example, innovation activity stages may

Table 6.1 Comparison of the relative costs (per cent) of each innovation activity.

Innovation activity	Charpie Panel	Mansfield	Statistics Canada	Israel
R&D	15–30*	46†	59‡	47
tooling and manufacturing facilities	40–60	37	31§	18
manufacturing start-up	5–15	9	6	15
marketing start-up	10–25	8	2	20

Sources: Data in columns 2–4 are from Stead (1976, p. 8) and data in column 5 are from Horesh and Kamin (1983, p. 22).

* Charpie Panel: research/advanced development, basic invention, engineering and designing the product.

† Mansfield: applied research, preparation of project requirements and basic specifications, prototype or pilot-plant design, construction and testing.

‡ Statistics Canada: R&D, product and design engineering.

§ Statistics Canada: capital, tooling and industrial engineering.

overlap and also they do not have to occur in any particular time sequence (Mansfield *et al.* 1977, p. 69). Variations in relative cost structures provided by the four sources for Table 6.1 may be explained to a degree by differences in industry mixes and the market size of firms. Some innovations are expected to have much larger market areas than others, thus increasing significantly their absolute and relative cost shares for tooling, capital expenditures, manufacturing and marketing start-up (Stead 1976, p. 9).

The significance of the non-routine decisions made by entrepreneurs within the various innovation activity stages will tend to be influenced considerably by the degree of uncertainty associated with various types of innovation, as shown in Table 6.2.

One would expect that within each of the six categories of innovation the degree of uncertainty would tend to be reduced as the innovation process proceeds due to a learning effect. A conceptualization of states of uncertainty and risk suggests a lowering of the level of risk as the innovation process continues towards the point of innovation and even beyond to the points on the product cycle where both product and process innovations cease to occur (Utterback & Abernathy 1975). Of course, the more radical the innovation the

Table 6.2 Degree of uncertainty associated with various types of innovation.

(1)	true uncertainty	fundamental research, fundamental invention
(2)	very high degree of uncertainty	radical product innovations; radical process innovations outside firm
(3)	high degree of uncertainty	major product innovations; radical process innovations in own establishment or system
(4)	moderate uncertainty	new 'generations' of established products
(5)	little uncertainty	licensed innovation; limitation of product innovation; modification of products and processes; early adoption of established process
(6)	very little uncertainty	new 'model'; product differentiation; agency for established product innovation; late adoption of established process innovation in own establishment; minor technical improvements

Source: Freeman (1982, p. 150).

higher level of risk one would expect throughout the innovation and post-innovation processes.

It is also useful to think of different kinds of uncertainties and complexities associated with a specific innovation process such as those related to the innovation technology, marketing, the economic organization of the firm as well as location decisions. It is not possible to do more than mention these relationships here, although a few tentative comments are made with respect to location and site decisions that are associated with the innovation process.

Location decisions

If we examine the innovative activity stages, we may be able to identify a stage when the firm has to make some type of location decision. If we relate the innovative activity stage (Table 6.1) and the type of location decision to the type of innovation (Table 6.2) we may be able to identify the degree of uncertainty and complexity involved in making the location decision. When a firm decides to carry out basic and applied research and development work, it has to decide *where* this will be done as well as what kind of research and developmental work it should undertake and what level of investment to make over what period of time.

The decision to proceed with the innovation process has locational dimensions. For example, where should applied research be performed? Should the prototype product be made and the pilot plant be built at the same location as where the applied research is done? Where will the manufacturing start-up for the new product take place?

Multi-product, multi-regional firms rather than small firms are the major innovators and are responsible for most of the more radical and major innovations (Brunner 1974, Thomas 1981). Nevertheless, small and medium-sized firms, in some industries, are significant sources of radical innovations (Rothwell & Zegveld 1982). The location strategies of large multi-regional, multi-product firms, however, will inevitably be different from those of single plant firms (Vernon 1974). Classical location theory is unable to explain the vital aspects of the location decision of these dynamic multi-regional, innovative firms and whose inter-firm differences bring into question the validity of using, in an unmodified form, the representative firm concept. Clearly there is need for an alternative behavioural location theory which can be integrated with a viable behavioural theory of the firm (Krumme 1969). A revised behavioural location theory needs to address location decision making by firms which have multi-regional or multi-national plant distributions, innovations in different stages of development and many products in different stages of their life cycles. It is encouraging to note that these problems are being addressed in the contemporary literature on the subject (Granstrand 1978, Thwaites 1978, Goddard 1980, Malecki 1981, Marshall 1982, McConnell 1982, Taylor & Thrift 1982a,b, Oakey 1983, Scott 1983).

Innovative firm behaviour

The previous discussion highlighted what appear to be critical kinds of decisions made by firms engaged in innovative activities (Cohn 1980, Maidique 1980, Slater 1980, Teece 1981, Horovitz & Thietart 1982, Miller & Friesen 1982). These decisions have a great influence on the future wellbeing of the firms as manifested in their patterns of growth or decline. If we wish to have a better understanding of the behaviour of innovative firms as they deal with critical kinds of decisions, then we badly need to know more concerning the identity and nature of these critical non-routine decisions and the decision-making processes that are used. There are also deficiencies in our knowledge of the nature and influence of factors considered in making such decisions.

Non-routine decisions in the innovative process

When faced with non-routine decisions regarding their future, we may perceive the behaviour of the firms in an industry to be influenced by the distilled memory of the history of each member firm. Some of the experiences from the past and present are represented, appropriately or not, in the current rules of the firms. When making decisions regarding their future wellbeing, firms attempt to synthesize past and present flows of information, generated within the firm and from external sources, concerning the present and future decision environments of the firms (Piatier 1981).

The 'decision environment' or 'selection environment' (Nelson & Winter 1977) of a firm is determined partly by conditions within the firm which influence its behaviour. The characteristics and behaviour of other firms in the industry also partly determine the nature of a firm's decision environment. In addition, conditions external to the firm and its industry play an important role in determining the decision environment of a firm. Such external conditions include product demand and factor supply conditions and those that influence other information flows to the firm. Inevitably there are inherent weaknesses in the information flows from the past, present and future decision environments of the firm as well as deficiencies in the firm's ability to process, evaluate and utilize the information correctly. These are only a few of the factors which, for the firm, introduce varying degrees of uncertainty with respect to the outcome of a non-routine decision regarding its future.

Nelson and Winter (1982b) have stressed the usefulness of the concepts 'organizational routine' and 'search' for the development of an evolutionary theory of economic change. They believe that at any time you examine an organization, such as an innovative firm, you will find that built into the organization is 'a set of ways of doing things and ways of determining what to do' (Nelson & Winter 1982b, p. 400). Of course, these organizational routine behaviours will not be sufficiently appropriate for dealing with a non-routine situation or new and changing conditions in the decision environment of the firm. In such situations the firm's wellbeing will be dependent on how effectively it can adapt its current organizational routines.

The term 'search' denotes 'all those organizational activities which are associated with the evaluation of current routines and which may lead to their modification, to more drastic change, or to their replacement' (Nelson & Winter 1982b, p. 400). Of course, many of these 'search' activities are, in effect, 'organizational routines'. However, these heuristic search processes also manifest 'a stochastic character both from the point of view of the modeller and the point of view of the organization that undertakes them' (Nelson & Winter 1982b, p. 400).

These three notions, 'decision environments', 'organizational routine' and 'search', provide a foundation for the development of a conceptual framework for understanding the behaviour of a firm when it deals with non-routine decisions such as those related to innovative activities. For example, the heuristic search process may be used in connection with the choice by a firm of R&D strategies and projects (Nelson & Winter 1977).

It would appear that the framework would also have utility in understanding the behaviour of the firm as it deals with the economic organizational dimensions of the innovation process. The technical success of the new product is of no consequence if the right kind of organizational structure and management practices are not in place to ensure the commercial success of the innovation (Slater 1980).

Exploratory use of this conceptual framework may be made in seeking a better understanding of the non-routine location decisions which result from their innovative activities. Business economists have accumulated much information about decision rules and strategies. These seem to be used widely by different kinds of firms in different industries when facing on-site expansion or plant relocation or new plant location decisions (Biggadike 1979). Some of these location decision rules and strategies appear to be strongly influenced by the organizational structure of the firm and by the composition of the group responsible for the 'search' and by the individual or committee that has final responsibility for making the location decision (Schmenner 1982).

Innovation and the growth of the firm

A major thesis of this chapter is that innovations may provide a competitive edge and increased growth prospects for innovative firms and industries. In addition, the presence of innovative industries or their component firms or establishments in a region enhances both the competitive position and economic growth prospects of the region.

Nevertheless, in light of what has been said earlier concerning the uncertainties and complexities that are so much a part of the innovation process, one must not believe that innovation is the automatic, unfailing means of achieving economic success in firms and regions. The majority of innovations are commercial failures (Rothwell 1977, p. 41). An innovation may be a technical success and a commercial failure in the innovator firm but a commercial success in the 'imitator' or 'counter-puncher' firm (Hoffman 1976).

In this section of the chapter, attention is concentrated on innovation activity generated within a firm and on the growth and regenerative implications of this innovation activity for the firm. Of course, all innovations that are incorporated in a new product over its innovative time-path are not always the product of the innovator firm (Von Hippel 1976). Other innovative firms frequently provide process innovations and intermediate product innovations to the innovator firm during stage I and especially stage II of the innovation life cycle for a radically new product. There is, therefore, an important interdependence between innovative firms.

In addition, the inter-firm and inter-industry flows of innovations embodied in new products and processes inject into the economy what are thought to be very important input and output quality multiplier effects (Thomas 1969). They are also believed to have significant impacts on the growth of productivity in the firms and industries connected to this innovation input–output flow network. Unfortunately, these 'spill-over' innovation effects have not received much attention in the literature, but they do represent worthy research challenges (Nadiri & Bittros 1978, Scherer 1982).

Industry and product life cycles

Before concluding it is worth commenting briefly on how innovations contribute to the establishment of a competitive edge and the long period growth prospects of a firm. These contributions are made through the creation of new products (and processes) and economic efficiencies in production. The literature on industry and product life cycles provides useful insights in dealing with this question (Magee 1977, Abernathy & Utterback 1978, Vernon 1979, Gort & Klepper 1982). Product and industry life cycle notions are, however, highly speculative and are based on information obtained from studies of a limited number of high technology industries such as electronics. Research on these and related concepts continues and interesting results are being reported in the literature. Healthy scepticism and constructive criticism with respect to the use of these life cycle frameworks have already had beneficial impacts (Rothwell 1976, Walker 1979).

Industry and product life cycles are based on the assumption (and limited empirical evidence) that the commercial life of a specific new product (single product industry) is finite. Product enhancement and product changes may well extend the commercial life. Nevertheless, sooner or later the product's life ends. The connection between this life cycle phenomenon and the concept of secularly declining industries (single and multiple product) is evident. Regions and firms are faced with the regenerative problem if their economic viability is to continue. They must be able to introduce new products which hopefully will be commercial successes. We do not know the relevant time-path, however, during which the regenerative problem is real, for a particular region or firm, but we do know that the firm's life cycle need not coincide with the life cycle of one of its products.

The expansion path of a commercially successful product innovation follows the general S form. Factors such as the degree of newness of the product, competition from substitutes, and changes in consumption functions of purchasers may influence the precise form of the specific product's expansion path (de Kluyver 1977, Goldman 1982).

Utterback and Abernathy (1975), in their dynamic model of innovation, specify that initially after the commercial entry of the new product, innovative firms, in the new product industry, concentrate on innovative activities which hopefully will enhance the new product in terms of its quality, design, strength, etc. In time, within the new product industry, innovations which increase the economic efficiency of the production of the new product will tend to dominate those innovations that contribute to product enhancement. If the product remains in production long enough, at some point product and process innovation ceases or virtually ceases (Utterback & Abernathy 1975). Subsequently, factors other than technology tend to have a greater influence over the commercial viability of the product. The concept of a 'product–process matrix', articulated in this model, has been used in the development and assessment of corporate strategies (Hayes & Wheelwright 1979a,b, De Bresson & Townsend 1981).

The product life cycle notion suggests that initially the firm's competitive position in the new product market is primarily influenced by the qualitative characteristics of its product. Demand for the new product tends to be relatively price inelastic and unit costs are relatively high. Over time embodied process innovations contribute to a significant improvement in cost efficiency in the production of the new product and to the productivity of the innovative firm (Thomas 1981, p. 15). These contributions subsequently tend to result in reductions in the price of the product.

This pattern of development seemed to hold in innovative industries in six major OECD countries between 1963 and 1970. However, it may be that the relatively large increases in the price of products from these industries during the period 1970–77 reflected increasingly greater product quality rather than lower costs of inputs (Pavitt 1979). In other words, there appeared to be a relatively greater emphasis on product innovation rather than process innovation in these innovative industries as a whole in the 1970–77 time period.

Conclusion

The dominant explanatory variable for the process of long run growth and structural change in the early 1950s was capital. Before the end of that decade, however, the scene was set for a major 'take-over' by technical innovation as the 'new causality'. The transfer of theoretical focus from capital to technical innovation was examined briefly in the early part of this chapter. Certain mechanical macro-economic relationships and associations between technical innovation and economic growth and structural change were then discussed. It was concluded that neo-classical macro-economic growth theories do not provide an appropriate articulation of the innovation time-path because they do not provide an adequate understanding of the process of innovation within a temporal framework. Furthermore, they do not provide coherent explanations for the dynamic causal impacts of innovation on rates and direction of economic growth and on changes in the composition of industries.

The literature suggests that a considerable strengthening of the body of macro-economic growth theory will result from a strengthening of its micro-foundations. This point of view was accepted, and an examination was carried out of some of the micro theoretic foundations for the process of innovation. An attempt was made to open up the innovation 'black box' so as to throw light on the mechanism underlying the process of innovation. Attention was therefore focused on causal chains linked to the innovation event as well as causal chains which linked innovation to various economic effects such as growth, product change and increased production cost efficiencies within the innovative firms.

Schumpeter's concept of behavioural competition provided an organizing principle for conceptualizing the process of innovation. Attention was focused primarily on the pre-commercial entry stage of the innovation time-path for a radically new product. Major emphasis was placed on the provision of conceptualizations of the behaviour of the firm as it encounters and deals with various kinds of 'uncertainty of outcome' problems along the innovation time-path. For this purpose ideas derived from Usher's theory of invention and Schumpeter's conceptualization of innovation and the role of the entrepreneur were most helpful.

By definition innovative firms were perceived as being engaged in the process of innovation. Some of these firms carried out activities which resulted in inventions. The process of invention and innovation in the firm was viewed as connected sets of routine and non-routine decisions and behaviour. Attention was focused on non-routine phases which required non-routine decisions on the part of the firm's decision makers. This non-routine behaviour was perceived as being composed of varying amounts of unlearned insight and high skill learned behaviour provided respectively by the entrepreneurs and managers of the firm (Schumpeter 1971, p. 35).

The process of innovation creates problems of uncertainty for the firm. The firm, in other words, is uncertain about the results which follow from decisions it makes in connection with the innovation process. For example, a decision to develop and introduce a radically new product will be accompanied by considerable uncertainty on the part of the firm regarding whether or not the product will be commercially successful.

The behaviour of the firms faced with these kinds of uncertainty problems in the process of innovation needs further study. For this purpose the theory of heuristic search seems to provide useful guidance. Eventually, through the use of heuristic search strategies, we may come closer to identifying the non-routine elements of a problem which require non-routinized solutions.

Although the conceptualizations presented in this chapter clearly need further development, refinement and testing, they nevertheless provide useful insights and information concerning the time-path or process of innovation in innovative firms. Clearly the task of providing ways of achieving a better understanding of how, why and where innovation occurs in firms, industries and in geographic space remains an important challenge. This challenge must be met successfully if we are to develop better theories which explain the process of economic growth and structural change.

Note

1 I wish to thank Gunter Krumme for his helpful comments. This material is based partly upon work supported by the National Science Foundation under Grant No. SES-8411682. Any opinions, findings, and conclusions or recommendations expressed in this publication are those of the author and do not necessarily reflect the views of the National Science Foundation.

References

Abernathy, W. J. and J. M. Utterback 1978. Patterns of industrial innovation. *Technological Review* **80**, 40–7.
Abramovitz, M. 1952. Economics of growth. In *A survey of contemporary economics* **II**, B. F. Haley (ed.). Homewood, Ill.: Irwin.

Baker, N. R. and D. J. Sweeney 1978. Toward a conceptual framework of the process of organized innovation technology within the firm. *Research Policy* **7**, 150–74.
Biggadike, E. R. 1979. *Corporate diversification: entry, strategy, and performance.* Division of Research, Graduate School of Business Administration, Harvard University, Boston.
Brunner, E. 1974. Some shortcomings in the economic analysis of technological change. *Omega* **2**, 33–41.
Bruton, H. J. 1960. Contemporary theorizing on economic growth. In *Theories of Economic Growth*, B. F. Hoselitz (ed.). Glencoe, NY: The Free Press.
Burns, A. F. 1934. *Production trends in the United States since 1870.* New York: National Bureau of Economic Research.

Chenery, H. B. and T. Watanabe 1958. International comparisons of the structure of production. *Econometrica* **26**, 487–521.
Clark, C. 1940. *The conditions of economic progress.* London: Macmillan.
Cohn, S. F. 1980. Characteristics of technically progressive firms. *Omega* **8**, 441–50.

Dasgupta, P. and J. Stiglitz 1980. Uncertainty, industrial structure and the speed of R&D. *The Bell Journal of Economics* **11**, 1–28.
De Bresson, C. and J. Townsend 1981. Multivariate models for innovation – looking at the Abernathy–Utterback model with other data. *Omega* **9**, 429–36.

de Kluyver, C. A. 1977. Innovation and industrial product life cycles. *California Management Review* **20**, 21–33.

Denison, E. F. 1962. *The sources of economic growth in the United States and the alternatives before us.* New York: Committee for Economic Development.

Elster, J. 1983. *Explaining technical change.* Cambridge: Cambridge University Press.

Ewers, H. J. and R. W. Wettmann 1980. Innovation-oriented regional policy. *Regional Studies* **14**, 161–79.

Fisher, A. G. B. 1933. Capital and the growth of knowledge. *Economic Journal* **43**, 379–89.

Freeman, C. 1977. Economics of research and development. In *Science, technology and society: a cross-disciplinary perspective*, I. Spregel-Rosing and D. de S. Price (Eds). Beverley Hills, Calif.: Sage.

Freeman, C. 1982. *The economics of industrial innovation.* Cambridge, Mass.: MIT Press.

Goddard, J. B. 1980. Technology forecasting in a spatial context. *Futures*, April, 90–105.

Goldman, A. 1982. Short product life cycles: implications for the marketing activities of small high-technology companies. *R&D Management* **12**, 81–9.

Gort, M. and S. Klepper 1982. Time paths in the diffusion of product innovations. *The Economic Journal* **92**, 630–53.

Granstrand, O. 1978. Coordination of multinational R&D: a Swedish case study. *R&D Management* **4**, 1–7.

Hahn, F. H. and R. C. D. Matthews 1965. The theory of economic growth: a survey. In *Surveys of economic theory*, **II**. New York: St. Martin's Press.

Hayes, R. H. and S. C. Wheelwright 1979a. Manufacturing process and product life cycles. *Harvard Business Review* January–February, 133–40.

Hayes, R. H. and S. C. Wheelwright 1979b. The dynamics of process–product life cycles. *Harvard Business Review* March–April, 127–36.

Harcourt, G. C. and N. F. Laing (eds) 1971. *Capital and growth.* Baltimore, Md: Penguin.

Heertje, A. 1977. *Economics of technical change.* London: Weidenfeld and Nicolson.

Hirschman, A. D. 1958. *The strategy of economic development.* New Haven: Yale University Press.

Hoffman, W. G. 1958. *The growth of industrial economies.* New York: Oceana Publications.

Hoffman, W. D. 1976. Market structure and strategies of R&D behaviour in the data processing market – theoretical thoughts and empirical findings. *Research Policy* **5**, 334–53.

Horesh, R. and J. Y. Kamin 1983. How the costs of technological innovation are distributed over time. *Research Management* March–April, 21–2.

Horovitz, J. H. and R. A. Thietart 1982. Strategy, management design and firm performance. *Strategic Management Journal* **3**, 61–76.

Jones, H. G. 1976. *An introduction to modern theories of economic growth.* New York: McGraw-Hill.

Kamien, M. I. and N. L. Schwartz 1982. *Market structure and innovation.* Cambridge: Cambridge University Press.

Keynes, J. M. 1936. *The general theory of employment, interest and money.* London: Macmillan.

Kohn, M. and J. T. Scott 1982. Scale economies in research and development: the Schumpeterian hypothesis. *The Journal of Industrial Economics* **30**, 239–49.

Krumme, G. 1969. Notes on locational adjustment patterns in industrial geography. *Geografiska Annaler* **51b**, 15–19.

Kuznets, S. S. 1930. *Secular movements in production and prices.* New York: Houghton Mifflin.

Kuznets, S. S. 1952. Comments on M. Abramovitz, 'Economics of growth'. In *A survey of contemporary economics*, B. F. Haley (ed.), **II**: 180. Homewood, Ill.: Irwin.

Link, A. N. and J. E. Long 1981. The simple economics of basic scientific research: a test of Nelson's diversification hypothesis. *The Journal of Industrial Economics* **30**, 105–109.

McConnell, J. E. 1982. The internationalization process and spatial form: research problems and prospects. *Environment and Planning A* **14**, 1633–44.

Magee, S. P. 1977. Multinational corporations, the industry technology cycle and development. *Journal of World Trade Law* **2**, 297–321.

Maidique, M. A. 1980. Entrepreneurs, champions, and technological innovation. *Sloan Management Review* Winter, 59–75.

Malecki, E. J. 1981. Science, technology, and regional development: review and prospects. *Research Policy* **10**, 312–34.

Mansfield, E., J. Rapoport, A. Romeo, E. Villani, S. Wagner and F. Husic 1977. *The production and application of new industrial technology.* New York: W. W. Norton.

Mansfield, E. 1981. Composition of R&D expenditures: relationship to size of firm, concentration, and innovative output. *Review of Economics and Statistics* **63**, 610–5.

Marshall, J. N. 1982. Organisational theory and industrial location. *Environment and Planning A* **14**, 1667–83.

Miller, D. and P. H. Friesen 1982. Innovation in conservative and entrepreneurial firms: two models of strategic momentum. *Strategic Management Journal* **3**, 1–25.

Nadiri, M. and G. Bittros 1978. Research and development expenditures and labor productivity at the firm level. In *New developments in productivity measurement*, J. Kendrick and B. Vaccara (eds). New York: National Bureau of Economic Research.

Nelson, R. 1959. The simple economics of basic scientific research. *Journal of Political Economy* June, 297–306.

Nelson, R. R. and S. G. Winter 1977. In search of useful theory of innovation. *Research Policy* **6**, 36–76.

Nelson, R. R. and S. G. Winter 1982a. The Schumpeterian tradeoff revisited. *The American Economic Review* **72**, 114–132.

Nelson, R. R. and S. G. Winter 1982b. *An evolutionary theory of economic change.* Cambridge, Mass.: Harvard University Press.

Oakey, R. P. 1983. New technology, government policy and regional manufacturing employment. *Area* **15**, 61–5.

Organization for Economic Cooperation and Development 1971. *The conditions for success in technological innovation.* Paris: OECD.

Pavitt, K. 1979. Technical innovation and industrial development. *Futures* December, 458–70.

Perroux, F. 1955. Note sur la notion de pole de croissance. *Economie Appliquée* **7**, 307–320.

Piatier, A. 1981. Innovation, information and long-term growth. *Futures* October, 371–82.

Rosenberg, N. 1982. *Inside the black box: technology and economics.* Cambridge: Cambridge University Press.

Rostow, W. W. 1952. *The process of economic growth.* New York: Norton.

Rothwell, R. 1976. *Innovation in textile machinery: some significant factors in success and failure.* SPRU, Occasional Paper Series, *No. 2.* Science Policy Research Unit, University of Sussex.

Rothwell, R. 1977. *The management of successful innovation in the firm.* Proceedings (December), The School of Business Studies, Liverpool University.

Rothwell, R. and W. Zegveld 1982. *Innovation and small and medium sized firms.* London: Frances Pinter.

Schelling, T. S. 1982. *Micromotives and macrobehavior.* New York: Norton.

Scherer, F. M. 1982. Inter-industry and technology flows and productivity growth. *Review of Economics and Statistics* **54**, 627–34.

Schmenner, R. W. 1982. *Making business location decisions.* Englewood Cliffs, NJ: Prentice-Hall.

Schumpeter, J. 1950. *Capitalism, socialism and democracy.* New York: Harper and Row.

Schumpeter, J. 1971. The instability of capitalism. In *The economics of technical change,* N. Rosenberg (ed.). Baltimore, Md: Penguin.

Scott, H. A. 1983. Industrial organization and the logic of intra-metropolitan location: I. Theoretical considerations. *Economic Geography* **59**, 233–50.

Solow, R. M. 1956. A contribution to the theory of economic growth. *Quarterly Journal of Economics* **70**, 65–94.

Solow, R. M. 1957. Technical change and the aggregate production function. *Review of Economics and Statistics* **39**, 312–20.

Slater, M. 1980. The managerial limitations to the growth of firms. *The Economic Journal* **90**, 520–8.

Stead, H. 1976. The cost of technological innovation. *Research Policy* **5**, 2–9.

Taylor, M. J. and N. J. Thrift 1982a. Industrial linkage and the segmented economy: 1. Some theoretical proposals. *Environment and Planning A* **14**, 1601–13.

Taylor, M. J. and N. J. Thrift 1982b. Industrial linkage and the segmented economy: 2. An empirical reinterpretation. *Environment and Planning A* **14**, 1615–32.

Teece, D. J. 1981. Internal organisation and economic performance: an empirical analysis of the profitability of principal firms. *The Journal of Industrial Economics* **30**, 173–199.

Thomas, M. D. 1964. The export base and development stages theories of regional economic growth: an appraisal. *Land Economics* **40**, 421–32.

Thomas, M. D. 1969. Regional economic growth: some conceptual aspects. *Land Economics* **45**, 43–51.

Thomas, M. D. 1981. Growth, change, and the innovative firm. *Geoforum* **12**, 1–17.

Thwaites, A. T. 1978. Technological change, mobile plants and regional development. *Regional Studies* **12**, 445–461.

Usher, A. P. 1954. *A history of mechanical inventions*. Cambridge, Mass.: Harvard University Press.

Usher, A. P. 1971. Technical change and capital formation. In *The economics of technological change*, N. Rosenberg (ed.). Baltimore, Md: Penguin.

Utterback, J. M. and W. J. Abernathy 1975. A dynamic model of process and product innovation. *Omega* **3**, 639–656.

Vernon, R. 1971. *Sovereignty at bay*. New York: Basic Books.

Vernon, R. 1974. The location of economic activity. In *Economic analysis and the multinational enterprise*, J. H. Dunning (ed.). New York: Praeger.

Vernon, R. 1979. The product cycle in a new international environment. *Oxford Bulletin of Economics and Statistics* **41**, 225–67.

Von Hippel, E. 1976. The dominant role of users in the scientific instruments innovation process. *Research Policy* **5**, 212–39.

Walker, W. B. 1979. *Industrial innovation and international trading performance*. Greenwich, Conn.: JAI Press.

7 The regional dimension to technological change in Great Britain

J. GODDARD, A. THWAITES and D. GIBBS

Introduction

The advanced industrial nations are facing a major crisis of structural change brought about by a period of rapid internationalization of production coinciding with the beginnings of a major technological revolution based on microelectronics (OECD 1985). The consequences of these changes have been felt very unevenly within countries – some regions have gained new investment while a large number of others have witnessed a scale of disinvestment unprecedented in the recent past. Notwithstanding the increasing crisis in many areas, regional policies, which during the expansionist era of the 1960s had a place within the armoury of national economic policy as a means of overcoming inflationary pressures emanating from congested regions, are being gradually abandoned or relegated to the domain of social policies designed to ameliorate the consequences of macro-economic change in the most severely affected areas.

In this policy vacuum a multiplicity of *ad hoc* initiatives, many promulgated by local authorities, and designed to bring about indigenous development based around new and small businesses, have emerged as one means of freeing areas from a dependence on international capital. By and large these local initiatives, while closely related to the real problems and opportunities of particular areas, have not been connected to national non-spatial programmes designed to address obvious obstacles to structural change – for example in terms of skills and training, research and development, finance for innovation and information about new technology. The local initiatives are generally under-resourced in financial and human terms and are unable to draw upon the considerable power of central government in such areas as public purchasing, market behaviour and inward and outward investment. A major mis-match is thus developing between the needs of localities and their capacity for action.

The central thesis of this chapter is that the structural challenge facing an economy like that of the UK is not only national but regional. Indeed we contend that just as regional industrial policy was recognized as an important adjunct to macro-economic policy in the 1960s, so too a wide ranging programme to overcome local obstacles to technological change should be central to addressing the national problem of the 1980s.

The macro-economic context for assessing new technologies, investment and employment growth has been clearly set out by Freeman in Chapter 5 of this volume and more fully expounded in a recent report for OECD (Soete & Freeman 1985). This Schumpeterian perspective suggests that the real economic and employment benefits of the new technologies arise with their widespread diffusion to all sectors and by implication all regions of the economy. In the early stages of a technological revolution the benefits are likely to be limited both in terms of enterprises and regions; large gaps will appear between best practice capital and labour productivity and that prevailing elsewhere in the economy. Thus Soete and Dosi reveal a marked contrast between the growth in both labour and capital productivity in the UK electronic industry in the period 1954–80 as compared with most other sectors of the economy (Soete & Dosi 1983). Elsewhere Soete and Freeman (1985, p. 61) argue that

> 'the radical nature of the new technology – its widespread cross-industry application, the lack of reliable, easily accessible information on profitability within the specific user's environment . . . provides a set of powerful retarding factors leading firms to postpone investment decision until the technology has matured and become a technologically less risky investment' (OECD 1985).

From the point of view of this chapter it is important to emphasize that when investment does occur it is introduced into new products and processes which are installed into particular workplaces (which may or may not be synonymous with enterprises) and these are embedded into specific geographic environments. It follows that policies designed to stimulate the diffusion of new technology by reducing the level of uncertainty about investment must take account of this geographical reality.

A further key feature of Freeman's analysis is the emphasis it gives to the interaction between the technological, economic and institutional systems in bringing about revolutionary transformations. He argues that in the downswing a mis-match develops between the emerging technological capacity and what is actually realizable given existing institutional and market conditions. In the case of information technology (see Ch. 5),

> 'fundamental changes in the education and training system, in industrial relations, in managerial and corporate structures, managerial styles, capital markets and financial systems, the pattern of public, private and hybrid investments and the legal and political framework are all required to ensure the widespread diffusion of the new technology'

Also, investments in the infrastructure of information technology, especially telecommunications, is a fundamental condition for its widespread adoption (Goddard et al. 1985, Gillespie et al. 1985).

From a regional perspective it seems reasonable to postulate that many of these 'mis-matches' have a very clear geographical manifestation. Labour skills are far from mobile and are by and large developed in local labour markets, and are very much influenced by the legacy of previous rounds of industrial investment. Areas where skills developed based around heavy engineering may be able to make the transition to electro-mechanical technologies but will need a heavy investment in training to embrace those parts of pure electronics where the emphasis is upon mental rather than physical skills. Moreover, the training capacity in local institutes of higher education is likely to reflect the needs of earlier periods and take a long time to adjust. In terms of management information, the enterprise's scanning of its business environment will be strongly conditioned by existing personal contact networks which are likely, for simple time and geographic considerations, to have a strong local orientation. Information reaching enterprises in areas dominated by outmoded technologies consequently may not embrace the latest technological knowledge. Lastly in the context of the information technology revolution, a lack of demand for telecommunication services arising from a failure to use the ability of this technology to provide access to an international store of technological knowledge may lead to an under-investment in the infrastructure that is likely to be a necessary condition for the next upswing.

Drawing these examples together and following Schmookler (1966) who defined the technological capacity of an economy as 'the accumulated body of knowledge weighted by the number of people who have access to that knowledge', we would suggest that there are significant regional variations in technological capacity or 'the regional ecology' of technological change (Lambooy 1984) within Britain. In the following section of the chapter we review our evidence on regional variations in the incidence of product and process innovation and the importance of one factor, research and development capacity, in accounting for these variations. The evidence we present moves through the innovations spectrum from significant to incremental product innovations and finally to process innovations.

Regional variations in rates of innovation in the UK

Researchers at the Science Policy Research Unit (SPRU), University of Sussex, have recently updated and extended to 1980 an earlier databank of significant innovations introduced into Britain in the postwar period (Townsend *et al*. 1982). The data covers nearly 2300 innovations occurring in over thirty sectors of manufacturing industry defined at the level of Minimum List Heading (1968). While not exhaustive these sectors represent a broad spectrum of British industry and cover a significant proportion of UK manufacturing output and employment. Table 7.1 illustrates the regional trends in innovation between 1945 and 1980. It shows that the South-East exhibits a share of significant innovations well above its share of manufacturing employment and more narrowly of manufacturing establishments. In contrast the 'development areas' have a decreasing share of significant innovations and by the last period this is considerably below what might be expected on their basis of employment and number of establishments.

Table 7.1 Trends in shares of substantial innovations by area.

Years	South East	Non-assisted outside the South East	Intermediate areas	Development area
1945–59	36.7	27.5	19.1	17.5
1960–69	31.2	28.4	24.8	14.8
1970–80	34.0	24.9	30.3	10.6
	(33.1)	(26.0)	(28.5)	(11.9)
total, 1945–80	33.7	27.0	25.5	13.7
N =	770	616	583	313
percentage of manufacturing employees	24.9	30.6	24.6	19.9
percentage of establishments	31.0	29.6	23.4	15.9

Source: Townsend *et al*. (1981). PA 1003 HMSO.
Figures in brackets denote standardization of sectors to produce comparable statistics with earlier time periods.

Table 7.2 Percentage of innovations of foreign origin by receiving area.

South East		Non-assisted		Intermediate area		Development area		Great Britain	
Foreign	Total	Foreign	Total	Foreign	Total	Foreign	Total	Foreign	Total
42.9	33.7	16.2	27.9	23.9	25.5	16.6	13.7	100	100
							$N =$	504	2282

Source: Townsend *et al.* (1981), Table 8.4, p. 83.

The Sussex study also reveals that the area to benefit most from the transfer of substantial foreign technology into Britain is the South East, which received approximately 217 innovations by this means (Table 7.2). On the other hand, the development areas have also benefited from this, largely it would seem at the expense of the non-assisted areas outside the South East. This perhaps reflects the high levels of foreign inward investment to the development areas which makes possible technology transfer within corporations. It also suggests that foreign-owned firms do not see any difficulties in transferring and successfully operating new technologies in the development areas (Haug, Hood & Young 1983).

While substantial innovations are perhaps of enormous value to innovating firms and industries and have far-reaching effects upon other industries and consumers, less significant and incremental changes can be very important to the future of individual enterprises and establishments within enterprises. Such changes can lead to product differentiation and the maintenance or enhancement of market shares. It is therefore not only the major technological changes which are important to the continued advance of industry in an area but also crucial updating and differentiation of locally produced goods. In the following paragraphs we provide evidence of regional variations in product innovations (defined as products 'new' to the establishment over the period 1973–77) in Great Britain.

The data were obtained from interview and postal surveys of 60 per cent of the establishments in three generally innovative industries well represented in all regions of the country – Metal Work Machine Tools, Scientific and Industrial Instruments, and Radio and Electronic Components. This survey, carried out by us at the Centre for Urban and Regional Development Studies, will be referred to as 'the Innovation Survey' in the following pages. The findings of the survey have been published by Thwaites et al. (1981).

Table 7.3 shows that the South East region recorded the highest incidence of product innovation while those establishments located in the development areas were on average less innovative than their national counterparts. Within these areas the least innovative set of establishments were operating from within the Northern region and the most innovative plants were operating in the circle of small commuter towns surrounding but not in London. Further analysis indicates that the spatial variations in product innovation are small within that set of establishments which form part of a larger group whereas the most noticeable difference is between performances in the independent single plant sector or enterprise 'indigenous' to specific areas. On this evidence the development areas appear therefore to suffer from a local enterprise problem, rather than from the effects of external control.

Table 7.3 Establishment location by status: incidence of product innovation (percentage of establishments innovating).

Area	Single plant innovation (%)	Group plant innovation (%)	Total innovation (%)
South East	85	91	88
non-assisted outside the			
South East	74	88	82
intermediate	76	87	82
development area	55	87	73
Great Britain	78	89	84

Source: Thwaites *et al.* (1981).

Although the presence of innovation is important to local economic advance, *where* the development of these innovations occurs may be a better indicator of longer term potential within a community. Hence, 'in-house' product development may more accurately reflect the innovative and resource base of industrial establishments than the mere introduction of new or improved products developed elsewhere. The survey reveals that 83 per cent of establishments claiming a product innovation also claimed that the major development work had been performed on site with the remaining respondents (109 cases) obtaining their products from 'elsewhere'. This latter group may be termed 'dependent' establishments.

The 'dependent' establishments consisted of 10 per cent of single plant enterprises and 22 per cent of group establishments that obtained their product innovations from some source external to the plant. Establishments located in development areas, and in particular the North, were more inclined to 'import' new products than were establishments located elsewhere (Table 7.4). While the 'dependence' of independent enterprises upon external sources for innovation

Table 7.4 Percentage of establishments with external sources of product innovation by region.

Total Great Britain (%)	South East (%)	Non-assisted (%)	Intermediate (%)	Development (%)
17	13	17	15	33

Source: Thwaites *et al.* (1981).

proved higher in development areas than elsewhere an even more marked difference was observed for group establishments in different locations. One-third of development area group plants import technology compared with less than one-fifth of similar plants located in the South-East with the majority of these sources lying in the same corporation.

Of the plants claiming an externally developed innovation nearly 50 per cent come from abroad in particular from the USA; the South East is the greatest beneficiary from this inflow of new products from the US. Within Britain 60 per cent of external sources noted were in the South East and only 8 per cent in the development areas. In addition, of thirty products developed in the South East and transferred to another location for production 57 per cent were transferred to other South East manufacturing plants and only 18 per cent to development area locations. Within the UK there is therefore very little inter-regional transfer of technology.

The preceding analysis has suggested that in quantitative terms the South East has some advantage in the development and manufacture of new products; it is also the chief beneficiary from the transfer of new products into Britain from abroad. Further examination reveals that these advantages are enhanced when the quality of innovations are considered. To achieve this evaluation each innovation mentioned by respondents in the survey was categorized with the help of industrial experts as to whether it was 'high,' 'medium' or 'low' technology. Table 7.5 describes the distribution of locally developed product innovations within independent enterprises according to the technological classification. The table clearly suggests that few enterprises indigenous to the development areas develop their own

Table 7.5 Independent enterprises by on-site development of technology and location.

Area		High	Medium	Low	Total
South East	number	35	35	46	116
	%	30	30	40	
non-assisted	number	3	16	20	39
	%	8	41	51	
intermediate	number	5	13	14	32
	%	15	41	44	
development	number	1	4	11	16
	%		25	69	

Source: Thwaites *et al.* (1981).

high technology products; when innovation does occur it is more likely to be low technology.

Firms may be made competitive by the introduction of new manufacturing processes which reduce the costs and/or improve the quality of existing products. These processes are usually embodied in new machinery of various types, machinery which itself may be the result of product innovations on the part of their manufacturers. The adopter usually purchases the new machinery 'off the shelf' from a sales representative of a supplier and only limited research capacity may be needed in order to incorporate the technology into the customer's own production.

A further perspective on the spatial aspects of technological change in Britain can therefore be obtained by identifying selected products and examining the pattern of take-up amongst potential adopters. Table 7.6 reveals the extent of regional variations in the adoption of five advanced process innovations in 1234 establishments in nine metal-working industries. The data are drawn from a survey which we shall refer to as 'the Diffusion Survey', carried out in the Centre for Urban and Regional Development Studies and reported in Thwaites et al. (1982). The techniques are computerized numerical control (CNC) of metal cutting, removing and joining machinery, microprocessors for the control of manufacturing processes, such as assembly, monitoring and inspection, and the use of computers for the coordination of production and design. By way of comparison with the earlier studies the incorporation of microprocessors into products as a product innovation is also included.

It will be at once apparent from the table that the regional variations in rates of process innovation are far less significant than those recorded for product innovation either in the studies reported previously or when the adoption of, say, CNC is compared with the incorporation of micro-processors into products in this survey. Moreover, examining the cumulative proportion of adopters over time suggests that for certain techniques like CNC the development areas led the South East in 1978 in the proportion of firms that adopted the techniques, a finding probably reflecting the influence of regional capital subsidies in bringing forward the purchase of new equipment.

The influence of research and development

While there are many factors at work we would suggest that regional variation in the commitment to R&D is one of the most important explanations of the low rate of product innovation recorded by industry in the development areas (Alderman et al. 1983). Employment of R&D workers demonstrates a commitment to technological

Table 7.6 Adoption of new technology by assisted area status.

	CNC	Computers in commercial use	Computers in manufacturing and design	Microprocessors in manufacturing processes	Microprocessors products
				Percentage of respondents in each area having adopted	
development areas	21.3	60.9	28.2	10.1	13.9
intermediate areas	25.4	70.3	31.1	12.6	20.2
non-assisted areas	27.0	64.5	29.8	11.6	22.4
South East	24.5	62.6	22.8	11.4	22.7
Great Britain	24.8	64.3	28.3	11.3	20.1
spatial variation coefficient*	22.9	14.6	29.3	22.1	43.8

Source: Thwaites *et al.* (1982).

* Calculated as: $\left(\dfrac{\text{maximum \% } - \text{ minimum \%}}{\text{mean \%}} \right) \times 100.$

advance and clearly increases the chance of success in product innovation. It is therefore not surprising that the Innovation Survey revealed a very strong link between *on-site* R&D and product innovation; indeed 89 per cent of the establishments recording a product innovation had some R&D effort in the establishment in question. Plants with no R&D on site were a far less innovative group.

Further examination reveals that establishments and in particular small independent enterprises located in development areas are less likely to carry out R&D activities on-site as compared with similar enterprises located elsewhere and particularly in the South East of England. Again it is the independent enterprises indigenous to development areas which do not appear to pursue technological advance so rigorously or systematically as their southern counterparts. But even within establishments that are part of a large group there appears to be a greater commitment to R&D in the South East: 50 per cent of such plants in the North employed less than five R&D workers compared with 23 per cent in the North West and 18 per cent in the South East. The regional variations in the mean size of R&D employment per establishment indicated in Table 7.7 suggest important implications for the aggregate level of technological expertise present in the economies of more and less prosperous areas.

A manufacturing establishment can supplement, or to some degree substitute for, its own research effort by using sources of technical information from outside the plant. The dynamic establishment will be expected to exploit these possibilities for technological advance. The Innovation Survey results suggest a clear difference between manufacturing establishments which are part of a larger group and those which are the sole location of the company in the extent to which external technical contacts take place. As a whole, single site companies record a lower level of external contact; however, the one-third of establishments which were part of a group record 'other locations within the group' as their principal source of external technical information. This intra-group transfer of technical information was of particular importance to manufacturing plants located in the development areas. In fact, contacts external to the

Table 7.7　Characteristics of R&D employment by establishment location.

Region	Number	Mean	Median	Maximum
North	40	9.7	4	60
North West	51	14.9	4	120
South East	55	21.2	5	300
total	146			

Source: Thwaites *et al.* (1981).

enterprise as a whole were much less likely in group establishments in development areas than in regions like the South East. This may be because of the lack of capability to absorb external information on the part of development area plants (i.e. a lack of R&D capability on site) and/or a scarcity of suitable information sources locally.

In terms of location, the South East region is the primary source of external technical information. In general, plants in development areas mentioned relatively few local useful technical contacts. They appear to prefer or are forced to use technical sources at a greater distance than are firms located elsewhere. Although, in general, independent enterprises with one manufacturing site are more locally orientated as regards technical information than are plants which are part of a larger group, this relationship does not hold in the development areas, again reflecting the possibly limited supply of suitable technical advice.

Technological change and employment

What do our findings so far imply for jobs in different regions? We would anticipate that a failure to introduce new products within the peripheral regions of Britain will indirectly result in a loss of markets and jobs. At the same time the introduction of new manufacturing processes could directly result in labour displacement. Our Diffusion Survey lends support to this suggestion with, for example, over 90 per cent of the establishments introducing CNC recording a decrease in average job time, a third a decline in setting up time of machines and a further third a reduction in inspection time.

In order to provide some indication of the employment changes associated with the introduction of new and improved products the respondents to the Innovation Survey were asked to estimate the number of jobs created or lost as a direct result of the changes in the year following the innovation. These estimates are compared in Table 7.8 for single and multi-site firms in the North and South East

Table 7.8 The mean employment effect of product and process innovation in the first year by region and plant organizational status.

	Product innovation		Process innovation	
	North	South East	North	South East
single	+0.25	+1.25	−0.50	+0.20
multi-	+6.00	+7.45	−6.53	−0.92
total	+4.30	+4.92	−3.81	−0.49

Source: Thwaites (1983).

Table 7.9 Estimated total annual regional impact of production and process innovation.

	North	South East
total employment change (annual average 1978–81)	−700 (−5.2%)	−4000 (−3.4%)
product innovation	+160 (+1.1%)	+3900 (+3.3%)
process innovation	−130 (−0.9%)	−290 (−0.25%)
total innovation effect	+24 (+0.2%)	+3600 (+3.1%)

Source: Thwaites et al. (1981) and Department of Employment.

regions. The table reveals that the North gains fewer jobs from product innovation but loses more jobs through process innovation than is the case in the South East, with the most significant losses accruing in multi-plant firms in the North.

The overall regional effects of these changes can be estimated by grossing up the sample to give an indication of the *possible* job gains and losses in the three sectors covered by the survey. Table 7.9 suggests that when account is taken of the different sizes of the three sectors in the two regions, the North has gained relatively fewer jobs from product innovation than the South East, but has lost more jobs through process innovation. Combining the two effects gives a marginal increase of employment in one year of 0.2 per cent of total employment in these industries. On the other hand, the South East gains 3600 jobs or 3.1 per cent of total employment. However, these changes need to be seen in the context of the *actual* trends in employment in the three sectors in the two regions. Table 7.9 shows that in the three years after the survey the North experienced an actual annual rate of employment loss of 5.2 per cent compared with a 3.4 per cent loss in the South East. These losses may be attributed to a wide range of factors; however, we may speculate that had firms in the South East also failed to innovate to the same degree as those in the North, then the former region may have experienced an equivalent rate of job loss.

Conclusion: problems and opportunities

The analysis that has been presented in the body of this paper has indicated important differences in patterns of technological innovation in Britain. The single most important cause of these differences would appear to be regional variations in innovative capacity as reflected in the distribution of R&D activity; the peripheral regions are generally dependent on the core area for sources of technological knowledge and do not seem to provide a supporting environment for innovation, especially amongst the smaller and medium-sized enterprises which form the focal point of many contemporary regional industrial development initiatives.

To overcome some of the many problems in the innovation environment in lagging regions a very thorough appraisal of the technological capacity of the local economy is required followed by the development and implementation of coherent strategies which address each of the local bottlenecks to the adoption of new technology. Given the rigidities amongst present institutional structures we would suggest that there is a need for new bodies whose specific terms of reference are to promote technological change within each region. The sort of tasks such a body might undertake related to new information technology are set out below. These tasks should form part of a well formulated strategy through which the area monitors developments, bids for resources, encourages and co-ordinates policy initiatives.

The following activities are indicative of the tasks involved:

(a) Keep abreast of infrastructure investments and new developments in technology and services. Lobby for investment and innovative projects (such as fibre–optic experiments and cable television networks), so helping to ensure that the area is well served and develops expertise in information technology (e.g. interactive cable services).

(b) Support the marketing of telecommunications services: publicity and awareness exercises, demonstration projects and resource centres.

(c) Lobby for tariff reductions to facilitate access to core regions.

(d) Co–ordinate and give greater publicity to existing initiatives, such as technology transfer; seek out and support new initiatives and projects, such as regional databases on goods and services, tourist facilities and export opportunities. Bid for new projects and 'top–up' resources to support innovation, in addition to those provided through national or European policies which are not regionally differentiated.

(e) Set up centres/agencies able to provide, at an accessible 'shop-front' location, a wide range of assistance on the adoption of information technology. This could include access to technical databases, access to facsimile, telex, etc., on a bureau basis also offering use and 'hands on' experience of automated office systems, microcomputers, etc. Such an activity would need field staff, especially to deal with technology transfer activities within manufacturing industry.

(f)   Demonstrations of telecommunications networking and the inclusion of its potential within promotional efforts to encourage inward investment. It is necessary to show enterprises the capabilities of telecommunications as an aid to branch managements and as a way of facilitating decentralization of some functions.

(g)   So far as information technology production is concerned, there is a need to identify specialisms which build on the industrial production strengths of the area and focus efforts on establishing these via indigenous development and inward investment. However, as far as possible competitive bidding for inward investment should be avoided.

(h)   Co-ordinate information on current and future skill requirements; support/lobby for training and re-training programmes.

Obviously, not all these proposals will be relevant to each region, and some regions may have specific needs which might be unsuitable for inclusion within an information technology strategy. However, it is worth noting that one of the strengths of an information technology strategy is that the technology is of such general applicability, and has such widespread impacts, that it can draw in a multiplicity of issues and concerns, cutting across boundaries of conventional policy areas.

The role of the provincial cities in carrying out these strategies in the less favoured and peripheral regions is undoubtedly crucial. They are the focal points of their regions, best able to take a leading role in the diffusion of technological awareness and change. Above all, they have the institutional infrastructures capable of supporting policies to stimulate information technology. Although these institutional resources have often become depleted – notably through the erosion of financial and business services – the provincial cities of Britain generally have higher education institutions, chambers of commerce, regional headquarters of the telecommunications services, local government and branches of central government. Many have regional development and promotion organizations as well. To successfully implement an information technology strategy, these institutions would have to work together and support each other.

These cities have some particular characteristics especially relevant to information technology. Certainly their educational institutions have much to offer information technology producers and users such as qualified manpower, training and R&D support. In many cases there remains considerable scope for greater involvement of these institutions in their local economies. The cities can offer environments conducive to the relocation of clerical work which has become more mobile with the spread of distance-independent data transmission services. Provincial cities often have plentiful supplies of clerical workers, low-cost accommodation and other services. The cities are very much more likely to be 'cabled' than small towns (let alone rural areas) and hence may have the opportunity of participating in the provision of 'value added network services', including city-wide information and interactive services between enterprises.

In a variety of situations the provincial cities would have to play a key role in establishing, leading and implementing the kind of strategy outlined above. They must show, by example, what information technology can offer and so set in motion a process of diffusion into their surrounding regions. The cities must service the activities of their hinterlands – such as agriculture or tourism – acting as brokers between hinterlands and markets elsewhere. In some ways new information technology may weaken the position of the cities, as hardware production favours greenfield locations and 'remote working' strengthens the attraction of locations outside the city. This makes it all the more imperative that strategies must be regional and the mutual dependence of city and region recognized.

Information technology is not a universal panacea for all the problems of lagging regions or old industrial areas. But it can offer them some new opportunities – in contrast to the apparently unavoidable and negative impacts on existing employment levels. A coherently structured strategy, sensitive to a region's specific needs, administered within the region – and drawing heavily on the resources of the provincial cities – could enable depressed regions to maximize the potential benefits of this new technology.

Note

1 This chapter draws heavily on research undertaken in the Centre for Urban and Regional Development Studies, University of Newcastle upon Tyne, over the period 1978–84. Neil Alderman, Tony Edwards, Andrew Gillespie, Peter Nash, Ray Oakey and Fred Robinson all made significant contributions to the research. Support was provided by the Economic and Social Research Council, the Department of Trade and Industry, the Department of the Environment and the European Commission. All responsibility for the text rests with the authors.

References

Alderman, N., J. B. Goddard and A. T. Thwaites 1983. *Regional and urban perspectives on industrial innovation: applications of logit and cluster analysis to survey data.* Discussion paper No. 42. Centre for Urban and Regional Development Studies, Newcastle upon Tyne.

Gillespie, A. E., J. B. Goddard, J. F. F. Robinson, I. Smith and T. Thwaites 1985. *The effects of new information technology on the less favoured regions of the Community*, Commission of the European Communities, Studies Collection, Regional Policy Series No. 23. Brussels: Commission of the European Communities.

Goddard, J. B., A. E. Gillespie, J. F. F. Robinson and A. T. Thwaites 1985. New information technology and urban and regional development. In *Technological change and regional development,* A. T. Thwaites and R. Oakey (eds). London: Frances Pinter.

Haug, P., M. Hood and S. Young 1983. R & D intensity in the affiliates of US-owned manufacturing in Scotland. *Regional Studies* **17**, 383–92.

Lambooy, J. G. 1984. The regional economy of technological change. In *New spatial dynamics and economic crisis*, J. G. Lambooy (ed.). Helsinki: Finn.

OECD 1985. *Employment Growth and Structural Change*. Paris: OECD.

Soete, L. and G. Dosi 1983. *Technology and employment in the electronics industry*. London: Frances Pinter.

Soete, L. and C. Freeman 1985. New technologies, investment and employment growth. In *Employment growth and structural change*. Paris: OECD.

Schmookler, J. 1966. *Invention and economic growth*. Cambridge, Mass.: MIT Press.

Thwaites, A. T., R. P. Oakey and P. A. Nash 1981. *Industrial innovation and regional development*. Final Report to the Department of the Environment. Centre for Urban and Regional Development Studies, Newcastle University.

Thwaites, A. T., A. Edwards and D. Gibbs 1982. *Inter-regional diffusion of production innovations in Great Britain*. Final Report to the Department of Industry and the EEC. Centre for Urban and Regional Development Studies, Newcastle University.

Thwaites, A. T. 1983. The Employment Implications of Technological Change in a Regional Context, in Gillespie, A. E. (ed.), *Technological Change and Regional Development,* London Paper in Regional Science **12**, Pion, London.

Townsend, J. F., F. Henwood, G. S. Thomas, K. L. Pavitt and S. M. Wyatt 1982. *Science and technology indicators for the UK: innovations in Britain since 1935*. Report prepared for SERC/SSRC Joint Committee, University of Sussex.

8 The electronics industry and regional development in Britain[1]

A. SAYER and K. MORGAN

Introduction

As the principal user and supplier of core technology for economic development in the foreseeable future, the electronics industry is the subject of great expectations in all advanced industrial economies. In Britain this interest is evident in the 'targetting' of the sector by the government in its industrial assistance and inward investment policies, and by the Scottish and Welsh Development Agencies and local industry and employment development schemes. The consequences of failure in this key sector would be dire for both national and regional development.

It is the connection between changes in this industry and British regional development that forms the focus of this chapter. The main questions we examine are as follows: What is the state of health of the electronics industry and what implications does this have for the sector's role in regional development? Does the industry provide, as some have hoped, a salvation or escape route for backward regions? What are the attractions and disadvantages of particular regions for the industry? And last but by no means least, what has it to offer labour in the regions?

The chapter consists of three sections: first, some theoretical preliminaries on how we think the above questions should be approached; secondly, the main empirical section, including a sketch of the special characteristics of the British electronics industry and its potential, brief assessments of recent developments in Central Scotland and the M4 corridor and a more extended analysis of electronics firms in South Wales; and thirdly, in the final section, we return to some more theoretical issues which have important policy implications.

Theoretical preliminaries

If the contribution of an industry to regional development is to be assessed, we must be clear about what we mean by 'regional development'. Unfortunately most commentators, be they policymakers or academics, pass over this problem, as if the enumeration of new enterprises in a region or such-like was an unproblematic index. The ambiguity of the concept can be brought home by means of a distinction between development *in* a region and development *of* a region. The latter would involve an improvement in a region's resources for labour, for skills, and in the quantity and quality of employment. Development *in* a region is clearest in cases of jobless growth in which company revenues and profitability grow but with stagnant or falling employment and local purchasing. The 'cathedrals in the desert' syndrome typified by the heavy industrial complexes of the Italian *Mezzogiorno* are perhaps the most famous example of this phenomenon.

The concept of 'jobless growth' is becoming more widely known now as scarcely a single SIC order reveals any net employment growth (Figs 8.1 & 8.2). However, few commentators appear to have thought through its implications for regional development. This failure generally allows development *in* a region to be presented as development *of* the region and hence obscures the problems faced by labour with respect to the changes. We intend to correct this oversight.

Our second theoretical preliminary concerns interdependencies involved in industrial change. We will deal with some of these in the final section of the chapter but at this point we want to emphasize *intra-firm* interdependencies in multi-plant firms. In such firms, the behaviour of a particular plant can only be understood within the context of the wider corporate system of which it is a part. Often this system takes the form of a hierarchical spatial division of labour, whether intra-national or international (Massey 1979); different stages of production and parts of companies are separated out and located in the most appropriate places. Usually the control and conception ('top-end') functions of the company are restricted to the main metropolitan region while ('back-end') production is widely distributed. This functional differentiation is reflected in the occupational profiles of a given industry in different parts of the country or, for the multinational firms, in different countries. The proportion of unskilled and semi-skilled workers is much higher in peripheral regions than in central regions, and the converse is true for management and technicians. However, many observers have been misled by these facts into imagining that the most prosperous regions have little basic production. This is certainly not true for electronics and

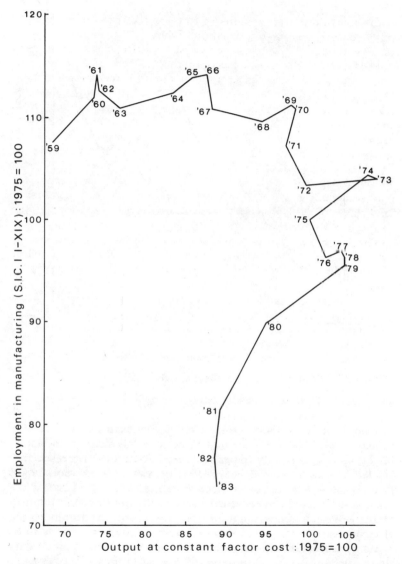

Figure 8.1 Jobless growth and decline in British manufacturing 1959–83.

Figure 8.2 Output and employment in electronics (Soete & Dosi 1983).

probably not for most other sectors either. For example, in electronic capital goods (MLH 367), while 55 per cent of Welsh workers are operators as against only 18 per cent in the South East, the respective *absolute* numbers are 222 and 10 195 (Brayshaw & Lawson 1982)! (Interestingly, the consumer electronics industry (MLH 365) is the most concentrated in the South East, despite its low skill requirements.) As can be seen from Figure 8.3, the South East dominates the electronics industry (MLH 363–367: telecommunications, components, consumer, computers and electronic capital goods), indeed its share has increased recently from 49.5 per cent in 1977 to 53.2 per cent in 1981.

While the concept of a hierarchical spatial division of labour does not entail the neglect of the dominance of production in central regions, many commentators have made this error, perhaps through the residual influence of crude 'centre–periphery' concepts.

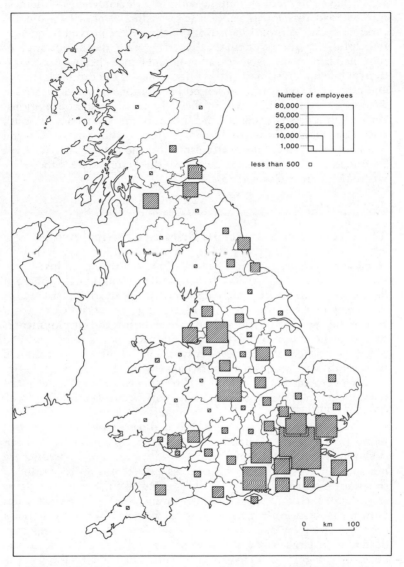

Figure 8.3 Employment in electronic engineering 1981, by county.

We might also comment briefly in passing on two other concepts, which have the merit of emphasizing interdependencies – the new international division of labour (e.g. Fröbel *et al.* 1980) and the product cycle (Vernon 1966). Both of these have proved frequently unhelpful, for they systematically exaggerate the importance of unskilled labour-intensive production and hence cheap-labour locations while underestimating the importance of the capital-intensive and high-skill and market-oriented production, which is located in advanced countries and, within these, in more prosperous regions. As a result it seems easier to find literature on electronics in South East Asia than in Western Europe, while within Britain Central Scotland seems to get more attention than the South East. We have examined some of the more pervasive theoretical stereotypes elsewhere (Morgan & Sayer 1983).

The electronics industry in Britain: a critical profile

In view of the strategic significance of the electronics industry it is now imperative that both its character and its contemporary phase of development are more widely appreciated. Its relative resistance to the generalized slump in manufacturing *output* is clear from Figure 8.2. Yet, the relationship between output and employment is such that the nature of this 'growth' industry needs to be qualified given the emergence of jobless growth, a phenomenon not confined to, though most pronounced in Britain (IMF 1982; Figs 8.2 & 8.4).

However, net employment decline conceals a profound social recomposition of the workforce along both occupational and gender lines. For instance, high-grade occupations (managers, scientists, technologists, technicians) have recorded net employment growth while lower grade occupations (especially operators) have been declining in numerical significance. Crude notions of de-skilling are not appropriate to capture this process: rather, it is more legitimate to speak of a polarization of skills (see Fig. 8.5). Secondly, it also seems appropriate to speak of a 'de-feminization' of the electronics industry (at least in Britain) because, in the period 1974–81, females accounted for over 80 per cent of total job-loss. This gender-specific decline is in large part a function of the 'collapse of work' in the operator category, a well-known occupational ghetto for females (SPRU 1982, Morgan & Sayer 1983).

Overall, the British electronics industry (in the strict sense, meaning the indigenous industry) is suffering relative decline; employment has fallen back to mid-1960s levels (350000) after peaking at 435000 in 1974 (Figs 8.2 & 8.4), and a trading surplus in 1975

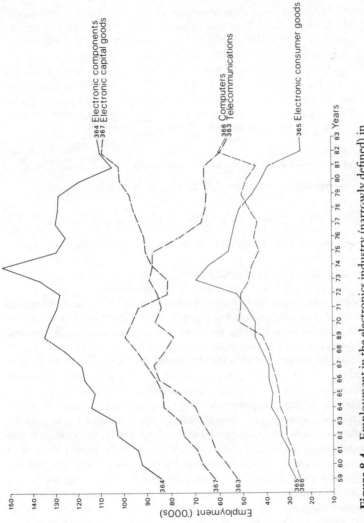

Figure 8.4 Employment in the electronics industry (narrowly defined) in Great Britain 1959–83 (Soete & Dosi 1983, and figures quoted in the Department of Employment Gazette).

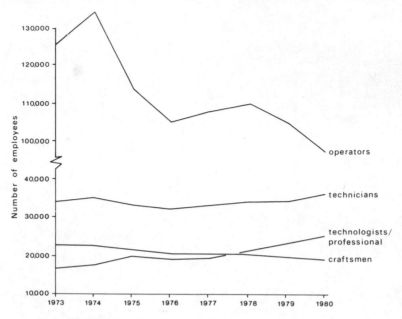

Figure 8.5   Employees in electronic occupations.

deteriorated into a deficit of some £1.5 billion in 1982. Moreover, the
two fastest growing subsectors (consumer electronics and information technology) largely accounted for this deficit. While the
indigenous industry is relatively strongest in the capital equipment
subsectors of defence and telecommunications, the former boasts
limited civil–commercial spin-offs, while the latter has suffered, *inter
alia*, from idiosyncratic national public procurement policies, with
the effect that export potential has not been exploited. Yet the
weakness of the whole of the British electronics industry is greater
than the weaknesses of its parts because the former lacks the benefits
of the technological complementarities between vigorous mass components, consumer and computer industries which are enjoyed by
the US and Japan. As a result technological dependence has increased
and Britain's record in generating major innovations in microelectronics has been very poor (Soete & Dosi 1983). Overall, this current
profile suggests that there is great cause for concern about this
strategic industry in Britain (NEDC 1983). Indeed, it is now difficult
to speak of a 'British' industry with respect to consumer electronics
and semiconductors and, given the influx of overseas telecommunications companies in response to liberalization, the composition of

telecommunications seems set to become radically transformed in the medium term. We therefore have to confront the damning paradox that although Britain is the most favoured offshore location for US electronics firms in the world, its electronics industry is still in relative decline. Whereas previously regional analysts have been concerned with external control in relation to the economies of particular regions, it now seems to us more relevant to consider its significance at the national level. Research into the diffusion and competitive effects transmitted from the overseas to the indigenous sector will become essential if we are to gain a deeper understanding of the long term cost–benefit effects on the national economy.

Corporate hierarchies and forms of regional development

We have already referred to the hierarchical spatial division of labour, the chief merit of which is to illuminate the *qualitative* dimension of uneven development: this dimension was always obscured when the regional problem was simply reduced to the restrictive conception of over-dependence on 'traditional industries' (as in McCrone 1976). Corporate hierarchies mean that we have to distinguish particular forms of regional development associated with the electronics industry. Clearly, the types of activities (e.g. control–conception–production) through which a region is inserted into wider national and international processes will have different effects within the region and will also set certain parameters as to what is or is not feasible given its position in the hierarchy. For illustrative purposes we now briefly examine some of these forms via three regional cases.

The (English) M4 corridor

The South East's increasing dominance of employment in the electronics industry has already been noted (although its dominance is even greater if more recent growth sectors like computer services is included because some 70 per cent of UK companies are based in this region). The non-metropolitan South East appears to account for most of the recent growth of employment in the region although the M4 counties do not display the burgeoning growth we have been led to expect from media and property development companies (see Fig. 8.3). Nevertheless, this 'region' is now a privileged location for a distinctive array of corporate HQs, public and private R&D facilities and national and international marketing functions: it has been fashioned by indigenous growth, intra-regional movement and overseas inward investment which, in not a few cases, has involved not production only plants but European management and R&D centres.

The apparent attractions of the M4 corridor are well enough known, at least in an impressionistic sense: they include a critical mass of highly skilled personnel, which enables incoming firms to recruit (though not necessarily to retain) labour for which there is an *international* shortage; access to good communications, especially Heathrow, which holds a premium for overseas companies; a core of government research establishments, proximity to which appears to be important for defence contractors; a rural work environment capable of sustaining elite life-styles; and a marked absence of trade union traditions, so that non-union company policies apparently coincide with non-union labour practices.

What most distinguishes the M4 corridor from Central Scotland or South Wales is its elite occupational structure and its dense decision-making network of activities which have the potential for spawning (and sustaining) new firm formation to an extent not readily apparent elsewhere. The vast corpus of recently established electronics firms claim to be locationally inert – immobility of professional staff being the most important reason – and, of those that do consider expansion in an assisted area, the major requirement is for a 'pool of low-cost labour' (DTI, 1982). While this elite occupational structure may not be numerically significant, its strategic importance stems from the fact that 'the critical future factor will be *personnel* and the corridor has the image and facilities to farm this important growth group' (Davies & Smyth 1983, p. 61). A further distinctive feature of the M4 corridor is its strength in subsectors of electronics which are still experiencing job growth – capital equipment, computers and computing services.

It is this specificity of the corridor which needs to be more widely appreciated, otherwise vulgar injections like 'Britain needs more Berkshires' (Anon., 1982) will continue to retail as feasible options for regional development generally. At bottom, such injunctions exaggerate the possibilities, but belittle the constraints, of the hierarchical spatial division of labour: and we need to remember that the leading edge of this hierarchy resides not in the corridor but in the USA and Japan.

Although the corridor is often referred to as an exemplar of development without aid, we ought not to forget that *public* investment in communications, R&D and military procurement together constitute powerful enabling conditions for 'take off': in short, the spatial effects of state policy are not to be exclusively identified with formal spatial programmes such as regional policy. The equipment budget of the Ministry of Defence (which in 1983 stood at some £7.2

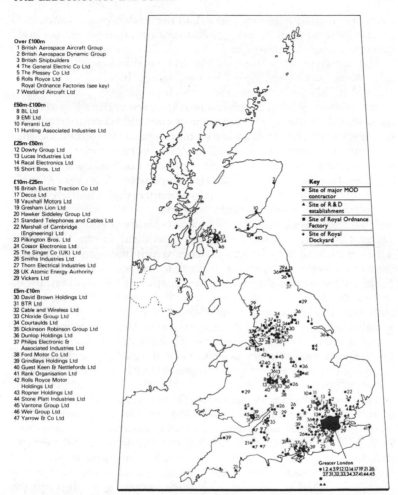

Over £100m
1 British Aerospace Aircraft Group
2 British Aerospace Dynamic Group
3 British Shipbuilders
4 The General Electric Co Ltd
5 The Plessey Co Ltd
6 Rolls Royce Ltd
  Royal Ordnance Factories (see key)
7 Westland Aircraft Ltd

£50m-£100m
8 BL Ltd
9 EMI Ltd
10 Ferranti Ltd
11 Hunting Associated Industries Ltd

£25m-£50m
12 Dowty Group Ltd
13 Lucas Industries Ltd
14 Racal Electronics Ltd
15 Short Bros. Ltd

£10m-£25m
16 British Electric Traction Co Ltd
17 Decca Ltd
18 Vauxhall Motors Ltd
19 Gresham Lion Ltd
20 Hawker Siddeley Group Ltd
21 Standard Telephones and Cables Ltd
22 Marshall of Cambridge
   (Engineering) Ltd
23 Pilkington Bros. Ltd
24 Cossor Electronics Ltd
25 The Singer Co (UK) Ltd
26 Smiths Industries Ltd
27 Thorn Electrical Industries Ltd
28 UK Atomic Energy Authority
29 Vickers Ltd

£5m-£10m
30 David Brown Holdings Ltd
31 BTR Ltd
32 Cable and Wireless Ltd
33 Chloride Group Ltd
34 Courtaulds Ltd
35 Dickinson Robinson Group Ltd
36 Dunlop Holdings Ltd
37 Philips Electronic &
   Associated Industries Ltd
38 Ford Motor Co Ltd
39 Grindlays Holdings Ltd
40 Guest Keen & Nettlefords Ltd
41 Rank Organisation Ltd
42 Rolls Royce Motor
   Holdings Ltd
43 Ropner Holdings Ltd
44 Stone Platt Industries Ltd
45 Vantona Group Ltd
46 Weir Group Ltd
47 Yarrow & Co Ltd

Key
● Site of major MOD
  contractor
▲ Site of R & D
  establishment
■ Site of Royal Ordnance
  Factory
✦ Site of Royal
  Dockyard

Figure 8.6 Arms companies paid £5 million or more by the MoD in 1979/80 (information taken from the Counter Information Services Report on the Arms Industry, 1982 CIS Anti-report No. 31).

billion or six times regional policy expenditure) is rarely considered as a form of industrial support. Yet non-assisted areas are the main beneficiaries of such contracts (see Fig. 8.6 and Morgan 1985). However, the question arises whether 'take-off' for the M4 corridor, or at least Berkshire, means recovery for the British electronics industry. Again we need to examine both the interaction between foreign inward investors and indigenous firms and the product and sectoral distribution of new plants and firms. Although we have yet to research these questions, existing information does not give strong grounds for optimism.

Central Scotland

If the core functions of the electronics industry in Britain are largely concentrated in the South East and its western M4 corridor, this does not mean that other regions are wholly engaged in routine production activities. Too often Central Scotland is characterized simply as a branch-plant location: the meaning being external control equals branch plant which equals routine assembly. However, Central Scotland cannot be subsumed under some undifferentiated 'periphery' and it seems more legitimate to see it as having an intermediate status, different from both the M4 corridor and South Wales. Currently, some 38000 are employed in the electronics industry in Scotland – largely concentrated in the central belt – and the most important segments are defence electronics (25 per cent), industrial, commercial and telecommunications (25 per cent), information systems (22.5 per cent) and components (17.5 per cent). However, despite the justifiable interest in the qualitative aspects of Scottish electronics, its quantitative importance in employment terms is rarely put into perspective; in 1981 employment in Scotland's electronics industry only amounted to 37 per cent of that of Greater London – and this after a decade of major job losses in the latter!

The 'Scottish' industry has been fashioned largely through inward investment from England and overseas: the indigenous sector accounted for only 10 per cent of employment in 1978. However, even though overseas multinational corporations do not perform their leading-edge R&D work in Scotland, their operations involve far more than routine assembly. US firms, for example, are frequently engaged in development work, adapting products to the nuances of the European market. While such work is of a secondary status compared to that of their parent, it can be quite advanced by the standards of the indigenous British civil electronics industry, so much so that 'branch-plant' status is not necessarily an index for routine assembly (Morgan & Sayer 1983). In other words, it is not enough merely to register the presence of 'branch plants' or 'R&D'. It is important to establish what *kind* of production and what kind of R&D if we are to assess their contribution to regional and national economic development: R&D in Central Scotland is unlikely to be the same or have the same effect as R&D in Silicon Valley.

Furthermore, the attraction of Central Scotland should not be reduced to its capital subsidies and (by European standards) its relatively low labour costs, as important as these have been. Increasingly important is the critical mass of firms already established and the small, but significant, pool of indigenous expertise in such fields as VLSI, opto-electronics and artificial intelligence within the Scottish universities. In one sense Central Scotland commands an advantage over the M4 corridor in that once key personnel are recruited, they are more easily retained and turnover is less of a problem in comparison with the corridor.

Nevertheless, it is the predominance of production activities that distinguishes Central Scotland from the corridor. The overseas sector remains poorly integrated, with multiplier effects which afford little secondary employment and, perhaps most important for long term prospects, a significant indigenous sector has not developed. What is notable about indigenous firms (e.g. Rodime) is that to keep abreast of international leading-edge innovation, they feel obliged to expand *outside* Britain (in the USA in this case) soon after birth.

This latter phenomenon has now become common in British electronics. It shows that although technological expertise and superiority is neither totally immobile nor unchangeable it is nevertheless massively concentrated in the USA and, more recently, in Japan. In other words, the mere fact of British ownership in electronics does not remove its technological dependence and the locational restrictions that this entails.

South Wales

If the 'branch-plant' stereotype needs to be somewhat modified as regards Central Scotland, its essentials are far more visible with respect to South Wales. Since total Welsh employment in the electronics industry in 1981 was only 14000, South Wales occupies a marginal position in this industry in terms of both the level and status of the employment. It has neither the limited R&D platform nor the small indigenous sector evident in Central Scotland, and its primary attraction lies largely in it being the subsidized end of the English M4 corridor. (However, its accessibility to southern England allows a number of firms to 'retreat' over the Severn so as to remove themselves from labour poaching and the up-bidding of key personnel salary levels.) The electronics enclave has even lower local multiplier effects than in Scotland, while the currently installed overseas plants – which have proved more secure than their British counterparts over the last decade – now appear to have reached the limits of their (employment) growth (Morgan & Sayer 1983). Yet, it is worth recording that few of the plants surveyed were 'overspill' establishments producing standardized products, which is what might have been expected from the 'branch-plant' or 'product cycle' stereotypes. Most were engaged in producing products for the nuances of the UK or continental markets (e.g. televisions adapted with teletext facilities).

Compared to Central Scotland, South Wales has few advantages beyond regional aid, and perhaps accessibility, to offer firms. Most North American and Japanese-owned firms are using their South Wales plants as export platforms for the European and British markets. The electronics industry in South Wales has had to adjust to working in Britain's nearest approximation to a homogenous working-class region. As a result South Wales has more of a 'headless' occupational structure than Scotland, with relatively low numbers of technically skilled and managerial employees.

The electronics industry in South Wales: examples of corporate behaviour

In this section we focus on a selection of plants from our survey. The electronics plants in the survey constituted over 90 per cent of employment in electronics in South Wales. The research aimed firstly to situate the plants in the subsectors and competitive contexts in which they operate and secondly to discover their general characteristics and interaction with the regional context. The examples selected below are intended to illustrate some of the main types of sectoral and competitive context. These are then followed by a brief summary of general problems faced by firms and labour which arise in the regional context, particularly those relating to management and unions.

Consumer electronics

The position of the indigenous consumer electronics industry deteriorated rapidly during the 1970s largely because of the superior product, process and marketing performance of Japanese companies. Domestic producers were unable to meet the demand induced by the 'Barber boom' (the trade deficit increased by over 100 per cent between 1972 and 1973) thus preparing the ground for an influx of Japanese direct investment in the UK (see Sciberras 1980, Morgan & Sayer 1983). Employment in the subsector fell from 69000 in 1973 to 25000 in 1981, leading to additional job-loss in the indigenous components sector as well. (This is an example of technological complementarities working in reverse.) *National* employment decline was offset in South Wales through new investment by four

Japanese companies which, in 1982, had a combined employment of 3650.

Among these new entrants, some very different effects were evident both within the plants and in terms of the latter's impact on their local labour markets. The most extreme contrast was between a wholly owned Japanese subsidiary (company A) and an Anglo–Japanese joint-venture (company B) whose shares of the UK television market were 6 and 16 per cent respectively in 1982.

The strategic aim of company A was one of *gradual* expansion: to strengthen the plant's competitive position in the long term, and to develop advanced technology products in its own right. Modest progress had been achieved in all these areas and, of all the Japanese CTV companies in Britain, company A had progressed furthest in exploiting development research on teletext and viewdata: the results were already being incorporated into products and exported to Japan. Although its process technology was not as advanced as its home plants, company A had introduced automatic insertion equipment from the outset despite the fact that volume did not justify its introduction: product *quality* appeared to be the principal rationale for its use. Furthermore, the status of this plant had been upgraded with the addition of a TV-tube facility which supplied in-house needs for 30 per cent of its European sales for this key component. Output had expanded annually since start-up (with the exception of 1983) and, while this was expected to continue for both UK and EEC markets, employment (960 in 1983) would remain broadly stable because of increased automation and productivity growth. Within its local labour market this plant was perceived as a 'novelty', principally because it had declared itself against any redundancies. So, in terms of received notions, this plant, now in its tenth year of production, could in no way be subsumed under the insecure 'branch-plant' syndrome.

Company B, though very much a marriage of convenience for both partners, represented a desperate bid to remain in the market on the part of the English plant, whose record on investment in process technology, product development and marketing had been little short of abysmal despite it being part of a large, diversified engineering group. At the start of the joint-venture in 1979, the time-economies of set production were well above the UK industry average of around 6.1 person-hours per set. Since 1979 output has doubled, time-economies of set production have been reduced from 9 hours to 2 hours in 1984 and employment in 1985 will have fallen from 1740 in 1979 to around 1200. The bulk of components (60 per cent) are still secured from Japan and attempts to produce some components in-house have been abandoned for both cost and technical problems.

The vast differences in the management practices of the partners in the joint venture have resulted in considerable corporate conflict, indeed it represents a poor advertisement for Anglo–Japanese co-operation and a justification for the Japanese preference for wholly owned subsidiaries on greenfield sites. In terms of both internal results and the impact on the local labour market, the plant – despite its semi-indigenous status – has proved extremely insecure from the point of view of labour.

Overall, the security of employment in the wholly-owned Japanese plants must be assessed against the larger (non-local) job-*loss* in the indigenous TV and components industries. Despite such relative job security in South Wales, it has been a great disappointment to the regional development authorities that some of the Japanese companies have not introduced their new generation, mass-market products (VTRs) into the region. This suggests that, in assessing the effects of 'external control', we should focus on product markets as well as labour markets.

Electronic components

The indigenous electronics components industry has fared better than that of consumer electronics but, while output has increased rapidly since 1970, so too has the trade deficit – especially in key components such as integrated circuits – although this is stabilizing as overseas exporters set up production facilities in the UK. However, rapid output growth has been combined with considerable advances in output per person which is in part responsible for the decline in employment from 132000 in 1970 to around 107000 in 1981. The past decade has witnessed a rapid change in component technology with, above all, the pervasive growth of microelectronics.

Six plants were examined in this subsector and the two cases reported here represent specific responses to the dominant trends in the industry, particularly as regards technological and product innovation, corporate status, employment and maturity.

Company C is the only major employer in our survey with its headquarters in South Wales: it has been operating in the region for 34 years. A decade ago this company was still very much a producer of electromechanical components, almost entirely reliant on the consumer electronics end market. Since the latter was a 'boom or bust' market (induced in part by 47 fiscal changes affecting credit terms in 25 years), the company consciously sought to diversify in 1965. A combination of foresight and necessity (in the shape of recession after 1973 and the falling number of components in TVs) stimulated a bold diversification strategy. By 1981 its traditional consumer market accounted for only 7 per cent of turnover, while electronic subsystems for the Ministry of Defence accounted for 12 per cent and professional and industrial equipment markets represented a further 23 per cent.

This diversification strategy was greatly facilitated by a licensing agreement with a US electronics company (which, up until 1982, controlled 20 per cent of company C's equity) and by a series of acquisitions in targeted products and technology (two of these four acquisitions have been along the English M4 corridor). The major obstacles to this diversification have been associated with the recruitment of managers and R&D teams since incumbent personnel proved unable to make the transition to new technologies and product markets: recruitment problems were attributed in no small way to the received image of the region as one of 'coal, steel and militancy'.

Symptomatic of the hierarchy discussed earlier, the R&D work for company C's most innovative product (a microprocessor-based control system for the automotive industry) was performed at its Berkshire facility where its advanced engineering centre is based. Despite its HQ base in South Wales, company C has been obliged to adapt to this prevailing hierarchy by locating some of its most advanced R&D work where the expertise is currently most concentrated.

Interestingly, *product* diversification was accompanied by a *spatial* diversification so that its fastest growing activities are based not in its three plants on the coalfield but, increasingly, in two plants in south-east Wales – within the Welsh Development Agency's 'golden triangle' around the M4 in Gwent – and in its two plants in Berkshire. Spatial diversification has also been stimulated by its recent emphasis on small plants (optimum size of 300 employees) and its attempt to seek out non-coalfield labour markets with more flexible labour practices (see later). However, new employment growth in these less mature plants has not been nearly sufficient to offset the job-loss associated with diversification and recession: total employment peaked at 3500 employees in 1974 and fell to 1960 in 1983 and, of all the plants, the *HQ plant* bore the brunt of this job loss. Company C has undoubtedly been very successful in corporate terms but, in the context of jobless growth in this subsector, corporate health is not wholly synonymous with regional health.

Company D is of interest both as a unique venture in itself and as an illustration of the constraints and demands of the spatial division of labour in the electronics industry. Established in 1978 in an attempt to provide Britain with an indigenous source of mass market semiconductor products – a market from which domestic firms had retreated to concentrate on customized products – this company hopes to catapult itself into advanced product markets. For this purpose, company D felt obliged to position its initial R&D and production facilities in the USA, because this combined leading-edge semiconductor firms and (equally important) a highly sophisticated end-user sector, as well as a major pool of process engineers, of which there was a chronic international shortage. This locational behaviour speaks volumes about the perceived status of Britain as an environment in which to develop truly leading-edge innovations in this field; it also illustrates the fact that indigenous ownership does not, of itself, eliminate technological dependence.

Company D has three major sites: R&D and production facilities in the USA; a British management and R&D centre in England; and its main volume production plant in South Wales. Currently, its employment in the USA stands at 750, while some 650 are employed in the UK, though some 900 are expected to be engaged in South Wales alone by the end of 1984. Unlike most plants in the region, company D has been able to buy its way out of the constraints imposed by its local labour markets. This, together with the attractions of working with advanced technology, has enabled company D to recruit key personnel from all over the UK to its South Wales plant. As yet it is too soon to assess the performance of the venture as a whole or its South Wales plant in particular. The company was expected to make its first profit in 1984 and although its output was split equally between the UK and the USA, the latter accounted for £35 million of its total £37 million turnover.

Despite its propitious start, in terms of both technological innovation and market shares, company D faces formidable problems. The semiconductor industry is increasingly being dominated by large multinational corporations – induced in part by the exponentially increasing costs of product design and equipment – and by alliances among semiconductor firms and between these and user firms (e.g. IBM and Intel). Currently, company D is without any such alliance and is in desperate need of investment funds to finance future growth prospects for established products and for product development; its future is extremely uncertain.

'Home computers'

The British 'home computer' industry is often taken to be the most robust in Europe and, in view of the dramatic growth of such small firms as Sinclair Research and Acorn,[2] it might appear to present opportunities for advanced technology-based small firms, currently canvassed as the 'vehicle for regeneration via innovation' in the older industrial regions (see Rothwell 1982). The home computer market, which only began in earnest in 1980, has certainly mushroomed and trade estimates suggest that it grew in value terms by between 40–50 per cent in both 1982 and 1983. In terms of market growth and the opportunities for small innovative firms, it is sometimes compared with the youthful US semiconductor industry of the 1960s. However, the market is rapidly maturing and established computer firms – who initially treated home computers as 'toys', and thus not worthy of consideration – have belatedly entered this lower price end of the market (about £500 per computer).

Three firms in our survey had some engagement with home computers, two of which were subcontract assemblers for other firms, and one (company E, the sole concern of this section) which 'produced' its own model.

Company E, a diversified off-shoot of an established company in South Wales, has its HQ in the region and in 1983 its employment stood at 270. Though barely two years old, its first model proved extremely successful with unit sale of 82000 (65000 in the UK) in its first 16 months. Nevertheless, its position was highly precarious for a number of reasons: fierce price-cutting; the inability to attain volume production fast enough to compensate for declining (and already low) margins, hence constant cash-flow problems; undercapitalization; short product life cycles (no more than two years) meaning that new products had to be developed as soon as others were launched on the market; and the failure to be inserted into a wider marketing system, and management feeling that the future belonged to those (such as IBM) who were able to combine low cost production with marketing strength.

Furthermore, this company was totally dependent on more powerful subcontractors who supplied the central processing unit, the cassettes and cartridges and the cases. As yet, this company was not an integrated producer: bought-in materials accounted for over 80 per cent of the ex-factory cost of each home computer. However, company E is something more than an assembly-only operation because it combines assembly with an in-house development team (11 engineers backed up by 17 technicians) which is seen as its greatest asset. Currently, company E is attempting to move into more powerful, versatile machines for business and professional use. As regards the home computer, success will depend on its ability to develop software and peripherals because these will have trebled the sales potential of hardware in 1985.

Company E encapsulates many of the problems confronting the 'small firm sector' generally and added problems associated with recruitment of key technical personnel in peripheral labour markets. Furthermore, its future survival seems certain to entail a loss of independence since it needs to overcome chronic under-capitalization and access to a wider marketing system.

Telecommunications

Of the major changes wrought in this industry over the past decade, two of the most significant have been the transition to fully electronic exchanges (e.g. System X) and, secondly, the conspicuous growth of the market for private exchanges (PABXs) and associated information technology products spawned by the convergence of telecommunications, computing and office equipment. British companies have traditionally been cossetted as regards the first market for public exchange equipment because of its protected status; the market for private exchanges and 'peripheral' products has traditionally been far more competitive and international in character, and here indigenous firms are much less prominent. The liberalization of telecommunications in the UK has already created a more competitive environment for British firms and, as already indicated, liberalization has been an important factor in attracting overseas telecommunications companies into the UK.

Three plants from this subsector were included in our survey, two very much caught up in the transition in switching technology and the third, an overseas company, which had achieved rapid growth in PABX markets. The former (plants F and G) were branches of diversified British companies which had operated in the region for over forty years. They shared an identical corporate status (as overspill factories with little autonomy) and both concentrated on the more mature switching equipment within their companies (i.e. Strowger, Crossbar, TXE2 and, more recently, TXE4A). Clearly, these plants constitute the very stuff from which the 'branch-plant' stereotype is made.

What is most interesting about plants F and G is that they have lived with and survived the threat of closure for nearly a decade as the market for mature switching equipment contracted. Their survival can be attributed to delays in the introduction of System X which conferred an unanticipated longevity on the older technology. But, also important, was the fact that these (largely female) workforces were among the most flexible and disciplined in their companies. Nevertheless, plant F was to have been closed in 1981 but survived because it was transferred from the company's switching to its transmission division, thus producing different products, and because a tutored labour force was preferable to expansion in the West Midlands, where industrial relations were more troublesome. Plant G, whose company is more dependent on TX exchanges, continues to concentrate on its traditional activities and, unless its function is redefined, as with plant F, its future is doomed. Not surprisingly, employment has halved in both plants since 1975.

The third member of this subsector (plant H) represents a stark contrast to the cases of plants F and G in terms of its technological status, corporate role and product market. This North American company established a facility (in 1981) in the UK for two reasons: the UK was its largest market for PABXs in Europe, and the liberalization of UK telecommunications presented it with opportunities not available elsewhere in Europe. South Wales was selected because it combined regional development grants with access to London and proximity to British Telecom, its major customer.

In one sense plant H does not conform to the 'branch-plant' stereotype: the South Wales facility is its HQ for Europe, the Middle East and Africa, as well as housing its European R&D and marketing centres. In fact, plant H provides an example of *research* and *development* being precisely what it suggests, rather than a 'black box' in which what is performed is not R&D but, rather, secondary or adaptive *development* work. Unlikely as it may seem, South Wales is one of its three R&D centres and the only one outside North America. The company practises a decentralized R&D strategy so as to tap international expertise and national strengths, to enable it to respond rapidly to new markets and to adapt its products to the specificities of different markets. South Wales is used as a base to recruit and retain UK software engineers because it was felt that the UK had an international reputation in this field.

The unusual corporate and technical status of plant H was such that it proved to be the least 'headless' plant in our survey: managers, scientists, technologists and technicians – the majority externally recruited – accounted for nearly 30 per cent of its total employment of 660. The firm's location off the coalfield near the border meant that it was not subject to the same labour-market constraints as many of the other plants, especially in recruiting key personnel. Its occupational profile was clearly 'responsible' for the (60:40) dominance of male over female employment.

As a new plant it is expected to increase employment to around 800 but not beyond this ceiling. This is not just because of technical scale factors but also because 'small' size is most conducive to manageable social relations. The former is already pervasive, while the latter is fast becoming the received wisdom among managers.

South Wales: some general considerations

Drawing on our survey work as a whole, a number of more general points need to be summarized:

Jobless growth

The combination of output growth with stable or declining levels of employment does not appear to be a temporary phenomenon caused by recession or spare capacity. Managers within the electronics industry identified jobless growth as the most disturbing characteristic of this industry so far as *labour* was concerned. Significantly, a major exception to this trend – apart from very recent new entrants still in the process of building-up employment – was a plant engaged in R&D and customized (software) products, with little or no opportunities for economies of scale. To the extent that the M4 corridor is over-represented in such activities, it seems likely that jobless growth will be less pervasive – and this probably accounts for the steady growth in such subsectors as capital goods and computer services (see Fig. 8.4). If this is so, the potential for jobless growth is unevenly distributed in the hierarchy of the spatial division of labour.

Regional multiplier effects

One of the most forceful criticisms associated with the 'branch-plant' stereotype is that of low multiplier effects, and this was confirmed in our survey. The relative absence of an indigenous small–medium firm sector, together with the fact that plants invariably relied on intra-firm sources or established sources outside the region, meant that both demand- and supply-side factors conspired to produce limited secondary effects within the region. Although indigenous firms expressed a preference for local purchasing, they too were more dependent on external sourcing than might have been expected.

Branch plant status

The most important point we would want to establish here is that 'branch plant' status does not of itself necessarily signify either insecurity or the absence of R&D. On the first issue, there can be a number of different forms, depending on sector, size of firm and, crucially, whether the plant is engaged in overspill production of standardized products or is a less dispensable unit in a wider system of production; it was this latter which predominated in our survey. Secondly, it is not the absence of R&D personnel but the predominance of routine occupations which typified the plants in our survey – although this former stratum is probably more pronounced in branch plants in the electronics industry. However, despite the heroic assumptions of some proponents of 'regional innovation policy', R&D functions are less sensitive to public policy than is often realized (Haug *et al.* 1983).

Innovation

The extent of (and the potential for) local innovation was largely related to incremental *process* innovation, while indigenous *product* innovations were typically of a cosmetic quality. This is largely consistent with the conclusions of other work (Oakey *et al.* 1980). Although the South Wales plants were often the last to benefit from new technology transfer within their respective multi-plant firms, they are still the major source of innovation in the region.

Indigenous potential

Indigenous potential might be defined as the capacity of a region to capitalize on a combination of different sources of new employment like new firm formation, innovation and inward investment. Clearly, regions such as South Wales are largely dependent on the third source, especially with respect to the electronics industry, whereas the M4 corridor combines all three. However, it is hopelessly superficial to suggest that South Wales ought to become more entrepreneurial because in large part even the necessary conditions – socio-occupational composition, sectoral structure, firm size, intra-firm hierarchies – are so manifestly absent. It is precisely for this reason that macro-policies designed to tap 'entrepreneurship' (e.g. small firm support) are spatially biased in effect if not by design – the manifold conditions for 'entrepreneurship' are not uniformly distributed in the (space) economy. Hence regions like South Wales and northern England in particular are in many ways structurally disenfranchised from neo-market macro-policies. However, the social and institutional conditions necessary for 'entrepreneurship' are not in themselves sufficient conditions: the latter involve general sectoral and economic circumstances which are usually unrelated to the characteristics of particular localities.

Labour and management: a 'modern' industry in a 'traditional' industrial region

It ought to go without saying that regional (re)development often entails a profound *social* recomposition of the (employed) workforce and its 'ways of life'. The tutoring of a workforce is one of the foremost priorities of management in a new location, especially in labour markets hitherto unaccustomed to industries with little or no pedigree in a region. Nowhere does this have more force than in South Wales, which has traditionally been the closest approximation to a working-class region in the UK.

On the basis of our work at least, it seems that firms entering a region for the first time are in a potentially privileged position in being able to introduce new management priorities and establish new terms and conditions of employment. As such, multi-plant firms, especially overseas firms, should be seen not simply as bearers of technical assets but, also, as bearers of new forms of *social* organization, which interact with, and modify, pre-existing forms in the area. These socio-cultural forms of capital make a genuine material difference to regional development, and specifically, to the experience of work and to labour's responses. The fact that overseas new entrants have a marked advantage over indigenous multi-plant firms in these *social* terms stems from the fact that organized labour lacks the purchase of existing involvement and, above all, the precedent. Whereas innovative social arrangements would, in the case of a multi-plant British firm, challenge precedents in all its plants, an overseas new entrant is not encumbered in this way.

Generally, overseas new entrants were not afflicted by the traditional (and interdependent) management-labour characteristics associated with many of the longer established British plants in our survey (itemized in Morgan & Sayer 1983). Among the most distinctive characteristics of the more recent (largely overseas) new entrants were the following:

(a) Management knowledge of, and involvement in, the labour process is much greater, and shopfloor control proportionately weaker.

(b) Despite greater surveillance and often more intensive work rates, industrial relations are usually less dispute-prone, in part because communication is more frequent and less inhibited by status differences (although it has to be said that industrial relations in the industry in this region have generally been dispute-free, despite images of labour intransigence).

(c) Recruitment policy tends to be more carefully geared to the particular needs of the plant and is seen as a means of improving productivity and lowering absenteeism.

(d) Simplified pay structures and less multi-unionism reduce demarcation and enable greater flexibility in job allocation, which again makes for higher productivity.

(e) Day to day communication with the workforce bypasses unions, and quality circles and other methods are employed to tap employee knowledge in problem solving.

(f) A conception of 'skills' – rarely formalized – was evident which referred not to *technical* qualifications but to behavioural qualities as regards 'good company employees' (e.g. attendance, adaptability, responsibility and company identification).

These socio-cultural characteristics – most closely associated with wholly-owned Japanese plants – are now becoming an accepted part of conventional management wisdom, in principle if not in practice, as a result of the demonstration effect and the enabling context of recession.

However, management–labour practices are interdependent and pre-existing labour traditions impart their own effects on incoming plants. For instance, South Wales was perceived as 'one of the most heavily unionized regions in Western Europe' and, of the plants surveyed, only three were non-unionized, so there is little evidence of an enclave of non- or anti-unionism that has been emerging in Central Scotland's 'new towns'. While this may be legitimately read as an index of the persistence of a labourist culture, unionization in itself does not betoken 'militancy' or 'activism' because management itself often viewed it as a means to an ordered environment and a number of plants have been 'unionized' before employees were actually recruited. Nor should unionization itself be seen as antithetical to innovative forms of management–labour practices because South Wales (along with the South West) has been used by the EETPU to experiment with its 'single union–no strike' agreements. These agreements have an ideological significance far greater than their number might suggest, principally as a demonstration effect. In this, and in the wider precedents that have been established in the overseas sector, the unions are aware that they have conferred social (and hence competitive) advantages to such firms – in order to gain recognition – which longer established firms have been unable to achieve, although the recession itself has wrought some profound changes.

Further theoretical and policy implications

By way of conclusion we shall now draw out some further theoretical points which were implicit in the preceding empirical section. As we hope to show, these are by no means merely of academic interest but have profound policy implications.

What kind of 'game' is regional development?

As we saw in the case of the TV plants, positive changes in one region are often offset by larger negative effects elsewhere. Making one set of firms or a particular region more competitive usually means making others less so. If the industry is characterized by jobless growth, then new plant openings or expansions in one place will provide fewer jobs than are displaced elsewhere. In such cases, from the point of view of labour this amounts to a negative sum game though gains may be possible in a few localities. However, from the point of view of capital in general and the rate of surplus value or level of labour productivity, it is a positive sum game producing increased efficiency, though not necessarily greater profits. Successful individual capitals will experience development *in* their regions but overall development *of* regions will not take place.

In addition to these (usually non-local) negative effects of competition we might add another hidden negative effect in the form of opportunities foregone elsewhere in the economy through the subsidization of particular industries and regions. (As we shall see later this probably *doesn't* take the form of prosperous regions subsidizing backward ones.) At the present time it is usually those on the right of the political spectrum who are concerned about these negative effects of subsidization of capital but we see no reason why the left should not also be concerned – however difficult to measure, the costs are real enough.

Both these kinds of negative effects are consistently ignored by the majority of policymakers, and unfortunately some academic commentators. But the problem is compounded by further oversights.

The 'new technology non-sequitur'

This concerns a pervasive error in reasoning about the effects of new technology. Now it is surely true at the present time that although a region or firm may lose jobs by adopting new technology, the consequences of non-adoption are likely to be even worse. The non-sequitur lies in the common supposition that this means that the adoption of new technology will therefore solve the regional problem. It's a bit like saying that because living on the dole is even worse than living on a low wage, that low wages are good for you.

Our pointing out this common non-sequitur does not mean that we are anti-new technology. We are not. It's just that we don't suppose that it will solve the regional problem.

While on the subject of new technology, it is perhaps worth noting that Academia has not been immune to the 'ideology of hi-tech' with its implicit assumption that hi-tech necessarily means high skills, high wages, job creation and prosperity. While such an assumption may be useful to industrial and property development agencies for advertising purposes (in the hope that it will become a self-fulfilling prophecy in their locality), it hardly bears scrutiny.

'Britain needs more Berkshires': the fallacy of composition

The new technology non-sequitur is usually backed up by a further erroneous argument which belongs to a general class known by logicians as the 'fallacy of composition': if anyone should doubt the benefits of new technology let them look at Silicon Valley, California, or, in this country, Berkshire. (Actually the reality of the former is very different from its glossy image – Pacific Studies Center 1977;

Anon. 1980; Saxenian 1983 – while recent employment growth in electronics in Berkshire has come nowhere near offsetting the employment decline of other sectors.) The fallacy lies in the assumption that, for any system, what is possible for a few individuals at a particular time must therefore be possible for all individuals simultaneously. The 'success' of Berkshire can supposedly be reproduced in other regions on a major scale, and simultaneously. This is rather like saying that because a few people who are born poor can rise from rags to riches that all the poor can do so simultaneously. And the root of the error goes back to the failure to take note of the interdependencies mentioned earlier: there are simply not enough 'front-end' activities to go round for every backward region to benefit; increases and decreases in competitiveness are necessarily related within the same industry and some integral parts of electronics currently rely on features of regional *backwardness* (e.g. low wages) for their survival.

On treating industries as black boxes

It should have been clear from the earlier discussion of the British electronics industry that the contribution of a sector to national and regional development depends on the particular characteristics of that industry both internationally and in Britain itself. Whichever of the three routes development takes, it is limited and shaped by the characteristics upstream and downstream of the British electronics industry itself, by the British (and European) markets for electronics, by the role of the government with respect to the industry, and by the strengths and weaknesses of Britain's array of skills and technological capabilities, in particular its position with respect to technological complementarities and gaps. If we are to come to an effective assessment of the possibilities of electronics or indeed any other sector for regional development, we cannot afford to ignore these industry-specific characteristics in the hope that some *universal* model of the effects of new technology on regional development will suffice. It is one thing to count new enterprises and inward investments and correlate them with various policies and conditions, but to assess their effect we have to understand the industry to which they belong and their location within it.

Policy implications and conclusions

The above theoretical points have a crucial bearing upon the success or failure of policies.

The first area that comes to mind is regional policy. We accept that

Figure 8.7 Location of micro-electronics applications consultants licensed by the UK Department of Industry (Goddard 1983).

this has had some effect on development in electronics, although the reasons are more complex than is usually assumed: the significance of regional development grants, advance factories, etc., for firms depend on their type (e.g. size and capital intensity of the firm and whether it is expanding *in situ* or moving into the region). Also the motives of firms newly locating in assisted areas are characteristically mixed. Be that as it may, the main point to be noted is that with the growing predominance of jobless growth and the dropping of the regional employment premium, regional policy has become primarily an aid to development *in* rather than *of* the regions.[3] Its prime function – whether intended or not – has been to bolster the competitiveness of British industry internationally (Morgan & Sayer 1983).

As we have seen earlier, State *non*-regional policies can also have major spatial effects and with the major exception of transfer payments these more than compensate the more prosperous regions for lack of assisted area status. (While assisted areas benefit most in *money* terms if transfer payments are included in the calculation, the *functions* of the payments made under various headings must also be assessed: £100 million of support for R&D in a region has very different long term implications from £100 million in transfer payments for that region.) Figures 8.6 and 8.7 give just two examples of this inadvertent 'regional policy in reverse'; both are strongly related to the electronics industry. Two policy implications follow from the unintended spatial effects of policies: firstly and more obviously that State agencies should pay more attention to these hidden spatial effects and secondly that the solutions to regional problems are by no means restricted to the terms of reference of regional agencies such as the Welsh Development Agency or of regional policy, traditionally conceived. General national policies may have more effect on the regional problem than specifically 'regional' policies. For example, at the present time a reflation would provide the regions with a significant boost, although its benefits would probably be short-lived unless it was part of a package of changes.

Another major policy issue concerns new technology. Our argument was that although it has to be adopted (albeit preferably in such a way that its specific form can be negotiated), it cannot provide a solution to the regional problem. But if this is not a solution then what is?

A *part* of the answer would lie in the expansion of sectors in which employment is also likely to grow (e.g. construction, health, education, transport) for that would produce development *of* regions rather than merely development *in* them. One of the most extraordinary, and erroneous notions to have become current is that advanced technology or 'sunrise' sectors are the only ones capable of and legitimate for expansion. In its extreme form its corollary is the rather desperate attempt to lionize such figures as Sir Clive Sinclair, and to canvass new, small firm formation as the only feasible route for regional development. However, if development *of* regions is to be taken seriously as an objective, then the expansion and diffusion of advanced technology (both being highly skewed to the South East) necessarily has to be accompanied by promotional efforts to expand more widely dispersed labour-intensive sectors. In turn, the latter would have to be incorporated in a much larger package of changes, including reductions in working hours and even, dare we say, a re-evaluation of the nature of work and its rewards. Finally, it should be said that although we do not pretend to have fully developed solutions, there is no reason for taking refuge in inadequate, but familiar, formulas: a dilemma characteristic of an intellectual and social crisis.

Notes

1   This chapter arises from two research projects funded by the ESRC – one, just finishing, on the electrical engineering industry in South Wales, the second, started in March 1984, on the electronics industry in the M4 corridor.
2   This chapter was written in March 1984. By May 1985 Acorn had virtually collapsed and been taken over by Olivetti, while Sinclair had run into financial difficulties. Now no-one seriously entertains optimistic views of the industry's growth prospects.
3   Since writing this, regional policy has been amended to give greater priority to job creation.

References

Anon. 1980. Silicon Valley's black market in cheap labour. *Electronics Times*, 19 September 1980.
Anon. 1982. Britain needs more Berkshires. *The Economist*, 30 January 1982.

Brayshaw, G. and G. Lawson 1982. *Manpower and training in the electronics industry*. EITB RP/5/82. Watford: Engineering Industry Training Board.

Davies, H. and H. Smyth 1983. *The western corridor: the shape of future growth*. Unpublished report, SAUS, Bristol University.
Department of Trade and Industry 1982. *The location, mobility and finance of new high technology companies in the UK electronics industry*. Unpublished report prepared by J. Beaumont.

Fröbel, F., J. Heinrichs and O. Kreye 1980. *The new international division of labour*. Cambridge: Cambridge University Press.

Goddard, J. 1983. Industrial innovation and regional economic development in Great Britain. In *Spatial analysis, industry and the industrial environment, 3, Regional economies and industrial systems*, F. E. I. Hamilton and G. J. R. Linge (eds). Chichester: Wiley.

Haug, P., H. Hood and S. Young 1983. R&D intensity in the affiliates of US owned electronics companies manufacturing in Scotland. *Regional Studies* 17, 383–92.

Hymer, S. H. 1972. The multinational corporation and the law of uneven development. In *International firms and modern imperialism*, H. Radice (ed.). London: Penguin.

International Metalworkers Federation 1982. *The Electrical and Electronic Industries, Tokyo Conference.*

McCrone, G. 1976. *Regional policy in Britain*. London: Allen and Unwin.

Massey, D. 1979. In what sense a regional problem? *Regional Studies* 13, 233–43.

Morgan, K. 1985. Re-industrialization in 'peripheral Britain': state policy, the space economy and industrial innovation. In *The Geography of De-industrialisation*, R. Martin and R. Rowthorn (eds). London: Macmillan.

Morgan, K. and A. Sayer 1983. *The international electronics industry and regional development in Britain*. Urban and Regional Studies Working Paper no. 34, University of Sussex.

National Economic Development Council 1983. *Policy for the UK electronics industry*. London: NEDC.

Oakey, R., A. T. Thwaites and P. A. Nash 1980. The regional distribution of innovative manufacturing establishments in Britain. *Regional Studies* 14, 235–54.

Pacific Studies Center 1977. *Silicon Valley: paradise or paradox?* San Francisco: Pacific Studies Center.

Rothwell, R. 1982. The role of technology in industrial change: implications for regional policy. *Regional Studies* 16, 361–70.

Saxenian, A. 1983. The urban contradictions of Silicon Valley. *International Journal of Urban and Regional Research* 7, 237–62.

Sciberras, E. 1980. *Direct investment in the UK by Japanese enterprises.* Unpublished paper, Science Policy Research Unit, University of Sussex.

Soete, L. and G. Dosi 1983. *Technology and employment in the electronics industry*. London: Frances Pinter.

Science Policy Research Unit 1982. *Microelectronics and women's employment in Britain*. Brighton: Sussex University Press.

Vernon, R. 1966. International investment and international trade in the product cycle. *Quarterly Journal of Economics* 80, 190–207.

9 Technical change in the food industry: the impact of the Ishida computer weigher

J. SHUTT and B. LEACH

The purpose of this chapter is to provide a case study which illustrates the relationship between technical change and corporate restructuring in the food industry. We investigate the early impact of a major process innovation in the cereals and snacks industries – the introduction of Ishida computerized check weighing machines during the period 1981–4.

Our original concern was with the employment implications of the new technology and with the trade unions' response to technical change. Investigation centred on the impact of the new innovation on companies within the Greater Manchester conurbation. The corporate case studies quickly established that a regional study provides an impossible context from which to understand the origins and diffusion of a new innovation and from which to analyse the occupational, gender and geographical impacts.

Restructuring in the food industry

In the postwar period food companies have constantly implemented innovations which mechanize and automate production. In the 1960s manufacturers tended to concentrate on the cooking process in order to progress from batch to continuous production. The weighing and packaging process remained labour intensive and provided an important source of employment for women. Now, technical change is focusing on weighing and packaging innovations because of the impact of microelectronics. The result is that women's employment and working conditions are becoming more insecure and uncertain as technical change and a new round of investment allow full-time jobs to be converted into part-time and temporary ones.

The food industry is characterized by high levels of firm concentration – output is in the hands of a few major transnational companies. Stagnant growth in consumption and low levels of import penetration due to the perishable nature of the product are being accompanied by lower transport costs and faster distribution systems.

These features combine to produce intense competition between firms to increase market shares and to examine methods for reducing manufacturing costs. Continuous product innovations and increased investment in process technologies offer the only route to survival in the late 1980s. In one of our case studies the Ishida is being introduced as a defensive investment and it occurs in the context of a corporation which is being forced to rationalize and concentrate production on one or two key plants. The other case study involves a corporation which is expanding and engaged in offensive investment designed to ensure that it retains its position as the market leader.

Technical change: the Ishida computer weigher

The Ishidas (see Fig. 9.1) were first imported whole from Japan in 1981 by Driver Southall (part of Avery GEC) of Walsall. Driver Southall produces weighing/filling machines for powders and granules (e.g. tea, sugar) but the company was late coming into the field for weighing of piece goods like cereals. Enter the Ishida.

Ishida Scales Manufacturing Company Ltd of Kyoto, Japan, are a fourth generation family firm employing over 500 people. They developed their first computer weigher in-house in 1973, but for six years its export potential went unrealized, since the firm traditionally never exported. It is said that Driver Southall first saw Ishida by accident in 1980. Realizing its potential, they negotiated to become its sole West European distributors and are selling it to over 300 UK customers involved in everything from crisps to dry pet foods.

Ishida developed their computer weigher in response to a unique problem. The Japanese use a lot of small green peppers in cooking. The problem for Ishida came in trying to automate their packing, since the peppers come in a variety of shapes and sizes. This is a problem with many small piece goods, from crisps to frozen prawns.

The conventional system of weighing is to have a gravity feed trough controlled by a shutter which allows a certain amount into a weighing hopper. When the target weight (200 g) is reached, the shutter is automatically closed. This system is not too wasteful with standardized piece products (grains and powder, for example), but where piece weights are irregular, the piece 'in flight' which tips the weighing hopper above the target weight can lead to unacceptable

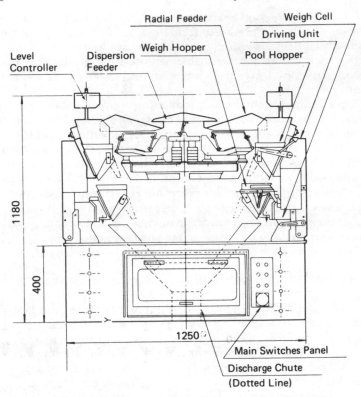

Figure 9.1 The Ishida computer weigher.

'give away' – in Figure 9.2 that means that the consumer will get a bag of 210 g weight when the stated weight is 200 g, i.e. 10 g 'free'.

For crisps, one way of overcoming the weighing problem was to remove raw material variation. Hence the popularity of extruded snacks based on powdered maize, and Smith's development and promotion of the square crisp (based on powdered potato). Short of genetic engineering to produce identical peppers, Ishida did not have the same option open to them. They approached the problem from a different angle altogether. Their machine uses a series of weigh–heads fed by a vibrator system which randomly disperse the product into one of the ten weigh hoppers (14 in the latest machine), arranged concentrically. The computer compares the static weights in the ten hoppers, and out of 1023 possible combinations (according to Driver Southall) selects that combination of hoppers closest to the target weight and discharges them to a packing machine below (Fig. 9.3). This system is much faster than previous systems, and it can cut 'give

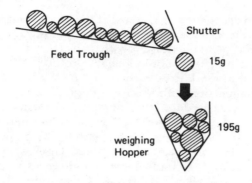

Shutter
Feed Trough
15g
195g
weighing
Hopper
TARGET WEIGHT : 200 grams

Figure 9.2 An example of a conventional weighing system. Against the target weight of 200 g, the weight of the products in the hopper is 195 g. If the weight of the product falling into the weighing hopper is 15 g, giveaway becomes 10 g (195 + 15 − 200 = 10) (Driver Southall Ltd).

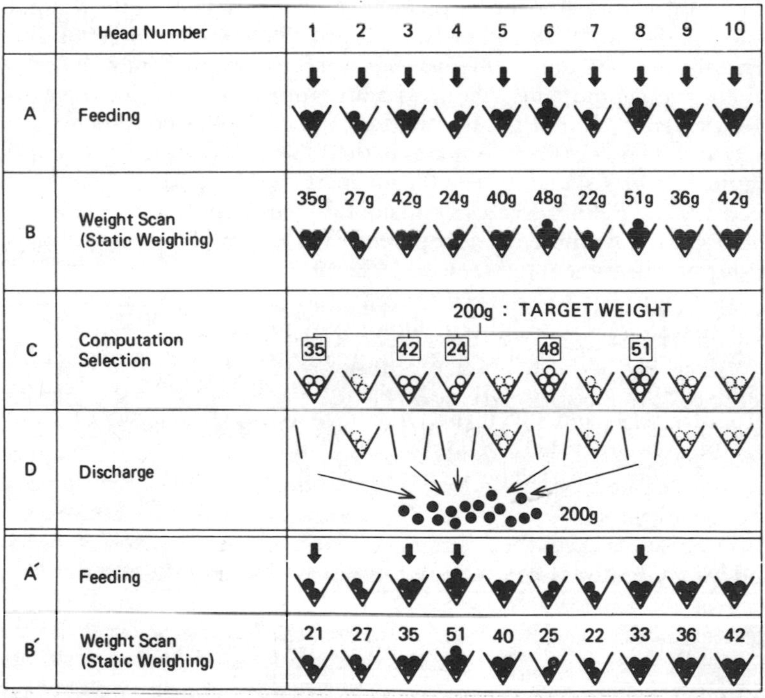

Head Number
1 2 3 4 5 6 7 8 9 10
A Feeding
B Weight Scan (Static Weighing)
35g 27g 42g 24g 40g 48g 22g 51g 36g 42g
C Computation Selection
200g : TARGET WEIGHT
35 42 24 48 51
D Discharge
200g
A′ Feeding
B′ Weight Scan (Static Weighing)
21 27 35 51 40 25 22 33 36 42

Figure 9.3 Computer combination weighing system (Driver Southall Ltd).

away' by up to a factor of ten. The cost of the Ishida is relatively small in relation to the increase in output, reduction in waste, reliability and streamlining of production. As with many technological innovations the Ishida weigher is not unique. A prototype check weigher was developed in the UK as early as 1967 by a Mr. A. Giles of Unilever in conjunction with Precision Engineering Products (Suffolk) Ltd. This team produced their first production machine in 1972 and later collaborated with Yamato Co. of Japan to produce computerized weighers. However, in the period 1981–84 in the UK it was the Ishida which dominated the computer check weigher market as it was installed by the leading crisps and cereals manufacturers including Smith's, Walker's and Tudor Crisps (now all owned by Nabisco PLC), Golden Wonder, Riley's and Kellogg's.

Cereals and snacks

Cereals and snacks are both sectors dominated by a small number of giant multinational corporations which originated out of the merger boom in the late 1960s and early 1970s. In 1982 the concentration and centralization of capital in the snacks sector reached new heights when the Monopolies Commission approved the takeover of Huntley and Palmer PLC by Nabisco Brands. Nabisco is the fourth largest food processing company in the USA and eighth in the world league. As was stated in *The Guardian* at the time, 'the takeover of Huntley and Palmer creates a considerable monopoly at a time when the present government, most prominently through privatisation, is trying to break them up' (Anon. 1982a).

Although data on market concentration is difficult to assemble, industry sources reveal that Kellogg's, Weetabix and Nabisco have between them 78.0 per cent of the ready to eat cereals market by value (Table 9.1). In crisps, Nabisco (Smith's, Walker's), United Biscuits (KP), and the Imperial Group (Golden Wonder) have a combined market share of 88 per cent (Table 9.2).

Both industries have been characterized by increasing demand for

Table 9.1 Market shares in ready-to-eat cereals by value (per cent), 1982.

Kellogg's	55.0	own label cornflakes	5.0
Weetabix	15.0	own label biscuits (bix)	3.0
Nabisco	8.0	own label muesli	4.0
Quaker	6.0	others	4.0

Source: Anon. (1983) (calculated from trade estimates).

their products throughout the last decade. For example, the average intake of breakfast cereals in the UK, boosted by the decline in cooked breakfasts, rose by 66 per cent from 1966 to 1979 (MAFF 1982). Similarly, crisp consumption increased by 25 per cent in the period 1975–82. Savoury snacks also showed a spectacular growth since they were virtually unknown before 1971 (see Mintel 1982).

However, as the economic crisis continues, household spending on food is declining and the 'recession-proof' tag has disappeared (NEDC 1983). With very little significant overall market growth expected, competition is intensifying, particularly from supermarket 'own brand' products. It is not surprising, therefore, that maintaining and increasing market shares preoccupies the leading companies and accounts for the vast sums they spend on advertising. In 1981, in an effort to halt market decline, the Smith's Food Group spent as much on advertising and printing as it paid in wages to direct factory employees and increased advertising expenditure in 1982. Also in 1982, Kellogg's budgeted to spend £15 million on advertising alone in the UK in order to protect its share of the market from 'own brand' products. Nabisco and Kellogg's are two leading American multinational companies and see themselves as world leaders in their respective sector of the food industry. Through extensive advertising on the one hand and a crash capital investment programme on the other, both companies have embarked on a new phase in the battle to expand and maintain market shares. For Kellogg's, this has involved plans to spend £120 million on capital investment in the period 1983–86, while Nabisco has already invested £17.5 million in one production centre at Beaumont Leys, Leicestershire, and intends to spend a further £30 million on the modernization necessary to boost the declining Smith's Food Group (see Monopolies and Mergers Commission 1982).

Table 9.2   Market shares by value, United Kingdom savoury snacks foods market, 1981.

	Crisps	Snacks	Nuts	Total
United Biscuits	27%	28%	49%	30%
Huntley & Palmer	21%	40%	21%	26%
Nabisco Brands	21%	8%	16%	17%
Imperial Group	19%	16%	4%	16%
RPC Foods	8%	4%	2%	6%
others	4%	4%	8%	5%
total market	£233 m	£96 m	£64 m	£393 m

Source: Monopolies and Mergers Commission (1982, p. 38).

Smith's Crisps – new workerless-flavour crisps?

The history of the UK crisps industry is poorly documented. Crisp production was started here in the early 1920s by Frank Smith in London, who used a recipe for a French speciality table dish. In the period until the 1960s there was no real national competition in the crisps market. Entry into the industry was relatively easy, markets were regional and local, and Bevan (1974) recalls that of the 800 or so very small manufacturers of crisps which existed in the late 1940s, many had established themselves using demobilization grants: 'The methods of production most of them used were so rudimentary that it is a wonder that the crisp survived at all in popularity' (Imperial Group, quoted in Bevan 1974, p. 2).

In the 1960s the structure of the industry began to change as the merger and acquisition boom combined with new advances in the crisp production technology. In 1963 Smith's took over Tudor Food Products, their main competitor in the North East. Golden Wonder was acquired by the Imperial Tobacco Group and they built two new factories as part of their expansion programme, at Widnes in 1962 and Corby in 1964. This firm began the process of introducing continuous frying cookers which were imported into the country from the USA. This innovation was linked to the requirement for a new form–fill–seal packing machine accompanied by new packaging film. Golden Wonder introduced the major innovation of cellophane film bags, which increased shelf life by up to six weeks, replacing the old waxed glassine paper and improving the quality of the product. Bevan points to the way in which the early introduction of the continuous fryer at Golden Wonder allowed the firm to develop a competitive edge over Smith's and allowed it to become a national producer by 1965:

> 'As Golden Wonder's new continuous frying process plants came into operation between 1962 and 1964 the consumers found that Smith's crisps were not of particularly good quality. Within two years Smith's were also introducing the new processing machinery, but in the meantime poor crisps and Smith's had already become popular association in the minds of consumers, and Golden Wonder had acquired a remarkably persistent reputation for producing good quality crisps' (Bevan 1974, pp. 291–2).

In this period the distinquishing feature of the two rising competitors in the crisp market (Walker's and United Biscuits) was also their early and heavy investment in these new technologies. Smith's Food Group on the other hand appears as a laggard and when defensive investment to recapture market shares began, it was accompanied by a major rationalization programme. Producing in

24 factories throughout the UK, a programme of factory closures began in 1964 and saw production concentrated at factories which were capable of accommodating the new production processes. Yet the investment programme was moderate and Smith's did not receive sufficient investment throughout the 1969–79 period to allow it to regain its market position. In 1979 the company was acquired by Huntley and Palmer Foods (previously Associated Biscuit Manufacturers) from its then owners (General Mills Inc.), as part of HPF's stategy of reducing its dependence on biscuit manufacture. Huntley and Palmer set up a committee in 1981 to evaluate the new group's assets and 'to recommend how premises, plant and equipment could be put to the most efficient use' (Monopolies and Mergers Commission 1982, p. 19).

By 1981 Smith's Food Group employed approximately 5000 full-time and part-time workers in eight factories (plus depots and offices), many of which were outdated. Walker's, with a similar market share, had only two factories. The Smith's Group profits were increasingly being squeezed by its competitors' ability to maintain profits while the real value of crisps sold dropped.

Smith's strategy for the 1980s

Once again Smith's was forced to embark on another round of defensive investment incorporating the latest process innovations – simultaneously investing in new machinery, closing down old factories and attempting to reduce labour costs. It was this second round of rationalization and new investment that brought in the Ishida. The first public hint of a changing strategy came in *The Sun* newspaper (Anon. 1981a) with the headlines '2000 crisp *men* go in shock closures' (italics added). Subsequently it turned out that only three of the eight factories were 'safe', and that even they stood to lose a high proportion (up to 60 per cent) of their workforce. Paulsgrove (Portsmouth) for example, the first factory in the Smith's Food Group to install Ishidas, reduced the workforce from over 400 to 180. At the same time production capacity increased by an estimated 44 per cent.

Twenty-five gram bags are cheap (10–12p) items, but as packing film is an expensive item, the bag must be as small as possible. With erratic bag filling this can lead to problems with bag seal, leading to a high proportion of rejects. With Ishidas, 25 g bags of crisps are a maximum of 0.5 g overweight compared with a previous 6 g maximum (Table 9.3). Although a ten-head Ishida costs £28000 and a 14-head £39000, more than double the previous weighers, customers generally expect the machines to pay for themselves in nine

Table 9.3   Crisp packing lines – old and new.

	Old	New	
weigher	Wrights (UK)	Ishida 10–head (Japan)	Ishida 14–head (Japan)
operation	gravity feed, mechanical weighing and discharge	vibration feed, static computer-combination weighing and discharge	same as Ishida 10–head
film wastage	17%, since many bags overweight and rejected	0.3% computer scan ensures no discharge unless target weight achieved, therefore no rejects	same as Ishida 10–head
product 'give-away' (25 g bags)	6 g	0.5 g	same as Ishida 10–head
bags per minute	46	55	80–85 single tube packer; 110–115, twin tube packet
cost	n.a.	£28 000	£39 000
quality control	manual sampling	auto printout on weight in each hopper before it goes into the bag	same as Ishida 10–head

Source: Driver Southall Ltd 1983.

months. A few weeks after the introduction of the Ishidas at Paulsgrove, the members of the National Joint Shop Stewards' Committee were told, 'Management now have definite knowledge that our competitors wanted to get hold of the Ishida machines. It was now necessary to place the order for another 20 Ishida machines. This has to be done by next Monday to avoid loosing our place in the queue' (NJSSC Minutes, December 1981).

Since that time, Smith's Food Group has accelerated its programme of closures and redundancies. Four factories have closed and 1500 jobs have been lost in the space of two years. (Fig. 9.4).

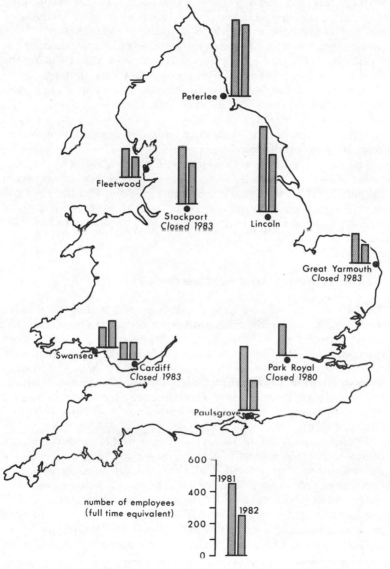

Figure 9.4 Smith's Food Group 1980–83.

At this time Golden Wonder appeared to be behind Smith's and Walker's in adopting the latest computer-weighing technology. Perhaps this was because they were on a different technology trajectory. Having established themselves as a new force in advanced cooking innovations in the 1960s, Golden Wonder appear to have continued the process of modifying cooking techniques throughout the 1970s. In 1975 for example, a decision was taken to update the Corby plant by spending £2 million on new fryers, updating other equipment and developing an Accumaveyor system (Darrington 1979). This removed another bottleneck in the frying process. At this time, with the range of flavours growing, it was necessary to switch from one flavour to another without stopping frying and so holding up the production lines.

The Accumaveyor was designed by Golden Wonder in conjunction with Driver Southall. Thus at the Corby factory, having spent the past 20 years improving crisp quality, Golden Wonder were still using manual check-weighing of individual packs with manual quality checks on random samples, until they too started to install the Ishidas.

Towards the automated crisp factory

The latest round of new capital investment is leading to massive over-capacity within the crisp industry, since output is increasing at a time when the recession is biting into household expenditure. Even if expenditure on crisps was to grow, it would appear that crisp production capacity already far exceeds likely demand. The Smith's shop stewards in Stockport put it like this: 'If all the new 40 Ishidas were installed at Peterlee, they could produce over 3000 million bags of crisps per year, compared with Stockport's 40 million a year' (Anon. 1982b).

The introduction of the Ishida is only one part of the development of the mechanized process which will ensure the eventual creation of the automated crisp factory. With the introduction of the Ishida the technology race is now on again and the logical outcome can only lead to further concentration of capital in the crisp sector. The UK production of crisps in 1981 was 3700 million packets per year, with more recent estimates in the industry of over 3900 million (Ministry of Agriculture and Fisheries 1983). To put it another way, in the UK about 7080 bags are produced per minute. Given the potential speed of 120 bags per minute of a 14-head twin-tube Ishida, a simple calculation suggests that, in theory at least, 59 Ishidas working 24 hours a day for 365 days of the year would be sufficient to cope with the existing UK demand for crisps. (An additional 24 would cope

Figure 9.5 Indices of sales of crisps by UK manufacturers, 1975–81 (information taken from the Business Statistics Office, MMC Study).

with the savoury snack market!) Even if practical problems of machine down-time are included, few more would be needed. Factories such as Peterlee or Walker's at Beaumont Leys now have large numbers of Ishidas, and between them they have the capacity to supply the major share of the UK market. For example, it was recently reported (Darrington 1983) that the new Walker's factory at Beaumont Leys has one line which costs £3 million and which produces 1200 × 48 pack cartons of crisps per count. This gives it a theoretical annual capacity of over 767 million bags of crisps – one-fifth of current UK demand. What is more, Walker's are near completion of their second line and plan another three. If this occurs, this one factory may be capable of meeting almost all the UK demand for crisps. Yet, while sales of crisps have increased by 25 per cent since 1975, their real value had declined by 25 per cent since 1976. Figure 9.5 illustrates the difficulties that crisp firms now face, while Table 9.4 summarizes the direction of change in the Smith's Food Group in August 1983.

Table 9.4 Smith's Food Group – closing down and moving out.

Factory	Location	No. of employees						Comments
		1981*				1982†		
		Full-time equivalent	Full-time	Part-time	Total	Total	Full-time equivalent	
Lincoln	Lincoln	540	95	546		641	367	main snack site; £15m investment planned but in doubt since Nabisco take-over)
Paulsgrove	Portsmouth	400†	65	246		311	188	crisp producer; first to have Ishida; workforce reduced by 100+ in first phase
Swansea	South Wales	130	41	262		303	172	makes Monster-Munch, Sizzles and Frazzles

Fleetwood	Lancashire	180	22	216	238	130	makes square crisps
Great Yarmouth	Norfolk	188	26	186	212	119	closed January 1983, despite firm offer from Adams and Dack
Stockport	Greater Manchester	358	43	419	462	252	closed March 1983
Peterlee	County Durham	480	97	694	791	444	biggest crisp producer; Ishidas installed 1982–83
Cardiff	South Wales	110	28	165	193	110	nut producer; closed December 1983
Park Royal	West London	197	0	0	0	0	closed 1980 after struggle by mainly Asian workforce for better redundancy terms

* Union estimates.
† Source: Nabisco Brands Press Reports.

The shopfloor response

It is the massive over-capacity within the sector which already exists
that has thwarted the plans of trade unionists to develop alternative
proposals to closures. For example, it was widely acknowledged by
shop stewards that the best Smith's crisps were produced at their
Great Yarmouth Factory. Marks and Spencers are said to have
insisted on being supplied with their own brand of crisps from this
factory. This ensured that the factory was profitable, yet despite this
the factory was closed. Investment and technical change means that
even profitable factories will be closed, simply because they are
surplus to capacity. Moreover, in this case Smith's were also determined to ensure that the factory plant was completely scrapped.
Despite an offer from Adams and Dack, a Norwich-based company
which planned to produce 'Canary' crisps (nickname of the local
football team, Norwich City), Smith's are reported to have insisted
on placing a covenant on the sale of the property prohibiting any
future purchaser from manufacturing crisps there.

Initial investigation would seem to confirm that the prime locational choices made by Smith's in their capital expenditure programme were influenced by the age of existing plants, their 'greenfield' status and their distributional potential. Factories which closed
were older conurbation plants with cramped conditions and little
room for expansion (Stockport and Park Royal), or were badly
placed for national distribution networks (Great Yarmouth). Those
factories where production is being concentrated are mainly modern
one-storey buildings providing ample room for expansion. While
trade union organizations at Peterlee and Plymouth may be weaker
than in the old conurbation plants, this does not seem to be the case
at Lincoln, and the evidence that this was a closure factor remains
inconclusive.

With the installation of the Ishidas at Paulsgrove, the unions at
Smith's Food Group were fully aware of the threat to jobs. As the
Great Yarmouth factory convenor said at a National Combine
meeting on 10 May 1982, following the announcement of the closure
of his factory, 'It is Ishidas which are closing factories; in one shift
they will produce as much as Yarmouth in a week.' Management
were not assured of being able to manage the closure and redundancy
programme while maintaining production. The Smith's Food
Group combine, the National Joint Shop Stewards' Committee, had
a full-time group convenor and representatives from all site and
unions, and it planned a campaign of opposition to the closures, led
by the main union, the Transport and General Workers' Union. As
well as the combine there was also the 'muscle' of what was known
as the Trunker Group. Unlike many other crisp manufacturers,

Smith's employed its own fleet of trucks. The truck depots (the Trunker Group) were closed TGWU shops, and if they went on strike, they had the ability to bring the group to a halt in a few hours (as manufacturers and retailers were unable to carry large stocks of crisps). The union's main strategy was to try to negotiate a new technology and job security agreement, while in the meantime maintaining the *status quo* (i.e. no introduction of new equipment without mutual agreement.).

Why did the trades unions fail?

Our research indicates a number of causes of the failure of the trades unions. First, they did not develop a perspective on the introduction of the Ishidas which transcended individual plants and allowed them to combat management control over the introduction of the new equipment. Information was released piecemeal to the unions, making it difficult for them to plan a long term strategy. For example, management talked of the 'continued refurbishment' of the Stockport plant in January 1982 and put forward the possibility of Ishidas being installed at Stockport and Swansea in March 1982. Two months later, on 5 May 1982, management announced the closure of the Yarmouth and Stockport factories. Secondly, the trades unions neglected basic organization. By the effort of a few individuals an effective national Smith's Food Group Combine had been established, but decisions were made which were frequently ignored or over-turned at branch level. Members were often given no information by the unions about what was going on, leaving management free to develop its own viewpoint to the workforce. Thirdly, while 80 per cent of Smith's Food Group workforce were women, many part-time, the unions' combine negotiators were overwhelmingly full-time males, with an over-representation of the depots as opposed to the factories. For example, out of eleven trades union representatives present when the closures were announced on 5 May 1982, only one was a woman.

For the unions the crunch came following the 5 May 1982 closure announcement. Either they were to take action then or to all intents and purposes abandon the struggle. A national mandating committee met on 10 May and passed a series of motions which included: opposition to the closure of Yarmouth and Stockport factories; refusal to accept the need for further loss of jobs; refusal to co-operate with management in any transfer of work until satisfactory negotiations had been completed; refusal to handle any new technology including computers; and opposition to transfer of work within the group outside normal quotas. These strong proposals were passed

The Trade Unions are demanding:

(a)   Investment in all Smiths factories,
      thereby keeping jobs in all the areas

(b)   Full and accurate information from the
      Company on their future plans

(c)   The introduction of new technology
      only after full consultation

(d)   No compulsory redundancies

(e)   Workforce to share in the productivity
      benefits through a shorter working week

Figure 9.6   Workers' demands (Anon. 1982b).

overwhelmingly by the mandating committee. The sites voted 4:1 for industrial action, but lack of basic organization at factory level and disunity over forms of action led to the crumbling of union resistance. By 28 July 1982 the opposition to closures had collapsed and sanctions were called off. Three months later, the Smith's Food Group convenor had left and in 1983 the factories closed without a struggle and without any of the Stockport workers' demands being achieved (see Fig. 9.6).

Most of the rationalization of the Smith's Food Group had thus been done before the completion of the 1983 Nabisco Brands take-over of Huntley and Palmer. The effect has been to ensure that crisp manufacturing has been removed from the UK's conurbations to greenfield sites which have the labour and land, storage and distribution potential which modern technology demands, thus confirming the pattern of locational change with which we are now familiar (Fothergill & Gudgin 1982). Job losses in the group will continue, as the recent announcement of the Cardiff factory closure and the following comment from the *The Financial Times* shows: 'Nabisco reckons it will have to pump some £95 million into the business over the next five years and lay off as many as 4000 employees to bring Huntley's operating efficiency to scratch' (Anon. 1982c). At the time Nabisco told the Monopolies Commission that it would be employing the following steps to offset the employment impact of its investment programme:

(a)   Consultations with the workforce and unions 'as far ahead of implementation of any particular stage as was practicable and not less than six months ahead.'

(b)   Greater use of natural wastage over the next four to five year period

(c)   Recruitment 'would largely cease'
(d)   Overtime would be reduced 'wherever practicable' so their full-time employment was not reduced by using overtime as a substitute
(e)   Temporary and seasonal workers would be the first to go.

In terms of future prospects: 'NBI acknowledge that the far reaching nature of its investment programme and the attendant improvements in productivity would have effects on employment greater than those which would accompany HPF's rationalization and investment plans as so far formulated' (Monopolies and Mergers Commission 1982, p. 56).

Cornflakes - the crunch to come?

Kellogg's operates in 20 locations throughout the world, supplying products to more than 130 nations. Its main product is ready-to-eat breakfast cereal and its main breakfast cereal manufacturing plant at Trafford Park, Manchester, is the second largest such factory in the world, producing 10.25 million packets of Corn Flakes and Rice Krispies per week. Kellogg's first started producing at Trafford Park in 1938 and 40 years of continuous production at one site, in an expanding product market, produced a strong trade union organization. In the late 1970s Kellogg's had already begun the process of decentralizing production away from Manchester as it introduced new products. Its Wrexham plant opened in 1979 producing Super Noodles, bran products and muesli. Then,

> 'in 1979 came the strike that put Kellogg's out of production for ten weeks. During it, briefly, Weetabix took over brand leadership. It was in that strike year that Kellogg's woke up to the Weetabix threat . . . Now, thanks, it is said, to greater determination, more concentration on the mainstream cereal business and a clear policy of spending big money on marketing, Kellogg's feels it has 'roared right back' (Anon. 1981b).

Kellogg's intensified its diversification policy but also took a global strategic decision to lower unit costs through plant modernization, greater commitment to research and development and by making heavier commitments in marketing expenditures. A decision was made to build a new 'high tech' manufacturing plant in London, Ontario, which when finished in 1984 is expected to be one of the most sophisticated food processing plants in the world. In addition to modernization at the Manchester plant, Kellogg's began to develop new cereal manufacturing facilities in Spain and South Korea (Fig. 9.7).

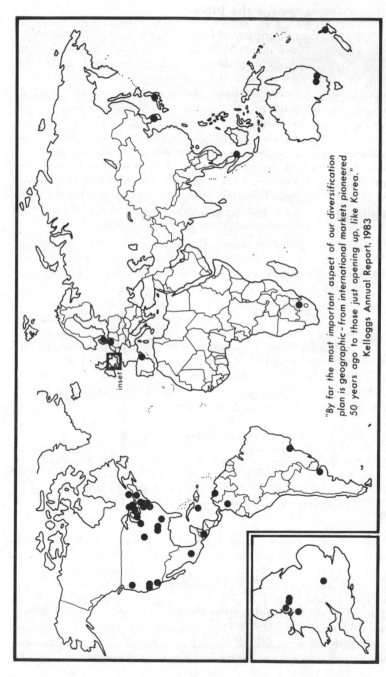

"By far the most important aspect of our diversification plan is geographic – from international markets pioneered 50 years ago to those just opening up, like Korea."

Kelloggs Annual Report, 1983

Figure 9.7 Kellogg's plant and subsidiary locations (information taken from Kellogg's annual report 1983).

Kellogg's strategy for the 1980s

In 1980 the Kellogg Company of Great Britain had commissioned a study by business consultants McKinsey & Co., in order to examine the case for re-equipment of their manufacturing units. This followed the prolonged dispute at the Trafford Park plant in 1979, which led management to doubt the wisdom of a strategy that concentrated too much production capacity in one particular location. While the consultants' report was never made available to the trades unions at the Trafford Park plant, there can be little doubt that it contributed to a stage-by-stage approach in the introduction of new technology and the restructuring of working practices at the plant. As Table 9.5 shows, over four years the workforce will have been reduced by approximately 435, the regular weekend shifts abolished, the packing lines re-equipped with Ishidas, and the concept of the disposable temporary worker introduced for the first time since the early 1970s.

Table 9.5 Job loss and technical change at Kellogg's in the 1980s.

Year	No. employees at Trafford Park	Comment	No. employees at Wrexham	No. employees (total UK workforce)
1980	2085		200	3465
1981	2079	360 redundancies declared with change of shift patterns from seven- to five-day cover)	231	3054
1982	1774	packing line requirement plan unveiled; job loss of 277 by end of 1984 predicted	264	2968
1983	1783	includes 200 temporary workers (contracts end October 1983)	270	no data
1984	1650	six Bag-in-Box lines installed	296	no data
1987 (est.)	1494	possibly include up to 400 temporary/ seasonal workers	342	no data

Source: Trade union estimates 1983, and Kellogg's Annual Reports.

Both unions and management agreed on the need for new technology and fresh capital investments. Many of the machines at Trafford Park were originally secondhand when installed in the 1930s. In January 1981 the company briefed the trades unions on the reasons for the introduction of new equipment:

'The current market position is not unsatisfactory, and Corn and Rice in particular have had a successful 1980. Recent studies, however, have indicated that our competitors are closing the gap through technological change and more efficient working practices. To protect our market share and ensure continued success, we have looked closely and urgently at our manufacturing costs and efficiencies. Only through an improvement plan of the scope outlined will we feel confident of meeting our targets for the remainder of the 1980s' (Kellogg's briefing notes, 6 January 1981).

Even before the new investment programme was announced, Kellogg's, disturbed by the effects of the ten-week strike, had already decided to take a tougher stance with the trades unions. The Company Public Affairs Manager told the *Financial Times* on 24 September 1980:

'In the past the Company's hourly paid workers got their information either on the grapevine or through the union. We are now asserting our right and duty to communicate. Unions still have a function in representing their members, that does not include communicating Company information. In future shop stewards will get such information on the basis of their function as employees rather than as officials of a trade union.'

Kellogg's American-style management has stressed the motto 'Kelloggs is People'. Clearly, rather than provide full information to the trades unions, the new style of management intended to weaken the role of shop stewards.

The trades unions' response to the Ishida redundancies

At Trafford Park, the main trades union is USDAW, which organizes the process workers, with 1400 members (nearly a quarter of whom are women). In addition there are 300 craft workers (all of whom are men), primarily organized by the majority craft union, the AUEW. In 1983, out of 15 USDAW shop stewards, two were women, and of nine on the negotiating committee, one was a woman.

When the company first announced their packing line re-equipment programme, USDAW's main concern centred on the 277 future redundancies for their members. Realizing the potential disruption that might occur, and bearing in mind the lessons of the bitter 1979 dispute, management has followed a policy of periods of pressure on the unions, eased for a while if there are any signs of industrial action. Together with this 'hard and soft' approach, management has made full use of the new policy of direct communications to the workforce through supervisors, the in-house journal and specially commissioned videotapes (viewed in company time). As in the crisps case, they have also been successful in playing off sections of the workforce against one another: hence the emphasis on the 'uprated skills of the line operators' (all men), as opposed to the redundancies among packers (of whom over 60 per cent are women) in the negotiations surrounding the introduction of the Ishidas and Ishida-based packaging lines.

The craft unions have traditionally been well organized at Kellogg's. Through a year-long overtime ban they eventually succeeded in June 1982 in negotiating a job security agreement, the key clause of which states: 'The company does not intend to make any Kellogg craft area employee compulsorily redundant as a result of the imminent changes in new technology'. While this agreement is by no means watertight from the union point of view, it is interesting to note that the management refused a similar agreement with USDAW workers. The reasoning behind this is quite simple. The craft workers had an overtime ban for over a year, until the company negotiated the job security agreement. The craft workers were determined and well organized, and the company needed their co-operation in installing and maintaining the new equipment. In contrast, the process workers were poorly organized, and nearly all of the jobs to vanish as a result of the introduction of the new machines were those of USDAW packers.

Kellogg's aim has been to reduce the work hours required to produce 1000 cases of breakfast cereals from approximately 73 to around 26. Already on the lines installed, average product 'give away' has been reduced from 20 g to an estimated 2 g. The company's plans, as outlined to USDAW in November 1981, called for the loss of 277 jobs, all but a handful of which were packers' jobs. Over 45 per cent of packers' jobs were to go. Although women are a minority in the factory, over 60 per cent of the packers are women. The line operators (all men) were to remain, and the assistant line operators (all men) were to be upgraded.

USDAW's difficulty in formulating an effective response, as judged by the acceptance of redundancies and re-introduction of temporary labour, was due partly to their complex structure. At factory branch level this made it almost impossible to develop a strong shop steward system. In particular, the key negotiating committee was not accountable to the shop stewards, since its members were elected by a mixture of secret ballot (branch officials) and show of hands at the Annual General Meeting (three others). Thus the shop stewards were without real power. Many members were unaware of who their shop steward was, and if they needed advice often went direct to negotiating committee members. Vacancies were often unfilled and stewards were left representing large constituencies of up to 160 members.

There have been other results of the introduction of new packing lines at Trafford Park apart from the loss of jobs for women. The attempt to move a workforce composed of possibly 1000 full-time workers, plus up to 400 temporary workers for the busy summer months, makes a significant deterioration in the terms and conditions of employment of the process workers. Many who previously had security of employment will now become seasonal workers, hired next season depending on demand and their previous work and sickness records, and without even the minimal protection afforded by the Employment Protection Acts. Trade union activity will increasingly pose great difficulties for such a workforce. All this has occurred against a background of Kellogg's doubling their sales between 1976 and 1981 (see Anon. 1983b), and increasing their profits from 1980 to 1981 by 60 per cent.

It would be difficult to conclude that the introduction of new technology here has secured the future for the workforce. Kellogg's hold a key position in an oligopolistic market, and its financial base is securer than most firms. The question inevitably arises as to whether or not the trades unions could have negotiated a different phasing in of the new technology. This approach would have started from the point of securing a share in the productivity of the new technology, examining the disproportionate effect on women's jobs, and the possibilities of retraining for key positions such as line operators, and examining the possibilities of shorter working hours.

Conclusions

We have focused on the automation of weighing and packing lines because it was one of the most labour-intensive areas in food processing and is ripe for automation. Crisps and breakfast cereals are not alone in being affected by the introduction of new technology in this area. For example, in biscuit manufacture, hand operations which include filling pre-made bags, weighing, weight adjustment and feeding bag-sealing machines are being replaced by automatic weighing, bag forming, packing and sealing. United Biscuits' largest biscuit factory, at Harlesden in North London, has cut its workforce by a third to 1130 since 1977. As part of this the workforce on each packing line has been cut down from fourteen people to two (Anon. 1982d).

Research by Birchall (1983) which examines technical change in UK biscuit manufacture confirms that process jobs have been reduced in the ratio of 3:1 and that full-time jobs have been converted to part-time ones after the introduction of the new equipment. This trend is also evident in the cereals and snacks industries. There can be little doubt that developments in weighing and packaging technologies are drastically reducing job opportunities and that women are bearing the brunt of job losses and being pushed back out of the workforce. But the actual level of job loss will depend on management and labour organization within each plant, on corporate status and firm size and on the forces of competition within the industries concerned. The two sectors investigated in this chapter are both characterized by oligopolistic production coupled to high rates of growth of output and fuelled by new technology which has also led to large numbers of redundancies. Both are reaching a stage where capacity will far outstrip demand. The counter-cyclical strengths of the food industry (under-performing the market in more buoyant times and out-performing the market in recession) are shown clearly in both crisps and breakfast cereals, but the signs are that the volume of growth may be reaching its limit and that even economic recovery would not significantly affect this. As the recent NEDC food report points out: 'The population is static, and UK consumers are generally eating as much as they need for nutritional and energy requirements. The management members' judgement is, therefore, that there is unlikely to be any significant overall growth in demand for the industry's products' (NEDC 1983, p. 2).

The studies indicate the wide range of options which large corporations have when introducing new technology. In cereals, production is being decentralized away from the Greater Manchester conurbation, while *in situ* change appears to be increasing the importance of the temporary part-time workforce for a key employer located in the inner city. In crisps, the decentralization process is also in evidence, but for different reasons. Moreover, with the rationalization process completed, the key company, Nabisco, told the Monopolies Commission that further redundancies would be concentrated on part-time staff first. The case studies examined here illustrate the uphill struggle facing organized labour in relation to technological change. In the current period, firms have been able to carry out a programme of redundancies and closures on their own terms with few concessions to the trades unions, despite the fact that dramatic output decline is not in evidence.

In order to make it possible to maintain or increase profits, manufacturers have no choice but to enter the new technology race to become a low-cost producer and pressurize competitors out of the market: a policy adopted by Kellogg's in cereals, Nabisco in crisps, United Biscuits and Associated British Foods in wrapped breads. Clearly the automated factory is still a long way off but the opportunities for further advances are increasing.

Researchers interested in examining the impact of technical change on jobs must confront a situation where the introduction of a new innovation like the Ishida rarely takes place as an isolated event. The introduction of new weighing machinery triggers off associated changes in technique along the production line and a variety of machinery combinations are possible in different contexts for some time after the new innovation is introduced.

In this case study, as Ishidas were being introduced in the early 1980s they were linked to a variety of packaging machines as product lines were being modernized. In crisps the most common machines were Woodman's vertical form–fill–seal machines; in cereals they were frequently attached to the R. A. Jones cartoning system. Within the last three years, however, a rival to the Ishida has already been produced with the advent of the 'Woodman Twin Tube Commander Unit' which provides an indication that a further new stage has evolved in the automation of the packaging process.

United Biscuits (Foods) Ltd has placed an order with the Woodman Co. Inc. for 30 Twin Tube Commander Units and 60 Clipper C Bag-makers. The machines are to be used to weigh and pack crisps, extruded snacks and biscuits, and it is said that in extensive trials of Woodman and competitive systems, United Biscuits found

'that productivity in terms of output per minute per unit of floor area was higher than competitive systems allowing reductions in numbers of machines and total line length, an important factor when updating existing plants. Woodman was also the only company offering a *total package of machinery including weighing and bag making equipment engineered as a unit from one source, this ensuring a perfect match and, most importantly, a clean smooth transfer of product weigher to bag down specially designed transfer chutes*. The correlation of discharged weights in the bag was significantly improved by the fact that the whole machine was designed as a total package, particularly on light weight snack products such as Potato Crisps' (Anon. 1984, italics added).

At the same time the flexibility of the situation is increased even further, when one realizes that many other microchip-based innovations may be coming on stream, simultaneously. Thus video techniques are being introduced into inspection and grading while light robots and laser- and computer-aided design, are all creeping in to increase the potential for faster accurate and automated weighing and packaging production. Darrington has recently observed that what we are witnessing is

'a radically new concept of automation, which is based on comparatively simple mechanical components which can be programmed to carry out a range of production activities under the control of sophisticated computer software. Many popular conceptions of flexible manufacturing systems are based on robotics, but in practice the scope is much wider than the simple imitation of human activities which is conjured up by this phrase' (Darrington 1983).

In the meantime the manufacturers will continue to spend vast sums of money on advertising to persuade customers to eat more expensive products that carry better profit margins and increase flexibility − extruded snacks such as Monster Munch rather than crisps, Crunch Nut Cornflakes rather than plain Cornflakes.

A new technology that started off with a problem packing green peppers seems to be ending up in large sectors of food manufacturing with a capacity that far outstrips demand and a large number of unskilled workers joining the 16 per cent of the population known in the trade as 'subsistence consumers' (Henley Centre 1982). In terms of industrial restructuring and a regional technology policy, it is clear that the suggestions which have been made (Edwards & Gibbs 1982) that we should encourage firms in peripheral areas to adopt process technologies as a way of *reducing* inequalities and uneven development appear increasingly untenable.

References

Anon. 1981a. 2000 crisp men go in shock closure. *The Sun* 16 July 1981.
Anon. 1981b. The saga of the cereals. *Marketing* 14 October 1981.
Anon. 1982a. Nabisco gets bid green light. *The Guardian* 21 October 1982.
Anon. 1982b. *Save our Stockport factory*. Anti-closure bulletin produced by Smiths' Joint Shop Stewards Committee, Stockport.
Anon. 1982c. *The Financial Times* 30 October 1982.
Anon. 1982d. A boring diet is bad for industry. *The Economist* **282** (No. 7228), 75.
Anon. 1983. Breakfast cereals. *Market Research (Great Britain)* **23**, 1–7.
Anon. 1984. United Biscuits chose Commander Weighers. *Confectionary Production* January, p. 80.

Bevan, A. 1974. The UK potato crisp industry, 1960–1972: a study of new entry competition. *The Journal of Industrial Economics* **12** (4), 281–97.
Birchall, D. 1983. Technical change in biscuit manufacture and its impact on jobs. In *The Impact of chip technology on conditions and quality of work*, P.

Kendall, A. Malecki, W. Alexander, A. Wallace and T. Wheatley (eds): 87–9. The Hague: Netherlands Ministry of Social Affairs and Employment (reprinted in 1983 by Metra Consulting Group Ltd).

Darrington, H. 1979. When it comes to the crunch. *Food Manufacturing* **54** (9), 77–81.

Darrington, H. 1983. What else from the potato? *Food Manufacturing* **58** (5), 28–9.

Edwards, A. and D. C. Gibbs 1982. Regional development, process innovations and the characteristics of the firm. In *Technology: a key factor for regional development*, D. Maillat (ed.). St Saphorin, Switzerland: Georgi Publishing Company.

Fothergill, S. and G. Gudgin, 1982. *Urban and regional employment change in the UK*. London: Heinemann.

Henley Centre 1982. *Manufacturing and retailing in the 80s – a zero sum game?* London: The Henley Centre for Forecasting.

Ministry of Agriculture, Food and Fisheries 1982. National Food Survey 1980. In *Household food consumption and expenditure annual report*. London: HMSO.

Ministry of Agriculture, Food and Fisheries 1983. *Statistics 1982/83: potato crisps and snack foods*. London: HMSO.

Mintel 1982. *Consumer spending: 10 year trends*. London: Mintel Publications.

Monopolies and Mergers Commission 1982. *Nabisco Brands Inc. and Huntley-Palmer Foods PLC, a report on the proposed merger*. London: HMSO.

National Economic Development Council 1983. *Review of the food and drink manufacturing industry*. London: HMSO.

10 The economics of smaller businesses: some implications for regional economic development

D. J. STOREY

At a time when local and national governments are placing greater emphasis upon small businesses as a source of new wealth and new jobs this chapter provides a personal 'state of the art' view of research by economists on the subject.

The first half of the chapter is concerned with the currently limited knowledge of factors affecting the establishment and performance of the small firm sector, defined in manufacturing as having less than 200 employees. It is shown that much of the work undertaken by economists has concentrated, for good reasons in the past, upon large enterprises. Even today much of the work undertaken by economists on 'small firms' is concerned with enterprises having significantly more than 200 employees, yet public policy is increasingly directed toward firms with between two and fifty employees. It is argued that only through a clearer understanding of the factors affecting the establishment and performance of small firms can public policy towards the sector become targeted more effectively.

The second half of the chapter is devoted to a consideration of the role of small firms in leading economic development at a local or regional level. Existing research, much of it by geographers, is reviewed from which it is clear that in the past new and small firms have, over a decade, made only a modest contribution to the creation of new employment and that it is in the prosperous areas that the contribution has been greatest. Finally it is suggested that if policies towards small firms are to be pursued, they should be more 'selective' than is currently the case in the UK.

Background

Major changes took place in the world economy during the 1970s. On balance these have led to more goods being produced by small

215

Table 10.1 Manufacturing employment in firms employing 1–199 workers (per cent).

year	1935	1958	1963	1968	1972	1976	1979
percentage (%)	38.0	24.0	21.3	20.8	21.5	22.6	23.1

Sources: Storey (1982), Allard (1983), Census of Production.

firms, thus reversing the increase in industrial concentration which took place in the manufacturing sector in the UK over the previous thirty years. These trends are clearly shown in Table 10.1

Several reasons have been advanced by the present author to explain these changes (Storey 1982):

(a) The rise in oil prices in the early 1970s made energy-intensive (and hence capital-intensive) forms of production more expensive. It gave a comparative advantage to smaller scale units.

(b) Increased energy prices led to a relative increase in transport costs, so reducing the attractions of having a single production unit. Instead it became more economic to have smaller production units spread more widely.

(c) Increased energy prices led to a slow-down in the rate of growth of world trade in the 1970s and the rise of protectionism. Since large enterprises are more likely to export, they were disproportionately affected by these developments.

(d) The growth in competition from Japan and Third World countries was particularly severe in industries where, in the UK large firms were dominant, e.g. motor cars, shipbuilding, textiles, electrical goods, etc.

(e) Increased incomes for those in work during the 1970s led to an increase both in the demand for services and for 'one-off' rather than mass-produced goods. In both cases these demands were more likely to be met by smaller firms.

(f) During the 1960s British economic policy was directed towards reaping scale economies at the plant level, but by the mid-1970s it became clear that managerial diseconomies were arising in giant enterprises.

(g) A minor role may also have been played by the Monopolies Commission in discouraging industrial concentration which was not viewed to be in the public interest.

(h) Finally technical change, and in particular the advent of the microprocessor, has enabled computer-based techniques to be developed and implemented by small firms. It would, however, be unwise to overstate the impact, to date, of such developments.

'Jobbers' and 'marketeers'

In assessing the response of small firms to these macro-economic changes the important distinction made by Lydall (1958) has to be borne in mind. Lydall distinguished between 'jobbers' and 'marketeers'. The jobbing business conventionally sells the bulk of its output to a single (usually large) firm. It frequently has only a single product and hence is closely allied to the fortunes of its customer. If that customer ceases to trade then the jobber is unlikely to continue in business because of a limited ability to switch to an alternative customer. Even if the large customer merely contracts the scale of its output then this can endanger the existence of the jobbing business. Thus a change in the fortunes of the large business sector can have a multiplier effect upon jobbing firms in the small firm sector.

The second type of small firm is the marketeer. Such a firm more closely resembles the textbook new firm since by definition it competes, rather than being complementary, with the large firm. In this sense it is simply a scaled-down version of a large firm.

Empirical work (Lydall 1958, Davies & Kelly 1971, Johns et al. 1978) has suggested that in the manufacturing sector the majority of small firms are jobbers, rather than marketeers. Furthermore, the work of Anthony (1983) on Japan has shown that, in an economy frequently highlighted as a model competitive economy, there are a higher proportion of jobbing small firms than in any other developed economy. This suggests that most small firms are neither an actual nor even a potential threat to large firms, nor is the presence of large numbers of marketeering small firms a necessary condition for a fast growing economy.

Research priorities and questions

There are three broad categories of research questions in dealing with small business at a national level which need to be raised and they parallel the development of a research understanding of large enterprises which was developed in the 1960s and 1970s. The first requires an understanding of the factors influencing the performance of small firms (performance questions). The second group of research questions concern the impact of policy instruments designed to influence the performance of small business (policy questions). Finally the ability of the public sector to deliver policy in the form in which it will be effective (institutional capacity questions) has to be investigated.

The remainder of this chapter will be devoted partly to an examination of current research on performance questions in small business and partly to questions of both policy and institutional capacity, using the example of economic development at a local or regional level.

Economists and small firms research in the UK

There are two major deficiencies in the work which industrial economists have conducted in the UK. Virtually all analysis of business performance according to size of enterprise has been conducted on large manufacturing firms. Clearly large manufacturing firms do have a major impact upon economic growth in the UK, but it must also be recalled that less than 10 per cent of all registered businesses are in the manufacturing sector (Ganguly 1982) and that more than 90 per cent of manufacturing businesses are small. The emphasis in research seems to be out of balance with the numerical importance of small enterprises.

In the past emphasis by economists upon large firms has been justified partly because of the absolute proportion of total manufacturing output, employment or investment in these enterprises, partly because of increasing industrial concentration and partly because of the absence of suitable data on the small firm sector. As noted earlier in Table 10.1 there is now strong evidence that the relative decline of the small manufacturing firm has been arrested or even reversed. Unfortunately, industrial economists concerned with the effect of enterprise size upon performance have either ignored such developments or have examined the performance of firms at the smaller end of the spectrum of large firms.

This ostrich mentality is best demonstrated in a recently published collection of essays edited by Levicki (1984) entitled *Small business: theory and policy*. The book contains a number of articles nominally on small firms written by reputable British economists better known for their work on industrial concentration and particularly on the role of large firms. For example, an article by Hindley on 'Economics and small enterprises' does not contain a single citation of work *published* after 1977, while the article by Utton, entitled 'Concentration, competition and the small firm', contains no citations whatsoever to work on small firms. Finally the article by Samuels and Morrish in discussing birth and death rates of firms quotes only the work of Singh (1971). As is well known, this last work is an examination of quoted companies, yet it is inferred that it is applicable to small companies. This type of analysis is dangerous for several reasons:

(a)   Since there are hardly any quoted manufacturing companies which are small (defined as having less than 200 employees), such research is misleading.

(b)   As noted above on several occasions, the world economy and the economy of the UK have changed fundamentally since the data quoted by some economists in their current work.

(c)   Public policy decisions on small firms are being made *now*. If policy is based upon outdated statistical material or on research which is not relevant to the size of business under consideration, then policy itself could be misguided.

(d)   A more likely outcome is that the lack of careful and relevant work on the sector will mean the vacuum is filled by ideologists able to convince public policymakers of their particular viewpoint. Perhaps the best example, in this context, of policy being influenced by the absence of existing empirical work, is the effect of misquotation of the work of Birch (1979) on job creation. By the time that the Birch work had been subjected to careful scrutiny by Fothergill and Gudgin (1979), Hamilton *et al.* (1981), and Storey (1980) for the UK and Armington and Odle (1982) for the USA, the 'results' had significantly affected the employment policies of governments in Europe and the United States.

Research priorities in performance questions

A number of factors affecting small firm performance have been studied and these are well summarized in Binks and Coyne (1983). For example, the willingness of an individual to offer himself as an entrepreneur has been empirically examined by Johnson and Cathcart (1979a). They argue that an individual is more likely to form his own firm if he previously worked in a small firm. A comprehensive theoretical statement of entrepreneurship broadly within the Neo classical framework has recently been offered by Casson (1982) and by Loasby (1982).

Entrepreneurship, however by its nature is multi-disciplinary and non-economists have devoted considerable attention to why certain groups appear both more willing to offer themselves as entrepreneurs and why some are more successful. Entrepreneurship has been examined as a function of social class (Scase & Goffee 1980, Gould & Keeble 1984, Lloyd & Mason 1984), motivation (McClelland 1961), religious beliefs (Weber 1904) and persecuted minority (immigrant) groups (Hagen 1962, Loebl 1978, Aldrich 1980).

Recent developments in the world economy, however, suggest three areas for priority in economic research in small business. All are designed to obtain a better understanding of the factors influencing small firm performance in order that public policy towards small business becomes more effective. The subject areas are given below, but not in any order of priority:

(a) The impact of macro-economic change upon enterprises of different size
(b) The impact of government polices upon different sized firms
(c) The relationship in small firms between profits and jobs.

On macro-economic changes and firm size, Allard (1983) has recently argued that the investment behaviour of small firms over the trade cycle differs from that of large firms. He suggests that while investment (buildings, plant and machinery and vehicles) per employee was always higher for large than for small firms, data for the 1970s suggested that it was large firm investment which was the more variable over the cycle - in downswings it declined more rapidly and in upswings it expanded faster than that of small firms. Paradoxically, however, the small firm is popularly (and politically) viewed as being more responsive to change (Bannock 1982, Conservative Political Centre 1983), and indeed the notion of entrepreneurship is one of identifying opportunities for profit which are unnoticed by others.

We therefore need to know how different sized enterprises perform over the trade cycle. Is it the small or the large firm sector that leads an economy out of recession? Does employment grow *pari passu* with investment or do their patterns differ? Is the relatively increased importance of small firms since the early 1970s merely a reflection of recession and hence a purely temporary phenomenon which will disappear once growth re-establishes itself in the world economy?

With regard to the second research priority, the impact of some government policies upon the small firm sector have been commented upon (Economist Intelligence Unit 1983), but priority should be given to studies which take aspects of government policy and identify whether these have a significant differential impact upon enterprises of differing size. Of popular interest, currently, are government purchasing policies which are thought to discriminate against small firms, but perhaps of greater relevance to economists are the operations of monetary policy. There is evidence (Binks 1979, Wilson Committee 1979) that small firms find it difficult to obtain loan capital. Partly in response to the comments made by the Wilson Committee, the Government introduced in 1981, as an experiment, the Loan Guarantee Scheme.

A most important question remains whether in the operation of monetary policy and conditions of tight credit an undue burden is placed upon smaller enterprises. Existing work on this subject by economists has again concentrated upon relatively larger firms. Davis and Yeoman (1974) concluded that 'Large firms possess an advantage over small firms and that [sic] advantage is particularly important in a severe credit squeeze'. Their conclusions were broadly similar to studies in the USA reported by Galbraith (1957) and Meltzer (1960). The data used in the Davis and Yeoman study again refer only to quoted companies and cannot be taken as representative of the small firm population according to the Bolton (1971) definitions.

How then does a *small* firm adjust to conditions of monetary squeeze? Does monetary policy have different effects upon different sized enterprises and, in particular, does the role of small firms as net receivers of trade credit change in conditions of squeeze?

With regard to the third research priority, now that public policy is firmly directed towards assisting the growth of small firms the basic relationships between growth, size of firm, profits and jobs needs to be closely understood. In the 1960s and 1970s pioneering work was undertaken at Cambridge and NIESR in understanding the factors underlying growth in large firms. The work of Prais (1976), Singh and Whittington (1971), Meeks (1977) and Hart et al. (1973) added significantly to our knowledge of both the extent of industrial concentration and of the factors which underlay it.

The limited work which has been undertaken on the small firm sector has not led to the establishment of clear relationships between the major economic variables, in part because of the heterogeneity of the sector. For example, Johnson and Darnell (1976) identified a positive but lagged relationship between unemployment and new firm formation rates whereas Binks and Jennings (1983) have identified the opposite relation. There is also no published UK empirical work linking profitability at an industry level with entrants to the industry, although the attempts by this author to relate these two variables using two major regional establishment databanks found no clear association. Indeed the strongest relationships seem to be between formation rates and the shedding of labour (Storey & Jones 1983).

The construction of data bases on small businesses that will enable work of a comparable quality to that produced at Cambridge and NIESR on the large firm sector more than fifteen years ago should be given a high priority. Only then will relationships between economic variables in the small firm sector be identified and a real contribution made to the development of public policy.

Small firms and regional economic development [1]

The shortage of detailed empirical work by economists on the UK small firms sector is serious because it has enabled those with an ideological commitment to small businesses to exert a disproportionate influence over public policy at a local and national level. Examples of this commitment include the measures to help small businesses, numbering in excess of 100, which the Conservative government has introduced since 1979, and the small firm initiatives introduced by local authorities, many of which are Labour-controlled. Such measures, while presented in the language of economics, i.e. new jobs, competition, etc. are, because of the lack of understanding of the small business sector, plunges into a sea of uncertainty, buoyed up only by the ideological life-jacket.

It is now apparent, even to those who in 1979–80 welcomed the additional support being given to the small firm sector on the grounds that it could create wealth and new jobs, that the effect, to date, has been small. From a regional standpoint there is a case that current policies to assist smaller businesses in the British regions have been a highly questionable use of public funds, but to understand this case requires a very brief review of the UK regional problem.

During the 1950s and 1960s it was recognized that the 'assisted areas' of Britain were characterized by having a high proportion of employment in declining industries such as coal, shipbuilding, metal manufacture and heavy engineering. A number of measures were therefore taken to offset this so-called 'unfavourable industrial structure'. Most involved the payment of subsidies to enterprises in more 'modern' industries to locate new factories ('branch plants') in the 'assisted areas'.

During periods of prosperity this strategy was modestly successful (Marquand 1980), but in the recession from the mid-1970s onwards many of these 'branch plants' began to exhibit high closure rates. Frequently the plants located in the assisted areas were 'marginal', so that when contractions in demand took place these plants were more likely to close than headquarters plants. Experience has demonstrated that it is an inadequate policy response to observe that a region has an unfavourable industrial structure and then merely attempt to diversify that structure by *bringing in* new industries without any *economic or commercial* logic underlying that location, and without taking account of the type of employment created.

In the past five years less emphasis has been placed upon bringing new industry into the 'assisted areas' and more upon helping the regions to help themselves through indigenous development. For example, in *Regional industrial development* the government says,

'Incentives . . . need to focus on encouraging new and indigenous development in the Assisted Areas, rather than simply transferring jobs from one part of the country to another' (HMSO 1983, para. 20). Elsewhere the government states, 'It is widely accepted that in the long run a region's economic wealth depends, amongst other things, on the creation and growth of new enterprises in actitivies which are likely to lead to a net increase in regional income' (DTI 1983, para. III:48).

These objectives have to be tempered by the results of research findings, mainly by geographers, on the contribution of new and small firms to employment in localities in the UK. Very broadly these results show that:

(a)   In *all* areas of the UK the new and small firm sector has made only a modest contribution to employment.
(b)   In the 'assisted areas' both the rate of formation and the expected impact of small firm policies will be less than in prosperous areas.
(c)   Despite their expected modest contribution, current policies to stimulate the sector are concerned to maximize the number of new firm births, rather than create employment and wealth in the small firm sector.

The contribution of new manufacturing firms to employment is clearly shown in Table 10.2 It takes the major studies of new firm

Table 10.2   Regional comparisons of new firm formation rates.

Area	Time period	Number of surviving new firms	Percentage of end year employment in new firms (%)	Standardized firm formation rate*
Cambridgeshire	1971–81	313	5.2	0.57
East Midlands	1968–75	1650	4.2	0.42
South Hampshire	1971–79	333	2.7	0.34
Norfolk	1971–81	208	3.5	0.30
Suffolk	1971–81	182	3.1	0.28
Durham	1965–78	236	4.4	0.25
Tyne and Wear	1965–78	486	3.6	0.17
Cleveland	1965–78	165	2.8	0.10
Scotland	1968–77	504	2.2	0.08

Sources: Gould and Keeble (1984); Durham County Council (1982), Cleveland County Council (1982), Tyne and Wear County Council (1982); Fothergill and Gudgin (1982); Mason (1982); Cross (1981).
* Firm formation rate divided by the number of years in the study.

formation in the UK and ranks the areas studied according to the final column index of standardized firm formation rates. The table shows clearly that the highest formation rates are in the more prosperous areas and that the low formation rates are in the least prosperous areas. Broadly the 'assisted areas' occupy the final four positions and the 'non-assisted areas' occupy the top five positions.

The third column of Table 10.2 shows the contribution which new firms made to the stock of employment. Thus in Cambridge-shire 5.2 per cent of jobs in 1981 were in wholly new firms created over the previous decade, and this is the *highest* of any UK area for which data are available. The importance of this statistic must be fully understood since it clearly shows that, in 1981, *even in an area where high technology small firms were very much in evidence, only five jobs in every 100 were in new firms created within the last decade.* It demonstrates that even in an area such as this the contribution made by new firms is negligible over a decade.

The formation rates in 'assisted areas' are approximately one-fifth that of Cambridge and new firms in such areas created about 2 per cent of the stock of jobs at the end of a decade.

National small firm policies are likely to have differential regional impacts since research into the factors affecting the formation rates and growth of new businesses have shown that:

(a) New firms are more likely to be formed by those working in an existing small firm (Johnson & Cathcart 1979a).
(b) Firms founded by those with managerial experience are more likely to show higher growth rates (Cross 1981).
(c) Firms founded by those with higher educational qualifications are more likely to show higher growth rates (Gudgin *et al.* 1979).
(d) Most new firms sell locally (Storey 1982).
(e) Most new firms are financed primarily from personal savings (Cross 1981, Storey 1982).
(f) Most individuals start their firm in the industry in which they were formerly employed (Johnson & Cathcart 1979b).

The regional implications of these findings can be shown by deriving a regional entrepreneurship index as shown in Table 10.4. The table takes the factors as shown in Table 10.3 and provides a regional index. For example, since an individual working in a small firm is significantly more likely to form his own firm than an otherwise comparable individual working in a larger firm then regions with more employment in small firms will, on balance, be expected to have a higher rate of new firm formation. Similarly, regions with a high proportion of the population having managerial

Table 10.3   Factors associated with high levels of entrepreneurship.

	Factors	High Entrepreneurship	Index
(1)	size of 'Incubator' firm	small firms	percentage of small firms in the region
(2)	occupational experience	managerial experience	percentage of population in managerial groupings
(3)	education	high levels	percentage of population with degrees
(4)	access to capital	easy access	(a) savings per head of population (b) house-owning population
(5)	entry into industry	low entry barriers	percentage of population in low entry barrier industries
(6)	markets	wealthy local markets	regional income distribution

experience or educational qualifications will be expected to create firms with more growth potential. Since it is possible to obtain regional data on the distribution of the factors listed in Table 10.3, it is possible to rank each region according to the presence of the factor. Where the factor has been shown to be positively associated with 'entrepreneurship' the region with the lowest ranking position scores 1 point and where the factor is negatively associated with entrepreneurship the region with the highest ranking scores 1 point. Hence regions with the *highest* total score are likely to be the major beneficiaries of national policies designed to assist small businesses.

Table 10.4 shows these regional results, clearly demonstrating that according to this regional entrepreneurship index, South East England followed by South West England are the areas most likely to benefit from small firm policies. The 'assisted areas' of the UK occupy the 'wooden spoon' positions, with Northern England, Northern Ireland, Scotland and Wales having significantly lower 'scores' than other UK regions.

The above regional index was constructed prior to data becoming available on the regional distribution of businesses registered for

Table 10.4 An index of regional entrepreneurship in Britain: rankings.

Region	Percentage in small manufacturing plants	Percentage in large manufacturing plants	Percentage going to degree courses	Percentage without qualifications	Percentage in administrative and managerial class	Percentage in manual class	Savings	Owner-occupied dwellings	Average dwelling price	Barriers to entry	Disposable income	Average score
Northern	2	1	2	7	4=	2	8	1	5	1	5	3.45
Yorkshire and Humberside	7	8=	6	4	4=	1	5	2	1	4	9	4.64
East Midlands	6	10	3=	6	8	3	10	5	2	6	6	6.09
East Anglia	8=	8=	1	8	7	9	4	6	6	11	8	6.91
South East	11	7	8	10	11	11	7	4	11	10	11	9.18
South West	10	6	5	9	6	10	9	8	8	9	4	7.64
West Midlands	3=	3	3=	3	9	4	6	3	7	7	10	5.27
North West	5	4	7	5	10	6	11	7	3	8	7	6.64
Wales	3=	2	10	1	2	7	3	n.a.	4	2	3	3.70
Scotland	8=	5	9	n.a.	3	5	2	n.a.	9	3	2	5.11
Northern Ireland	1	11	n.a.	2	1	8	1	n.a.	10	5	1	4.44

n.a. = not available

VAT. It is therefore interesting to compare the results of the VAT-based data for 1980 and 1981, which show that, apart from Northern Ireland, Wales had the lowest firm formation rate for new businesses of any UK region in 1980 and the third lowest, after Scotland and Northern Ireland, in 1981 (Ganguly 1982). Indeed there is a strong positive association between the theoretically derived index in Table 10.4 and birth rates as found in the VAT-based data (Whittington 1984). *In short this demonstrates that there are major regional differences in the rates at which businesses will be formed. Essentially, small business policy is regionally divisive since its biggest impact is in the most prosperous areas and its least impact is in the least prosperous areas.*

Implications for policy

While the impact of small business policy is very limited, and while the impact is almost certainly regionally divisive, this does not mean that the small business should be ignored as a source of new wealth and new jobs. What is of importance is to maximize the impact of public policy designed to assist the sector. Unfortunately, even on this basis, current UK government policy must be judged a failure.

If a public policy towards small firms is to be formulated, the following statistics have to be recalled (Storey 1985a, Ganguly 1983): Firstly, at least 30 per cent of new manufacturing firms close within four years; secondly the median employment in a firm which is ten years old is twelve workers; thirdly, one-third of all jobs created in new businesses are in 2 per cent of the firms which start; and finally the chances of a new firm having 100 employees within a decade are about 1 in 150. These statistics show that about one-third of new businesses close very quickly, the vast majority of the remainder are small and will always remain small and that major employment creation takes place only in a mere handful of firms.

If there is to be a policy to assist small businesses, then it has to be directed towards those few businesses and entrepreneurs who are capable of transforming the local economy. A policy of picking the winners, or at least avoid the losers, has to be adopted.

Two familiar but irrelevant criticisms of a selective policy should be discussed at this stage: firstly, that the public sector has a poor record at picking winners; secondly, that if the firms are successful they do not require assistance.

It is true that it is virtually impossible to isolate the Identikit entrepreneur when he starts his business. However, the present proposals would only apply to businesses that were three years old or more. By that time, our research has shown that the fast growth business is already significantly different from other new businesses

(Storey 1985a). It is at that point that the package of assistance could become available.

It is also argued that there is no need to assist 'fast growth' businesses since, by definition, they are prospering well. However, survey evidence shows that these fast growth firms *are* encountering many more problems than the normal business (Storey 1985b). They experience problems because their premises are too small, they have difficulty with finding new premises, with recruiting suitable labour, etc. In short they encounter problems *because* they are growing. It is they who need assistance and, if such businesses can grow slightly faster as a result of receiving the assistance, this can make a *major* impact upon employment and wealth creation.

Policy amendments

If public policy towards small business is to be directed towards having the maximum impact upon employment and wealth creation, it should comprise the following elements:

(a)   No assistance would be provided to start up businesses.

(b)   A comprehensive package of assistance would be available only to those businesses with worthwhile growth prospects. Assistance would include finance, advice and marketing assistance, using a 'hands-on' approach.

(c)   Only existing businesses would be selected, i.e. those which could demonstrate a track record.

(d)   To be selected for assistance a business would need to demonstrate that it was not merely displacing other local businesses. It would have to show a capacity to sell outside the region and preferably outside the UK.

(e)   Each Small Firms Service Office should have no more than ten firms on its books, but for those ten firms it should offer a 'total' service.

(f)   A *full* review of the operations of the Loan Guarantee Scheme, Business Expansion Scheme and Enterprise Allowance Schemes should be undertaken to evaluate the *net* job contribution which these schemes have made. Only when the schemes have been fully evaluated should a decision be made on their future.

(g)   All calls for a proportion of public tenders to be allocated to small firms should be rejected, unless it can be shown that this will lead both to a net increase in UK employment *and* to no increase in costs to the public sector.

Conclusion

This chapter has argued that public policy on small business is currently being developed well in advance of research findings. A panoply of forms of public assistance in the form of loans, grants, tax reliefs, advice, provision, etc., are now provided by national and local government but without any clear understanding of the expected results. In some respects the research community has failed to provide satisfactory guidance on these policies since its understanding of the motivations and aspirations of entrepreneurs is sketchy. There is, for example, no major empirical work on the small business sector which identifies the relationship between public subsidy provision and net job creation. The question remains, of course, whether, even if such work existed, it would influence an area of government policy which regards 'seat of the pants' and 'gut-feel' as positive virtues.

Note

1   This section is based on the author's evidence to the Select Committee on Welsh Affairs, Session 1983–84. 'The impact of regional industrial policy on Wales', Minutes of Evidence, pp. 257–61.

References

Aldrich, H. 1980. Asian shopkeepers as a middleman priority: a study of small businesses in Wandsworth. In *The inner city: employment and industry*, A. Evans and D. Eversley (eds): 389–407. London: Heinemann.

Allard, R. 1983. The importance and position of small firms. *The Economic Review* November, 19–24.

Anthony, D. 1983. Japan. In *The small firm: an international survey*, D. J. Storey (ed.): 46–83. London: Croom–Helm.

Armington, C. and M. Odle 1982. Small businesses – how many jobs? *Brookings Review* Fall, 14–17.

Bannock, G. 1981. *The economics of small firms*. Oxford: Basil Blackwell.

Binks, M. 1979. Finance for expansion in the small firm. *Lloyds Bank Review* October, 33–45.

Binks, M. and J. Coyne 1983. *The birth of enterprise*. Hobart Paper No. 98. London: Institute of Economic Affairs.

Binks, M. and A. Jennings 1983. *New firms as a source of industrial regeneration*. Mimeo., Nottingham University Small Firms Unit.

Birch, D. L. 1979. *The job generation process*. Cambridge, Mass.: MIT Program on Neighborhood and Regional Change.

Bolton, J. (Chairman) 1971. *Small firms: report of the Commission of Enquiry on Small Firms*. Cmnd 4811. London: HMSO.

Casson, M. 1982. *The entrepreneur: an economic theory*. Oxford: Martin Robertson.

Cleveland County Council. *Manufacturing employment change in Cleveland since 1965*. Middlesborough: Cleveland County Council, County Planning Department.

Conservative Political Centre 1983. *Moving forward: small business and the economy*. London: Conservative Political Centre.

Cross, M. 1981. *New firm formation and regional development*. Farnborough: Gower.

Davies, E. W. and K. A. Yeoman 1974. *Company finance and the capital market: a study of the effects of firm size*. Cambridge: Cambridge University Press.

Davies, J. R. and M. Kelly 1971. *Small firms in the manufacturing sector*. Committee of Enquiry on Small Firms, Research Report no. 3. London: HMSO.

Department of Trade and Industry 1983. *Regional industrial policy: some economic issues*. London: HMSO.

Durham County Council 1982. *Manufacturing employment change in Durham since 1965*. Durham: County Planning Department.

Economist Intelligence Unit 1983. *The European climate for small business: a ten country study*. London: EIU.

Fothergill, S. and G. Gudgin 1979. The job generation process in Britain. *Centre for Environmental Studies, Research Series No. 32*. London: Centre for Environmental Studies.

Fothergill, S. and G. Gudgin 1982. *Unequal growth: urban and regional employment change in the UK*. London: Heinemann.

Galbraith, J. K. 1957. Market structure and stabilization policy. *Review of Economics and Statistics* **29**, 124–33.

Ganguly, P. 1982. Births and deaths of firms in the UK in 1980. *British Business*, 29 January 1982, 204–7.

Ganguly, P. 1983. Lifespan analysis of businesses in the UK, 1973–82. *British Business*, 12 August 1983, 838–45.

Gould, A. and D. Keeble, 1984. New firms and rural industrialization in East Anglia. *Regional Studies* **18**, 189–202.

Gudgin, G., I. Brunskill and S. Fothergill 1979. *New manufacturing firms in regional employment growth*. Centre for Environmental Studies, Research Series no. 39. London: Centre for Environmental Studies.

Hagen, E. E. 1962. *On the theory of social change: how economic growth begins*. Homewood, Ill.: Dorcey Press.

Hamilton, D., L. Moar and I. Orton 1981. *Job generation in Scottish manufacturing industry*. Glasgow: Fraser of Allander Institute, University of Strathclyde.

Hart, P. E., M. A. Utton and G. Walshe 1973. *Mergers and concentration in British industry*. Cambridge: Cambridge University Press.

HMSO 1983. *Regional industrial development*. Cmnd 9111. London: HMSO.

Johns, B. L., W. C. Dunlop and W. J. Sheehan 1978. *Small businesses in Australia – problems and prospects.* Sydney: Allen and Unwin.

Johnson, P. S. and D. G. Cathcart 1979a. The founders of new manufacturing firms: a note on the size of their 'incubator' plants. *Journal of Industrial Economics* **28**, 219–24.

Johnson, P. S. and D. G. Cathcart 1979b. New manufacturing firms and regional development: some evidence from the northern region. *Regional Studies* **13**, 269–80.

Johnson, P. S. and A. Darnell 1976. *New firm formation in Great Britain.* Department of Economics, Discussion Paper no. 6. University of Durham.

Levicki, C. 1984. *Small business: theory and policy.* London: Croom-Helm.

Lloyd, P. and C. Mason 1984. Spatial variations in new firm formation in the United Kingdom: comparative evidence from Merseyside, Greater Manchester and South Hampshire. *Regional Studies* **18**, 207–20.

Loasby, B. J. 1982. The entrepreneur in economic theory. *Scottish Journal of Political Economy* **29**, 233–45.

Loebl, H. 1978. *Government financed factories and the establishment of industries by refugees in the special areas of England, 1937–61.* MPhil thesis, University of Durham.

Lydall, H. F. 1958. Aspects of competition in manufacturing industry. *Bulletin of the Oxford Institute of Economics and Statistics* **20**, 319–37.

McClelland, D. C. 1961. *The achieving society.* New York: Van Nostrand.

Marquand, J. 1980. *Measuring the effects and costs of regional incentives.* Government Economic Service Working Paper no. 32. London: Department of Industry.

Mason, C. M. 1982. *New manufacturing firms in South Hampshire: survey results.* Department of Geography, Discussion Paper no. 13. University of Southampton.

Meeks, G. 1977. *Disappointing marriage: a study of the gains from merger.* London: Cambridge University Press.

Meltzer, A. H. 1960. Mercantile credit, monetary policy and size of firms. *Review of Economics and Statistics* **42**, 429–37.

Prais, S. J. 1976. *The evolution of giant firms in Britain.* London: Cambridge University Press.

Scase, R. and R. Goffee 1980. *The real world of the small business owner.* London: Croom Helm.

Singh, A. 1971. *Takeovers, their relevance to the stock market and the theory of the firm.* London: Cambridge University Press.

Singh, A. and G. Whittington (in collaboration with H. T. Burley) 1971. *Growth, profitability and valuation: a study of United Kingdom quoted companies.* Department of Applied Economics, Occasional Paper no. 7, University of Cambridge.

Storey, D. J. 1980. *Job generation and small firms policy in Britain.* Centre for Environmental Studies, Policy Series no. 11. London: Centre for Environmental Studies. (Reprinted as part of minutes of evidence presented to the House of Lords Committee on Unemployment, 7 May 1980.)

Storey, D. J. 1982. *Entrepreneurship and the new firm*. London: Croom Helm.

Storey, D. J. 1985a. Manufacturing employment change in Northern England, 1965–78: the role of smaller businesses. In *Small firms in regional economic development: Britain, Ireland and the USA*, D. J. Storey (ed.). London: Cambridge University Press.

Storey, D. J. 1985b. The problems facing smaller businesses. *Journal of Management Studies* **22** (3), May 1985, pp. 327–45.

Storey, D. J. and A. Jones 1983. *New firm formation: a labour market approach to industrial entry*. Paper presented at the ESRC Urban and Regional Economics Study Group meeting, Reading.

Tyne and Wear County Council 1982. *Manufacturing employment change in Tyne and Wear since 1965*. Newcastle upon Tyne: Planning Department, Tyne and Wear County Council.

Weber, M. 1904. *The protestant ethic and the spirit of capitalism* (translated by T. Parsons). New York: Scribner.

Whittington, R. 1984. Regional bias in new firm formation in the UK. *Regional Studies* **18**, 253–6.

Wilson, Lord (Chairman) 1979. *The financing of small firms, interim report of the Committee to Review the Functioning of the Financial Institutions*. Cmnd 7503. London: HMSO.

11 Trends in small firm industrial relations and their implications for the role of the small firm in economic restructuring

J. CURRAN and J. STANWORTH

Introduction

The role that the small enterprise might play in the massive economic restructuring now taking place in Britain, particularly in spearheading technological innovation and the shift towards a tertiary economy, is receiving increasing attention. Much of this attention emerges in the form of highly optimistic pronouncements, especially from politicians, identifying a central role, even *the* central role, for the small firm. Small enterprises are defined as opportunity-seeking, risk-taking, organizationally flexible and employment-creating. Larger enterprises, in contrast, are often portrayed as anchored in the economy of the past, inflexible, risk-averse and, because of their capital–intensive strategies, negative contributors to employment.

Much in these optimistic views is questionable. There is more than a suspicion, for example, that they are often linked closely to currently fashionable ideologies (Bechhofer & Elliott 1981, GLC 1983) rather than to any rigorous evaluation of the role and status of the small enterprise in an economy undergoing complex and unprecedented changes. There is already a good deal of research and analysis on some aspects of these changes, for instance, on the economics of the small firm (Boswell 1973, Bannock 1981, Storey 1982), on the role of small firms in technological innovation (Rothwell & Zegveld 1982) and an especially detailed and continuing debate on the employment creation potential of small firms (Birch 1979, Fothergill & Gudgin 1979, Storey 1980, 1981, Woodcock 1983). Overall, it might be argued that, at best, these offer inconclusive support for the more optimistic views of the role of the small firm in current economic changes.

When, however, we turn to the social dynamics of the small firm and its relations to the issues of innovation, employment and economic restructuring, there is not only much less research analysis but much of what is available adopts a curiously one-sided perspective. The latter takes the form of an overriding concern with the owner–manager and his (much more rarely, her) problems, with a virtual neglect of any direct examination of the involvement of employees in the enterprise or the bearing this involvement might have on the issues in question[1]. Again, it might be suggested, this general lack of attention to the enterprise as a social entity is connected to the ideological emphasis on the individual entrepreneur as a lone creator of wealth almost as if others played no significant part in the process.[2]

An industrial relations approach to the small firm is a convenient and revealing way of both focusing directly on the enterprise as a social entity and of correcting this bias. But, in addition, the conceptual, theoretical and empirical concerns which constitute contemporary industrial relations studies also offer the means systematically to link internal social relations with a wide range of external influences. The latter affect enterprises of all sizes (although not usually, of course, in identical ways) and, by incorporating them into the analysis, a comparative dimension emerges setting the small enterprise alongside its larger counterpart. Such an approach offers, we would argue, an important contribution to the assessment of the role the small firm might play in economic change, innovation and employment creation in the 1980s.[3]

Industrial relations and the small firm

The industrial relations of the small firm[4] may be conveniently divided into two contexts: the internal and the external. The internal context concerns the characteristic patterns of employer–employee relations which arise within the small firm. The external context covers a wide range of influences which will have some impact on the internal context: the main influences to be considered are the character and changes in the wider industrial and economic structures, State policies and labour law, labour market patterns, trades unions and the wider ideological and political climate.

The analysis of the internal context of small firm industrial relations seems subject to a remarkably persistent myth which is counter to the bulk of research evidence. Broadly, the myth asserts that the small firm is a haven of tension-free employer–employee relations. Each communicates openly and easily with the other in a friendly, easy-going but efficient and highly productive atmosphere. Labour turnover is low, employers take a strong interest in their employees as individuals and help with their personal problems, while the employee feels strongly committed to the enterprise, willingly taking on tasks over and above any nominal job specification.

Support for this view of small firm industrial relations goes back at least to the 1950s (Acton Society Trust 1953, 1957, Revans 1956, 1958) but was perhaps most authoritatively reiterated in the influential Bolton Report (HMSO 1971, pp. 19–22). This has since been echoed by a string of published statements from the host of small business pressure groups such as the National Federation of the Self-employed and Smaller Businesses and the Association of Independent Businesses.

Critical analyses of the validity of these accounts have been made in detail elsewhere (Curran & Stanworth 1981b, Westrip 1982) but what is perhaps most surprising is that they co-exist with a small but increasing body of well conducted research which offers a contrary and somewhat more plausible view. For instance, as early as 1974, the Commission for Industrial Relations revealed that small firms experienced special problems in coping with the negotiation of wages and conditions of employees and that the much vaunted ease of communications between boss and employee might not be so open and free-flowing as was popularly assumed (Henderson & Johnson 1974). Subsequently, research by Newby (1977), Curran & Stanworth (1979b, 1981a, b), Scott and Rainnie (1982) and Stephenson et al. (1983) substantiated these doubts.[5]

To understand the patterns industrial relations are likely to take up in the small enterprise and at the risk of some over-generalization, given the wide variety of economic circumstances in which small firms occur,[6] it is necessary to explore further the internal social dynamics involved. Small firm owner–managers have been shown to have a distinct managerial style with clear implications for attitudes to industrial relations (Kets de Vries 1977, Scase & Goffee 1980, Chs. 5 & 8). Broadly, this managerial style favours a highly centralized and structured organization with a relative absence of defined procedures, role specification and forward planning. Owner–managers recognize a distinct separation of interests between themselves and their employees as well as a marked difference in the levels of involvement in the enterprise between the two. Small firm employers frequently express strong antipathy to trades unions (Henderson & Johnson 1974, p. 30, Scase & Goffee 1980, pp. 115–8, 1982, pp. 148–9), an antipathy which many small firm pressure groups have sought to capitalize upon (Hughes 1979, Westrip 1982).

In discussing small firm employee expressions of conflict much has been made of the relative absence of overt and especially collective expressions such as strikes (HMSO 1971, pp. 19 and 21, Shorey 1975, Prais 1978) with a more or less explicit argument that observed statistical variations are an indicator of the quality of internal social relations within the firm.[7] But, of course, strikes are only one form of conflict expression and given the considerable problems faced by employees and trade unions in organizing collectively in small firms, it should not be too surprising that strikes appear to occur less frequently in small firms as compared with large firms. It is much more relevant to look at individual expressions of employee conflict and particularly labour turnover since this is undoubtedly the easiest way for a small firm employee actively to demonstrate dissatisfaction with the conditions and rewards offered by the employer. Curran and Stanworth (1979a), for example, reported marked differences in levels of employment stability among small and large firm workers in the printing and electronic industries. High levels of labour turnover are in fact common in many industries with a high proportion of small firms, such as catering.

But statistical indicators of the above kind, however well based, are not ideal for analysing the quality of social relations within the small enterprise. Studies explicitly focusing upon the latter have repeatedly shown employee awareness of the differences in interests between employers and those they employ. Commitment to the enterprise is frequently tempered by feelings of not being taken into management's confidence or not being kept fully informed and with feelings of insecurity arising from perceptions (largely accurate) that a small enterprise is more subject to market forces than the larger firm (Curran & Stanworth 1979a, Scott & Rainnie 1982). In other words, the small firm shows tensions between employers and employees which are not easily reconcilable with the stereotypical harmonious characterization of the small firm.

Perhaps the central point to be made is that whatever differences undoubtedly exist between industrial relations patterns in small and large firms the typical small enterprise remains organized on a capitalist basis. Owner–managers are constrained to conform to market forces, including adjusting the number and types of people employed, while employees remain basically sellers of labour and skills no matter how long they work for a particular firm or how close the personal relations they develop with their employer (Newby 1975, Curran & Stanworth 1979b, Scott & Rainnie 1982). Indeed in some respects these forces and contradictions are often more apparent in the small enterprise since it usually has less opportunity to insulate itself from market forces or to develop internal resources and procedures to withstand the immediate effects of such forces.

If the stereotypical harmonious view of the small firm were accurate, it might be expected that in terms of economic restructuring, innovation and employment creation the small firm would be able to play a major and highly positive role. Structural unemployment plus that resulting from the recession would free large numbers of employees to opt for the attractions of the small firm. The open unstructured small enterprise would be in a position to respond rapidly to new opportunities including the adoption of new technology. However, the account of the internal context of industrial relations in the small firm offered above suggests that the potential of the small firm in these circumstances might be easily overstated.

For instance small firm employers might be seen at first sight to have adopted an organizational framework consistent with innovation since in many ways it resembles the organic model of Burns and Stalker (1961) widely accepted as highly suited to organizations coping with rapid technological and market changes. But a main feature of the latter is decentralized decision-making whereas, as noted above, a good deal of research on small business management strategies indicates highly centralized decision-making. In these circumstances high levels of innovation are likely to lead to an increase in uncertainty and insecurity among other members of the organization which, as already noted, is often relatively high in the small firm anyway. One possible response to high levels of innovation in any organization, it has been suggested (Bluedorn 1982), is high levels of turnover.[8] It might be expected that such tendencies are accentuated in the small firm, rendering internal relations even more stressful and undermining the firm's ability to implement innovation smoothly and successfully.

Innovation, particularly where it is closely linked to new technology, requires skilled labour and the current recession might be thought to have helped small firms recruit their share of such labour. But again there are complexities underlying any such assumed transition of labour from the economy as a whole to the small enterprise. For example, small firm employers are selective in their recruitment (Curran & Stanworth, 1979b), usually preferring cheaper, younger and non-trade union member employees. Skilled workers may often display some or all of the opposites to these attributes. But equally, small firms may not be all that attractive to skilled workers themselves as an alternative to working for a large firm. The latter will usually be able to afford a superior reward package (earnings plus fringe benefits including subsidized canteen, more generous pensions, etc.) to that of the small firm and especially the small firm investing heavily in expansion and new technology. A larger enterprise will also be more likely to offer an internal career ladder to skilled and able employees, whereas in many small firms there are few promotion opportunities even when the firm is expanding.[9]

Some support for the above may be derived from a recent Economists Advisory Group survey (Economists Advisory Group 1983) which reported that small firms were apparently finding the task of attracting and keeping good quality staff as difficult as had been the case five years previously.[10] Indeed, almost a third of respondents thought their labour problems had become worse in this period. Such a finding may also be thought likely where firms are attempting to recruit employees with high technology skills. Even in the current recession some areas of the economy are expanding rapidly and there are considerable shortages of skilled employees (particularly where this has been accompanied by cutbacks in government support for training) in some areas. Small firms will be in no better position to obtain such workers than previously under these circumstances.

Overall, therefore, an examination of the internal context of small firm industrial relations suggests that while we can expect small firms to play a role in the current restructuring of the economy, we should be aware of the constraints involved. The restructuring of the economy, introducing and adapting to new technology and recruiting employees who may have little experience of the small firm environment, adds to the normal problems of maintaining effective internal social relations within an economic unit which many claim to be at the mercy of increasingly hostile forces in an advanced industrial society.

The external context of small firm industrial relations

The external context of industrial relations in the small firm is if anything even more complex. Changes in the wider economic structure of a fundamental character are now widely recognized as occurring in Britain. De-industrialization and the shift to a tertiary based economy are well under way. The domination of the economy by larger enterprises is now more evident in Britain than in almost any other advanced free enterprise industrial society (Samuels & Morrish 1984, Utton 1984). Economists are not entirely in agreement on the implications of these changes for the survival of the small enterprise but recently there have been a number of suggestions that the role of the small firm in the economy is by no means exhausted.

For example, the argument that large firms have the advantages of economies of scale which gradually ensure that the small firm disappears or is pushed into a marginal role in the economy has been increasingly questioned of late. Technical economies of scale have been suggested to both favour and discriminate against the small enterprise. The Bolton Report (HMSO 1971) and Blair (1972) pointed out that a good deal of recent technological change in fields ranging from plastics to electronics has reduced considerably the size at which a plant may operate profitably. Moreover, while *firms* have undoubtedly grown in size in Britain since the 1930s, the size of *plants* (the unit where technical economies of scale are most likely to have their impact) has not. As one recent commentator has argued, an examination of the relevant data suggests that the industries where very large size plants are needed to fully exploit technical economies are relatively few and that elsewhere 'there is still enormous scope for plants, even in manufacturing, which employ fewer than 200 people' (Utton 1984, p. 8).

Further, the analysis of economies of scale has to be balanced with an analysis of *dis*economies. The latter have generally received much less attention since on the whole they concern phenomena very much more difficult to quantify than those emphasized in the analysis of economies of scale. In the main, diseconomies appear to be connected with organizational characteristics such as communications, flexibility and especially motivational problems which tend to occur wherever large numbers of people are brought together within a single bureaucratized impersonal enterprise.[11]

Much of the economic debate on concentration and economies of scale was concerned with established and mainly manufacturing industries and, without wishing to enter further into a highly complex area of analysis, it may be reasonably suggested that the broad conclusions to be derived from recent thinking tends to point towards the survival of the small enterprise but no dramatic change in its economic role. Areas where small firms continue to be pushed out as the economy changes seem to be balanced by emerging opportunities for small firms in other areas, perhaps best exemplified recently in the electronics and computer industries. On the other hand, as will be suggested below, these changes are far from neutral in their implications for industrial relations in the small firm.

But it is to the emerging tertiary sectors of the economy that more attention must be given simply because the indications are that these are more significant for the economy of the future. In knowledge-based industries, commercial and financial services as well as services more generally, there are fewer obvious economies of scale than in those spheres of economic activity which have dominated Britain's economy until recently. One important reason for this is that many tertiary activities are also people-centred; they involve the producer in direct contact with other people either on a continuing or single transaction basis. Either way the complexities involved make standardized, impersonal procedures difficult to evolve or, if they are developed, they often result in consumer apathy or resistance. Another reason for fewer economies of scale in tertiary activities is that a large proportion of the main assets required are intangibles – human creativity, knowledge and person-to-person skills.

These distinctive characteristics of the emerging tertiary economy do not rule out the large enterprise as the banking and insurance industries so clearly demonstrate. Yet they do offer openings to the small enterprise allowing it to compete more effectively with larger enterprises and, while no precise figures are available, it has been suggested that much of the renaissance in small enterprise in Britain recently has been in the tertiary sector. There are also increasing possibilities of joint small–large ventures which enable split economies of scale to be exploited with the larger enterprise covering mainly initial production and certain support activities while satellite small enterprises serve the individual consumer.[12]

In the emerging economy, therefore, it might be suggested that opportunities for small enterprise will continue to be generated at least at a level commensurate with that prevailing in the economy of the recent past. Some might argue more optimistically that the result might be an increase in the significance of the small firm in the economy, reversing the long term slow decline of most of this century. Taking the less optimistic view, it will still imply a change in the composition of the small enterprise sector, a change which will reflect shifts in the mix of the economy as a whole and may even be more marked for the small firm. Again, as will be shown below, these wider economic changes have considerable implications for small firm industrial relations.

The state and the small firm

State attitudes to the small enterprise in Britain have undergone a dramatic reversal over the last decade and a half. Traditionally governments in Britain have ignored the small enterprise and even in the postwar period where government economic intervention became increasingly pronounced, it was the larger enterprise that governments sought to influence. Small firms were difficult to reach administratively and macro-economic theory emphasized the importance of the large enterprise in influencing the performance of the economy as a whole. But from the beginning of the 1970s[13] there was a burgeoning State interest in the small enterprise. Small firms were increasingly seen as providing the seed bed for the large firms of the future, as important in innovating and, as unemployment increased, as generators of new jobs.

The increasing attention given to small firms was accompanied by policy changes designed to promote their fortunes. For instance, the 1974–79 Labour Government abolished capital transfer tax on businesses transferred within families. The 1979 Conservative administration greatly accelerated this trend introducing a Loan Guarantee scheme in 1981 and new tax incentives to attract individual investors to back small enterprises. By 1983 the Department of Industry was able to claim that the government had introduced almost a hundred measures to help the small business (Department of Industry 1983).

Unfortunately, much of this increase in positive help for the small business was vitiated in the eyes of small business owners by other changes seen as distinctly unfavourable, especially changes in industrial relations laws[14]. Owner-managers were especially incensed at the Employment Protection Act of 1975. This accompanied the Trade Union and Labour Relations Act of 1974–75, repealing the 1971 Industrial Relations Act which had been seen as largely favouring employers' interests.

The Employment Protection Act was intended to improve industrial relations especially by encouraging the extension of collective bargaining. It set up ACAS (the Advisory Conciliation and Arbitration Service) as a statutory body offering advice, a conciliation service and arrangements for arbitration. ACAS could also conduct enquiries and publish its findings. Where an employer refused to recognize a trade union, ACAS could recommend recognition which might be enforced. The powers of Wages Councils (which are important in many industries with high numbers of small firms) were extended to cover all terms and conditions of service. Pregnant employees were also given protection by law for the first time against dismissal on the grounds of pregnancy. The Act also extended unfair dismissal legislation already in being, to the discomfort of small firm employers.[15]

However, since 1979, Conservative administrations have attempted to reverse much of what the 1983 Conservative Party manifesto (promising further changes) described as the 'militants' charter of trade union legislation' passed in the 1970s which 'tilted the balance of power in bargaining throughout industry away from responsible management' (Bright et al. 1983, p. 29). In 1979, immediately after winning the General Election, the Conservatives doubled the qualifying period of service before an employee could seek redress for unfair dismissal from an industrial tribunal from six months to one year and to two years where the firm employed 20 or fewer workers.

In addition, those offered fixed term contracts of a year or more could be formally contracted out of the legislation (previously such contracts had to be for a minimum of two years). The Employment Act of 1980 with its linked codes of practice covered a wide range of employment and trade union issues including strikes, closed shop provisions, trade union membership and recognition, terms and conditions of employment and maternity rights. Specifically, the Act required industrial tribunals to take into account the size and administrative resources of a firm in deciding whether dismissal was unfair and relieved firms with five or less employees from the liability of reinstatement after maternity leave. Overwhelmingly, the effects of this legislation were to strengthen management power and weaken trade union and employee rights. The Employment Act of 1982 continues these processes.

The Government has pushed these trends further with the recent Trade Union Bill, which among other things insists on a secret ballot of all those who will be called upon to take part in industrial action. 'Action' in this context covers not only a strike but also a work to rule, an overtime ban or similar expressions of conflict. The union may be sued for damages and, as has been recently seen, its funds put totally at risk if it fails to heed a court injunction. Clearly, the aim of this Bill is to make it more difficult for trade unions to marshal their members in a concerted action in an enterprise and it may make it even more difficult to mount such an action where the enterprise is small.

In addition, uncertainty hangs over the future of wages councils which cover workers in low paid industries, many of which, as noted earlier, are also industries with a high proportion of small firms.[16] In any event, since 1979 the number of wages inspectors – responsible for ensuring that the various wages councils' orders are obeyed by employers – has been reduced so that employers now run much less risk of being detected if they, for whatever reason, fail to comply (Low Pay Unit 1983).

Overall, therefore, it might be suggested that the web of restrictions which small firm employers protested against so strongly in the 1970s and which they claimed restricted the employment-generating potential of the small enterprise as well as its ability to respond rapidly to the market and new technology, has been greatly reduced since 1979. These changes, together with changes in taxation, greater availability of finance and support services for small firms could enable the small firm to play a much fuller role in economic restructuring, pioneering innovation and job creation.

By the late 1970s, trades unions in Britain had achieved the highest density level (the proportion of the labour force who were trade union members) in their history. While overall this figure was about

54 per cent (Bain & Price 1983), the density for large firms was much higher. For instance, the Bullock Report (HMSO 1977, p. 14) reported that in 1974 in manufacturing establishments with over 200 workers, 89 per cent of employees were trade union members. In the public sector, with the odd exception, similar density levels were reported. It was, therefore, possible to argue that it might be expected that trades unions would begin to turn their attention to the remaining sectors of the economy which had so far resisted organization. These were small firms in otherwise well unionized industries or predominantly small firm industries with low overall levels of unionization such as construction and the services sector generally.

But clearly this is now much less likely. First, several of the highly unionized areas of the economy have been hit much harder by the recession than the economy generally leading to heavy losses of members (Department of Employment 1984, p. 18). The Transport and General Workers Union for instance has lost over a quarter of its members since 1979. This reduces the confidence and resources available for the relatively expensive task of organizing small firms and small firm industries. Secondly, the changes in the law outlined above have made gaining union recognition much more difficult. Thus, the provisions for ensuring employer recognition of a union for employee representation and bargaining purposes embodied in the 1975 Employment Act have been substantially emasculated or suppressed by post-1979 legislation. Thirdly, small employers' unwillingness to concede union recognition and formal bargaining rights has been greatly reinforced by these changes so that not only will unions have mounting difficulties in penetrating poorly organized sectors of the economy but they may lose the gains in membership made in the 1970s (Bain & Price 1983, pp. 32–3).

The position of the small business owner in the social structure

Finally, in the discussion of the external context of small firm industrial relations some reference needs to be made to what may be termed the wider social and cultural climate in Britain. For much of this century the *petit bourgeoisie* has been a forgotten class: neither of the main political parties actively sought their support or votes, Labour for ideological reasons and the Conservatives because they assumed such support was automatically theirs anyway. The Liberals, the party of the *petit bourgeoisie* in the 19th century were in decline for most of this period. In the economic realm the emphasis, particularly after World War II, was on the advantages of size. Occupationally, self-employment became a less considered alternative among those entering the job market and one with declining status (Bechhofer & Elliott 1976, 1981). By the beginning of the 1970s the small business owner class in Britain was unorganized, unheard and in numerical decline (HMSO 1971).

The late 1970s and the 1980s have seen a remarkable turn-around in the social and cultural climate and its implications for small enterprise. As a class, the *petit bourgeoisie* participated in the 'middle class revolt' of the 1970s, producing a number of pressure groups which had successes in gaining changes in taxation, employment and industrial relations laws (Hughes 1979, Elliott *et al.* 1982). The fragmentation of the political party system has made all parties much more sensitive to the aspirations of smaller groups within the electorate whose votes could be vital in winning elections.

The Conservatives in particular have striven to rebuild their links with the *petit bourgeoisie*. In 1976 the Party set up the Small Business Bureau with a regular newspaper, conferences and a network of local branches to ensure that small business owners felt they had a direct voice in the formulation of policy, particularly policy affecting their interests. But further, the Party itself shifted ground ideologically in the direction of the 'New Right,' which emphasizes the rolling back of the State, the toppling of monopolies, especially the nationalized variety, individualism, economic freedom (including especially freedom from the contraints of unionized labour), hard work, risk-taking and tax reductions. This ideological shift brings the Party much closer to the ideological outlook of the *petit bourgeoisie* itself which has remained largely unchanged since the 19th century. Symbolically, this rapprochement was crowned by the accession to the leadership of the Party of a person from a *petit bourgeoisie* background which has clearly powerfully shaped her political beliefs.

Economically, the decade of big business and concentration, the 1960s, has been followed by a period of increasing questioning of the virtues of size as the discussion of economies of scale earlier demonstrated. In fact it has become fashionable for large firms themselves to promote the interests of small enterprise with major companies such as Shell, Marks and Spencer and British Steel as well as the clearing banks offering help either directly or indirectly.[17] These, in turn, are swamped by the large numbers of official schemes to aid small enterprise (London Enterprise Agency 1980).

Numerically there is every indication that the number of small firms in the economy is on the increase though it is impossible to be precise (Curran & Stanworth 1984). This parallels the increase in the depression of the 1930s but there are also reasons to suppose that at least part of this increase will not disappear when the present recession retreats. For instance, the restructuring of the economy discussed earlier means that it is unlikely that much of the loss of manufacturing industry will be restored in an economic upturn so that areas of the economy where large size is favoured will not be so well placed as other areas such as services where small-sized enterprises are more competitive.

Overall, the four segments of the external context of small firm industrial relations – *the wider structure of the economy, State policies and industrial laws, trade union influences,* and *the social and cultural climate* – have all moved in favour of the small business owner–manager. Freedom to create new enterprises, add to existing activities and, most important, to create an internal industrial relations climate more closely in accord with what the typical small business owner–manager sees as ideal, have all been enhanced. It is the changes in this external context which have been greatest and this is why they have been given more space and attention here. They feed into an internal context of small firm industrial relations which in fact they seem to threaten to transform.

The implications for the role of the small enterprise in the remaking of the economy in this and the next decade, especially in innovation and employment generation, might be seen as obvious. The potential dynamism widely attributed to the small firm in these processes would at last be unleashed to enable the small enterprise to play a central role – if not *the* central role – in these processes. However, it might be argued that drawing these implications from the kind of analysis presented above comes from a failure to fully think through the arguments and especially to keep in mind the key point that, whatever may be happening to the small firm, it remains one part of a tripartite economy (the State economic sector, the large enterprise sector and small enterprise)[18] with which it has complex inter-relations and which is also undergoing change. Some of the changes for instance, which are central to the external context of small firm industrial relations, also have important consequences for the large firm sector.

Small firms, industrial relations and economic performance in the 1980s

There are two main reasons for caution in accepting the apparently obvious implications of the major changes in the external context of small firm industrial relations. First, the impact of the latter changes on the internal context of small firm industrial relations may be a good deal less than might be first thought so that their potential for transforming the economic role of the small firm may not be anything like as large as expected. Secondly, many of the influences which have changed in the external context of small firm industrial relations also have the potential for altering the industrial relations patterns of large firms. It will be argued below that the latter have a greater potential for exploiting such changes.

Of the changes in the four segments of the external relations context of the small firm discussed above, it is changes in State policies and industrial relations laws and trade union influences which might be thought to have the most liberating effects on owner-managers. It was the handicaps in these segments which produced the most vociferous protests from small business owner representatives in the 1970s and which were said to have the most stultifying effect on the performance of the firm. The changes in the remaining two segments, the economic structure of the economy and the social and cultural climate, while being seen to be important also, would undoubtedly be seen as secondary to these, albeit reinforcing their impact.

Yet, a careful analysis of the available evidence might well lead to the conclusion that the changes in State policies and industrial relations laws, and the influence of the trade unions will not have the effects ascribed to them. Thus, although small business owners have benefited from taxation changes since the mid-1970s and have been offered a wider range of formal sources of finance neither will have the magnitude of impact potentially possible. The benefits of taxation changes are undermined by the fact that small business owners already benefit greatly from their ability to avoid or evade tax (O'Higgins 1980, McLoughlin 1983).

Similarly, despite the existence of the Loan Guarantee Scheme and other new sources of business finance, research indicates that the majority of small firms – particularly established small firms – do not perceive any dramatic change in the availability of finance. In a recent survey, for example, just under 90 per cent of a sample of established small firm owners stated that publicly backed finance agencies and schemes had no impact on their businesses (Economists Advisory Group 1983, p. 8).[19] There are also considerable doubts about the willingness of small firms to borrow even where finance is easily available because of their unwillingness to accept any help which might compromise their independence (Hankinson 1982).

The host of advisory services set up by national and local government have also so far largely failed to have the intended effects. Small firms are simply unaware of their existence or unwilling to accept the help offered. For example, the Economists Advisory Group survey, noted above, reported that only a very small proportion of their sample were able to name any government assistance scheme without prompting, and an Association of British Chambers of Commerce survey (1983) talked of an 'advisory jungle' which, it argued, was largely directed to start-up small firms rather than to the much larger number of existing small firms. In fact there are suggestions that the help offered to new small firms may simply lead to these new enterprises displacing existing established small firms with little net benefit to the economy (GLC 1983, Ritchie 1983).

Changes in State policy on employment which, it has been argued, allow small business owners much greater freedom to employ whom they like, adjust the level and mix of their labour forces as needed, get rid of unsatisfactory employees and hence create an enterprise capable of creating more new jobs, may also have much less potential for change than is sometimes claimed. There is evidence to suggest that restrictions on employment practices were always a great deal less severe than small business pressure groups claimed (Westrip 1982, Williams 1983). As with taxation, there is also evidence that small firm owner–managers often ignore the law either deliberately or through ignorance (Ford 1982). Quite often the law appears to have been treated as simply one variable, but by no means the main one, in arriving at decisions on whether to recruit or discharge employees and in setting appropriate rates of pay and conditions (Ford 1982, Swaffin-Smith 1983). Relaxations in the laws in this area since 1979 therefore have much less potential for change than the relaxation itself implies.

A closer examination of the likely effects of the change in the remaining two segments of the external context of small firm industrial relations (the wider economic structure and the social and cultural climate) is best considered as part of the discussion of the second main reason suggested as important in assessing the future role of the small firm in the economy, namely the changes likely to occur in the large firm sector. As several recent discussions have suggested (Brown 1981, Bain & Price 1983, Brown & Sisson 1983, Daniel & Millward 1983) changes in the economic structure, State policies and industrial relations laws and trade union influences are having important effects on the large firm sector. In fact it can be argued that some of these effects are much greater in the large firm sector than in the small firm sector in real terms. For example, the relaxations in employment and redundancy laws since 1979 might well have had more effect on large firms since, on the whole, they were generally more legally conformist than small firms. Their very visibility ensured that compliance with the letter of the law was more likely, while the presence of trades unions ensured a greater likelihood of compliance with the spirit of the law.

The dramatic reversal in trade union bargaining power due to the recession, high unemployment and the collapse of so many industries where trade union membership was high, has meant an equal expansion of large firm management bargaining power. In addition, there have been shifts in large firms' bargaining strategies, e.g. from multi-employer to company agreements and from company level bargaining to plant level but with strategic decisions kept at company level. These changes have been interpreted as attempts to regain management control and 'the right to manage' (Brown & Sisson 1983, p. 11).

Structurally, as noted earlier, there is evidence that many large enterprises are shifting towards a multi-establishment pattern with the average employment level of the establishment tending to decline (Prais 1976, Utton 1984). It has been claimed that among the reasons for this decline in average size of establishment are that labour becomes easier to manage, labour becomes cheaper, and employee bargaining power is reduced (GLC 1983, pp. 13–14). This trend may still have some way to go since, as Utton (1984, p. 8) points out, compared to the median plant size in the USA and Germany, the UK figure is still high, suggesting that further reductions are possible without any infringement on technical efficiency.

In terms of the changes in the social and cultural climate discussed earlier, large firms may be expected to respond in at least two ways. First, the need to manage publicly in a socially responsible fashion, which many large firms found a helpful strategy in the 1960s and 1970s, may be reduced. The need to attract and retain employees in conditions of high employment might well have been aided by a socially responsible image. In the recession and in areas of the economy undergoing major restructuring, maintaining such an image is expensive, difficult and even unnecessary.

Alternatively, large firms may adopt a 'sophisticated paternalism' approach (Brown & Sisson 1983, p. 11). Taking advantage of the current weakness and unpopularity of trades unions, a strategy will be developed which avoids collective bargaining and, if possible, trade union recognition by using sophisticated personnel techniques. Some American and Japanese firms in Britain already use such approaches (Brown & Sisson 1983, p. 12). The advantage here is that as the economy emerges from the recession the firm will be in a strong position to resist any revival in trade union power and/or overt conflict on issues connected with wages and working conditions.

Overall, it may be argued that these changes in large firm industrial relations will in effect lead to a convergence in the industrial relations patterns of the small and large firm sectors of the British economy. The wider economy and society, including large firms, have shifted towards the patterns more typical of the small firm in the past. Small firm employers will have successfully ridden out the pressures on them to adopt 'modern' industrial relations practices which were prevalent in the 1960s and 1970s. The rest of the economy meanwhile has shifted from the industrial relations of high employment and labour shortages to the industrial relations of high unemployment and a return to an approximation of a *laissez-faire* economy.

However, for the small enterprise this convergence in industrial relations patterns is attended by possible disadvantages in relation to the role it plays in the economy as a whole. Thus, important advantages which the small firm tended to have over the large firm were in the areas of labour costs and flexibility. Theories of labour market segmentation have stressed that large firms tend to generate a primary labour market as a deliberate strategy. By paying higher wages they were able to cream the labour market, recruiting more experienced, skilled and stable workforces. Small firms, on the other hand, tended to occupy a secondary labour market, recruiting less skilled, less experienced and less stable employees who were also cheaper (Stoltzenberg 1978, Wilkinson 1981, Scott & Rainnie 1982). Internally, large firms, since they tended to be more unionized and bureaucratised, displayed greater rigidity in the usage of labour and especially in role demarcation.

Recession, economic restructuring and new technology render labour markets – internal and external – more fluid. Divisions between firms or within firms become less related to large firm needs to retain particular kinds of labour, minimize the value of specific kinds of experience and reveal the problematic nature of skill (Lee 1981, Penn 1983). The collapse in trade union bargaining power enables large firm managements to break down institutionalized internal rigidities in the usage of labour and to reform internal labour markets to bring them into line with current thinking on the effective use of labour. Relaxations in legal requirements on employers to treat employees in particular ways are an aid to this process since large firm employers were much more affected by such restrictions than smaller enterprises.

In short, some of the traditional advantages of the small firm in a stable, buoyant economy such as lower wage bills, not having to cope with trades unions' attempts to protect workers' interests and being able to use labour more flexibly, might be expected to become less apparent under conditions of economic restructuring and large scale innovation. On the other hand, in some areas such as those where there are shortages of particular kinds of workers as in computer-related activities, large firms may still tend to practice strategies in the form of reward packages and internal career structures designed to minimize labour shortages, thus handicapping small firms seeking to innovate or participate in expanding forms of economic activities.

Large firms and new technology industries show signs of displaying 'sophisticated paternalism' as a personnel strategy to minimize attempts of trades unions to break into these new areas as their older established areas of recruitment in the industry of the past shrink.[20] Again, this suggests convergence, a convergence in styles of personnel management which again removes claimed small firm advantages in treating employees as individuals rather than as impersonal units of labour. Large firms have the resources to create a very wide range of personalized labour-handling strategies well beyond the capabilities of most small firms.

Conclusion

In examining the role that small firms might play in the present restructuring of the economy, in innovation and in employment creation, by using the conceptual framework of contemporary industrial relations studies we have sought to offer a careful assessment of the opportunities and constraints involved. Clearly, small firms will have an important role in these processes and *some* small firms will have a central role as media comment already makes abundantly clear.[21] But the picture to be derived for the small firm sector as a whole has to take into account changes in the wider economic environment of the small firm, especially in the large firm sectors. Basically, the argument in this paper is for a convergence in industrial relations patterns between the small and large firm sectors of the economy which will have the effect of reducing some of the small firms' traditional advantages in reacting to change.

To the extent that recession and massive economic restructuring are, as some commentators argue, breaking down the institutionalized rigidities in organizational structures, working practices and management–worker relations built up over the long period of the first industrial revolution, firms right across the economy will be affected. Some – small and large alike – will simply go under. For the firms remaining, and for new enterprises created to respond to change, a more open, dynamic economic performance will be necessary to survive, but this is likely to be an across-the-board response also. Small and large firms will play their part in these processes, each drawing on their relative strengths and advantages. In other words, in the organizational ratchet effect likely to accompany widespread successful adaptation to change, small firms will play an important role in these processes but so also will large firms. There appears to be no good reason to suggest that the small firm will somehow change its relative position to come to occupy a far more central, let alone *the* central, role in these processes.

Notes

1 An official example of this bias was provided in a recent paper by a senior economic advisor to the Department of Industry (Rees 1983). This offered a detailed inventory of aspects of the small firm on which the Department would like to see further research. It covered the usual concerns with the personal attributes of small business founders, their financial problems, technological changes, urban policy, relations with local government, etc., but the only reference to the small firm employee and employment conditions was confined to a single sentence paragraph.

2 This is an ideological stance which has its reflection in the way some social scientists, and especially economists, analyse the small firm. See Bannock (1981) and Storey (1982) for recent examples. Even debate on employment creation has not focused directly on small firm employees as people with psychological and social characteristics. Instead, the tendency has been to treat employment as net additions or deductions from an abstract entity, the labour force.

3 We would not, of course, claim that such a contribution provides a complete assessment of these highly complex questions. Only through a multidisciplinary approach can an informed, rigorously argued set of predictions of the role of the small firm in the 1980s be offered. Economists, geographers and others, as well as sociologists and industrial relations specialists, all have a contribution to make to this analysis.

4 Much of the discussion of small firms is concerned with questions of definitions. To date no satisfactory or agreed definition has emerged and different writers adopt different approaches (Curran & Stanworth 1984, pp. 128–33). For the purposes of this paper, the small firm in manufacturing will be taken as one employing up to 100 employees but usually much fewer and in servicing firms employing up to 20 people. In retailing we follow Kirby (1985) who, following the Wilson Committee (HMSO 1979), defines the small firm as one with an annual turnover of under £200000 and usually operating a single outlet.

5 It should be pointed out that two well-known studies (Ingham 1970, Batstone 1976) offer findings and interpretations which are not consistent with the more recent research discussed here. Both, to differing extents, offer views of industrial relations in the small firm more or less consistent with the well publicised harmonious picture. However, the theoretical adequacy and methodological strategies of Ingham's work have been strongly questioned (Curran & Stanworth 1981a, b) and Batstone's findings may be interpreted as an example of small firm industrial relations in a particular community context which is unlikely to occur with any frequency in contemporary Britain.

6 Qualifications of the characterization to be outlined here are given later in the paper but a full delineation of the variations in small firm industrial relations patterns is not yet possible because of the rather patchy nature of the present research. However, it is suggested that the underlying principles of employer–employee relations described in this paper apply to a wide range of small enterprises with certain obvious exceptions such as small producer co-operatives.

7   It is noticeable that a more recent article in this tradition (Edwards 1981) takes a much more cautious line concluding that 'the size effect is no more than a general tendency. Part of the variance of a plant's strike-proneness can be explained by it, and by a small number of other variables. But the greater part of the explanation must lie elsewhere. . . . The greater part of the responsibility lies in the handling of industrial relations not in . . . structural influences' (Edwards 1981, p. 146).

8   Often combined with taking on new employees to cope with the special labour demands of innovation which cannot be met from within the existing labour force. Again, this might be further expected to add to the insecurity among employees and even resentment where new employees are given positions which existing employees see themselves as capable of filling.

9   Often there are only one or two levels of hierarchy between the shop-floor and the owner-manager directors. The latter level will often be closed, recruiting no further members or only recruiting from relatives of existing owner-managers or others with capital to introduce into the enterprise.

10 From the Bolton Report (HMSO 1971) onward small firm employers have repeatedly reported problems in obtaining suitable labour (Golby & Johns 1971, Boswell 1973, Curran & Stanworth 1979a, Scase & Goffee 1980, pp. 158–61) so, in some respects, it is not surprising that the situation has not changed recently.

11 The strong positive statistical association between size of plant and propensity to strike, discussed earlier, is one indication of motivational diseconomies which may be a cost of size although, again as discussed earlier, great care is required in interpreting statistics of this kind.

12 For a more fully developed version of this argument in relation to the recent expansion of the franchised small enterprise in Britain, see Curran and Stanworth (1983).

13 The publication of the Bolton Report (HMSO 1971) is usually taken as marking the turning point in government interest in the small business and there can be little doubt that, for whatever reasons, the report did have enormous success in arousing interest in the small firm among politicians and the mass media, and in raising the self-confidence and assertiveness of the small business community.

14 There were also other policy changes regarded by small business owners as unfavourable to their interests, such as the introduction of VAT in 1973 and the changes in the 1974 Social Security Amendment Act, which increased National Insurance contributions by the self-employed (see Hughes 1979), but it was the changes in employment legislation that arguably led to the most persistent lobbying for change.

15 The 1975 Employment Protection Act was merely the most discussed piece of legislation in the context of what small firm owner-managers saw as an ever-expanding network of legislative constraints on their freedom to manage their relations with their employees in the tradi-tional way. Other legislation which could be listed as contributing to these constraints would include: the Employment Protection Act 1970; the Contracts of Employment Act 1972; Sex Discrimination Act 1975;

and the Race Relations Act 1976, which set up the Equal Opportunities Commission and Racial Equality Commission; the Employment Protection Act 1978; as well as codes of practice and similar additional supporting orders which amend or clarify employment and industrial legislation (Clegg 1979).

16 For example, Ford (1982) reports that in the retail sector, hotel and catering, clothing manufacturing and hairdressing industries – all covered by wages councils – over 90 per cent of the firms are small.

17 The clearest example of this sponsorship is probably the London Enterprise Agency, funded by a number of Britain's largest companies, which has already given several thousand people help with developing their ideas for owning a small business.

18 In Britain these three sections of the economy are roughly the same size in employment terms. The ways in which they are integrated so that each forms an indispensable part of the continued functioning of a modern economy may be derived from the arguments offered by Miller (1975).

19 A finding supported by a recent survey by the Association of British Chambers of Commerce (1983).

20 In the electronics industry, where trade unions have so far not managed to make the kind of recruitment impact they achieved in manufacturing generally in the past, this kind of paternalism may have a longer history (Lawson 1981).

21 The attention given to Sir Clive Sinclair and the owners of other high flying small firms in the computer industry can easily lead to an over-assessment of the role of small firms in innovation more generally. In terms of employment creation it is noteworthy that Sir Clive subcontracts most of his manufacturing to existing large firms, thus preventing a drop in their labour forces rather than adding new jobs directly through small firm activities. Indeed, this type of link between small and large firms is another reason why the small firm role in economic restructuring cannot be discussed in isolation. As other industrial societies show, notably Japan, this type of co-operation may well become a distinctive feature of an advanced industrial economy.

References

Acton Society Trust 1953. *Size and morale: a preliminary study of attendance at work in large and small units*. London: Acton Society Trust.

Acton Society Trust 1957. *Size and morale, part II: a further study of attendance at work in large and small units*. London: Acton Society Trust.

Association of British Chambers of Commerce 1983. *Small firms – taking stock*. London: ABC.

Bain, G. S. and R. Price 1983. Union growth: dimensions, determinants and destiny. In *Industrial relations in Britain*, G. S. Bain (ed.). Oxford: Basil Blackwell.

Bannock, G. 1981. *The economics of small firms, return from the wilderness*. Oxford: Basil Blackwell.

Batstone, E. 1976. Deference and the ethos of small town capitalism. In *Working-class images of society*, M. Bulmer (ed.). London: Routledge & Kegan Paul.

Bechhofer, F. and B. Elliot 1976. Persistence and change: the petit bougeoisie in industrial society. *European Journal of Sociology* 17, 74–99.

Bechhofer, F. and B. Elliot 1981. *The petit bourgeoisie, comparative studies of the uneasy stratum*. London: Macmillan.

Birch, D. 1979. *The job generation process*. Cambridge, Mass.: MIT Program on Neighborhood and Regional Change.

Blair, J. M. 1972. *Economic concentration*. New York: Harcourt Brace Jovanovich.

Bluedorn, A. C. 1982. The theories of turnover: causes, effects and meanings. In *Research in sociology* 1, S. B. Bacharach (ed.). Greenwich, Conn.: JAI Press.

Boswell, J. 1973. *The rise and decline of small firms*. London: Allen & Unwin.

Bright, D., D. Sawbridge and B. Rees 1983. Industrial relations in the recession. *Industrial Relations Journal* 14, 24–33.

Brown, W. 1981. *The changing contours of British industrial relations*. Oxford: Basil Blackwell.

Brown, W. and K. Sisson 1983. Industrial relations in the next decade, current trends and possibilities. *Industrial Relations Journal* 14, 9–21.

Burns, T. and G. M. Stalker 1961. *The management of innovation*. London: Tavistock.

Clegg, H. A. 1979. *The changing system of industrial relations in Great Britain*. Oxford: Basil Blackwell.

Curran, J. and J. Stanworth 1979a. Self-selection and the small firm worker – a critique and an alternative view. *Sociology* 13, 427–44.

Curran, J. and J. Stanworth 1979b. Worker involvement and social relations in the small firm. *Sociological Review* 27, 317–42.

Curran, J. and J. Stanworth 1981a. A new look at job satisfaction in the small firm. *Human Relations* 34, 343–66.

Curran, J. and J. Stanworth 1981b. Size of workplace and attitudes to industrial relations in the printing and electronics industries. *British Journal of Industrial Relations* 19, 14–25.

Curran, J. and J. Stanworth 1983. Franchising in the modern economy – towards a theoretical understanding. *International Small Business Journal* 2, 8–26.

Curran, J. and J. Stanworth 1984. Small business research in Britain. In *Small business theory and policy*, C. Levicki (ed.). London: Croom Helm.

Daniel, W. W. and N. Millward, 1983. *Workplace industrial relations in Britain*. London: Heinemann.

Department of Employment 1984. Membership of trade unions in 1982. *Employment Gazette* 92 (January), 18–20.

Department of Industry 1983. *Summary of government measures of benefit to small firms*. London: HMSO.

Economists Advisory Group 1983. *The small firm survivors*. London: Small Business Unit, Shell UK Ltd.

Edwards, P. K. 1981. The strike-proneness of British manufacturing establishments. *British Journal of Industrial Relations* **2**, 135–48.

Elliott, B., F. Bechhofer, D. McCrone and S. Black 1982. Bourgeois social movements in Britain: repertoires and responses. *Sociological Review* **30**, 71–96.

Ford, J. 1982. Who breaks the rules? The response of small business to external regulation. *Industrial Relations Journal* **13** (3), 40–9.

Fothergill, S. and G. Gudgin 1979. *The job generation process in Britain*. London: Centre for Environmental Studies.

Golby, C. W. and G. Johns 1971. *Attitude and motivation*. Committee of Enquiry on Small Firms, Research Report no. 7. London: HMSO.

Greater London Council 1983. *Small firms and the London industrial strategy*. London: GLC.

Hankinson, A. 1982. *The investment problem: a study of investment behaviour of South Wessex engineering firms, 1979–1982*. Poole: Dorset Institute of Higher Education.

Henderson, J. and R. Johnson 1974. Labour relations in the small firm. *Personnel Management* **6**, 28–31.

HMSO 1971. *Small firms, report of the Committee of Enquiry on Small Firms* (The Bolton Report). Cmnd 4811. London: HMSO.

HMSO 1977. *Report of the Committee of Enquiry on Industrial Democracy* (The Bullock Report). Cmnd 6706. London: HMSO.

HMSO 1979. *The financing of small firms, interim report of the Committee to Review the Functioning of the Financial Institutions*, Cmnd 7503. London: HMSO.

Hughes, J. 1979. The self-employed and the small independent entrepreneur. In *Respectable rebels: middle class campaigns in Britain in the 1970s*. R. King and N. Nugent (eds). London: Hodder & Stoughton.

Ingham, G. K. 1970. *Size of industrial organization and worker behaviour*. Cambridge: Cambridge University Press.

Kets de Vries, M. F. R. 1977. The entrepreneurial personality: a person at the crossroads. *Journal of Management Studies* **14**, 34–57.

Kirby, D. 1985. The small retailer. In *The survival of the small firm*, J. Curran, J. Stanworth and D. Watkins (eds). Aldershot: Gower, in press.

Lawson, T. 1981. Paternalism and labour market segmentation theory. In *The dynamics of labour market segmentation*, F. Wilkinson (ed.). London: Academic Press.

Lee, D. J. 1981. Skill, craft and class: a theoretical critique and a critical case. *Sociology* **16**, 56–78.

London Enterprise Agency 1980. *Financial incentives and assistance for industry: a comprehensive guide*. Prepared by Arthur Young McClelland Mores & Co. London: London Enterprise Agency.

Low Pay Unit 1983. *Who needs the wage councils?* London: Low Pay Unit.

McLoughlin, J. 1983. VAT frauds cost up to £500m. *The Guardian* 21 May 1983.

Miller, S. M. 1975. Notes on neo-capitalism. *Theory and Society* **2**, 1–35.

Newby, H. 1975. The deferential dialectic. *Comparative Studies in Society and History* **17**, 139–64.

Newby, H. 1977. Paternalism and capitalism. In *Industrial society: class cleavage and control*, R. Scase (ed.). London: Allen & Unwin.

O'Higgins, M. 1980. *Measuring the black economy*. London: Outer Circle Policy Unit.

Penn, R. D. 1983. Theories of skill and class structure. *Sociological Review* **31**, 22–38.

Prais, S. J. 1976. *The evolution of giant firms in Britain*. Cambridge: Cambridge University Press.

Prais, S. J. 1978. The strike-proneness of large firms in Britain. *Journal of the Royal Statistical Society* **141**.

Rees, R. D. 1983. *Issues in small firms research of relevance to policy making*. Paper presented to the National Small Firms Policy and Research Conference, held at Durham University, December 1983.

Revans, R. W. 1956. Industrial morale and size of unit. *Political Quarterly* **27**, 303–10.

Revans, R. W. 1958. Human relations, management and size. In *Human relations and modern management*, E. M. Hugh-Jones (ed.). Amsterdam: North Holland.

Ritchie, J. 1983. *Predictable casualties: older small businesses under late capitalism*. Paper presented at the National Small Firms Policy and Research Conference, held at Durham University, September 1983.

Rothwell, R. and W. Zegveld 1982. *Innovation and the small and medium sized firm*. London: Frances Pinter.

Samuels, J. M. and P. A. Morrish 1984. An analysis of concentration. In *Small business, theory and policy*, C. Levicki (ed.). London: Croom Helm.

Scase, R. and R. Goffee 1980. *The real world of the small business owner*. London: Croom Helm.

Scase, R. and R. Goffee 1982. *The entrepreneurial middle class*. London: Croom Helm.

Scott, M. and A. Rainnie 1982. Beyond Bolton – industrial relations and the small firm. In *Perspectives on a decade of small business research: Bolton ten years on*, J. Stanworth et al. (eds). Aldershot: Gower.

Shorey, J. 1975. The size of the work unit and strike incidence. *Journal of Industrial Economics* **23**, 175–88.

Stephenson, G., C. Brotherton, G. Delafield and M. Skinner 1983. Size of organization, attitudes to work and job satisfaction. *Industrial Relations Journal* **14** (2), 28–40.

Stolzenberg, R. M. 1978. Bringing the boss back in: employer size, employee schooling and socioeconomic achievement. *American Sociological Review* **43**, 813–28.

Storey, D. 1980. *Job generation and small firms policy in Britain*. Centre for Environmental Studies, Policy Series no. 11. London: Centre for Environmental Studies.

Storey, D. 1981. New firm formation, employment change and the small firm: the case of Cleveland County. *Urban Studies* **18**, 335–45.

Storey, D. 1982 *Entrepreneurship and the New Firm* London: Croom Helm.

Swaffin-Smith, C. 1983. *The effect of recent employment legislation concerned with developing individual rights on management behaviour in small companies.* MPhil thesis. Council for National Academic Awards.

Utton, M. A. 1984. Concentration, competition and the small firm. In *Small business theory and policy*, C. Levicki (ed.). London: Croom Helm.

Westrip, A. 1982. Effects of employment legislation on small firms. In *Stimulating small firms*, D. Watkins, J. Stanworth and A. Westrip (eds). Aldershot: Gower.

Wilkinson, F. (ed.) 1981. *The dynamics of labour market segmentation*. London: Academic Press.

Williams, K. 1983. Unfair dismissal: myths and statistics. *The Industrial Law Journal* **12**, 157–65.

Woodcock, C. 1983. Behind a job creation myth, your guide through the maze of static data and gross flows. *The Guardian* 2 September 1983.

12 High technology small firms and regional industrial growth

R. P. OAKEY
and R. ROTHWELL

Introduction

It is clear from recent public policy statements, and from the considerable number of small firm-specific policy initiatives being introduced, that governments in the advanced market economies increasingly have laid greater emphasis on ensuring the wellbeing of small firms. This appears to be based on the belief in their potential for generating technological innovations, their potential for industrial regeneration of the so-called development regions and their ability to create new employment (Rothwell & Zegveld 1982). Interest in the employment-creating potential of small firms intensified following the publication of a report by Birch (1979) which claimed to show, in the United States between 1969 and 1976, that firms or establishments employing less than twenty people created 66 per cent of all new jobs; approximately 52 per cent of these jobs were created in independent firms. While Birch's results subsequently have been questioned by a number of informed policy analysts (see Storey 1980), they have nevertheless gained considerable acceptance among public policy makers in a number of countries.

Evidence on the contribution of small firms to manufacturing employment suggests that in most of the advanced market economies (a notable exception being Japan), their share generally has declined during most of the post war era. Comparative data suggest that small firms' share in national manufacturing employment has been generally lower in the United Kingdom than in any other advanced market economy (Rothwell & Zegveld, 1982). More recent UK data suggest, however, that between 1968 and 1978 the number of small UK firms (employing less than 100 workers) increased considerably, together with their share in employment (Bollard 1983). Despite this recent increase, small firms' share of manufacturing employment in the UK remains only at about 20 per cent of the total.

The above data do not necessarily suggest, of course, that small firms in the UK have been specially successful at creating new employment. Their increased share of total manufacturing employment, which has itself declined significantly in absolute terms, might be due more to a reduction in employment in larger firms than to any absolute increase in small firms. Certainly there exists considerable evidence to suggest that investment during the past two decades has shifted significantly towards rationalization and away from expansion, and we might suspect this shift to be more significant in the case of large firms (Prais 1976). Perhaps one of the major problems in using aggregated data of the type employed by Birch and Bollard is that while it differentiates between firms of different sizes, it fails to differentiate between *types* of small firm. The employment-creating potential of an infant Intel or Signetics would be considerably greater, we might suppose, than that of an equivalent-sized firm in textiles or leatherware. Thus, while a significant proportion of small firm employment might currently be in 'traditional' small firms – many of which will have been in existence for a considerable period – employment growth potential is likely to be considerably greater in small new technology-based firms.

Figure 12.1 shows the evolution of industrial output and employment (1950–1980) for the EEC, and for the USA (1960 = 100). What is interesting about these curves is their divergence from about 1965 onwards. An at least partial explanation for this divergence can be found in the different modes of evolution of US and European industry from the early 1960s onwards. In the first case we would contend that the USA moved more rapidly and to a greater extent than her European competitors into the 'new' industries of the postwar era (semiconductors, computer-aided design, electronics, etc.) Secondly, we would contend that the mode in which this structural industrial shift into new technology-based industries was achieved in the USA was different from that in Europe. Specifically, while large US corporations played an important part in basic invention and early innovation in these new areas of production, rapid diffusion came about via the vehicle of new technology-based firms (Rothwell 1984); many of these grew extremely rapidly and created a considerable volume of new employment. In Europe, in contrast, where production occurred at a later date, exploitation of the new technologies occurred mainly within existing large firms, which were able to enter production – albeit at a lower level – with the creation of fewer additional jobs.

A report for the Anglo German Foundation (Little 1977) confirmed that new technology-based firms (NTBFs) have played a

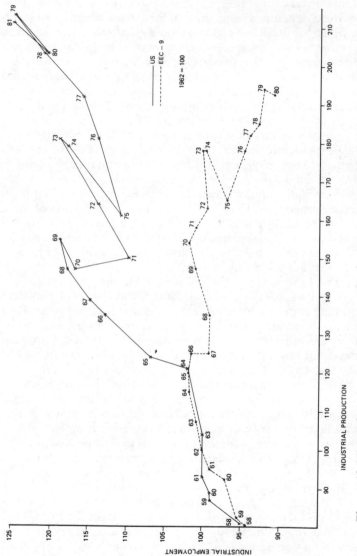

Figure 12.1 Manufacturing output and employment in the nine EEC countries and the USA (Rothwell & Zegveld 1982).

major role in the US economy, while their role in the UK and West Germany has been only small. In 1976 there were several thousand NTBFs in the USA employing in excess of 2 million workers. In the Silicon Valley area alone in 1974 there were 800 NTBFs with total annual sales of $2.5 billion. In the UK in 1976 the number of NTBFs was about 200 with total sales of £200 million. In West Germany the number of NTBFs was even less. Through its more rapid and proportionally greater shift into new, higher technology areas of production, US industry enjoyed the dual benefits of rapid job creation – mainly in fast growing NTBFs – and enhanced international competitiveness through production of the new product groups (Kelley 1978).

Innovation, firm size and employment

A number of studies have been undertaken in the USA (not all, unfortunately, covering the post 'oil crisis' period) which point to the superior employment generating potential of, in the first instance, young firms, many of which are high technology-based. The first study, undertaken by the American Electronics Association (1978), was a survey of 325 AEA member companies. In 1976 these accounted for $45 billion in revenues, 14 per cent of total US exports, employed 750000 people, paid $1.8 billion in federal corporate income tax and $700 million in state and local taxes, and spent $2.2 billion on R&D. Eighty-five per cent of the companies were founded after 1954.

The AEA study also looked at the job-generating potential of firms of different ages in the sample. Their results are shown in Figure 12.2 which gives the employment growth rate of firms in

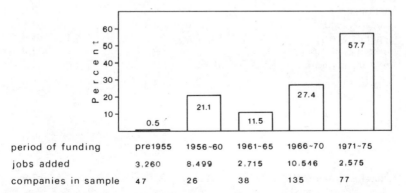

period of funding	pre1955	1956-60	1961-65	1966-70	1971-75
jobs added	3,260	8,499	2,715	10,546	2,575
companies in sample	47	26	38	135	77

Figure 12.2 Employment growth rates in 1976; young companies create jobs much faster than mature companies (Rothwell & Zegveld 1982).

1976 in different age bands. They can be summarized as follows:

(a)   Firms 10–20 years old had an employment growth rate 20–40 times the rate of firms more than 20 years old.
(b)   Firms between five and ten years old had an employment growth rate of 55 times that of the mature (more than 20 years old) firms.
(c)   Firms less than five years old had an employment growth rate on average 115 times that of the mature firms.
(d)   Although the mature firms had 27 times the total employment of the firms less than 20 years old as a group, the younger smaller firms created an average 89 new jobs per company in 1976, versus an average of 69 new jobs per mature company.

Thus, even though the total employment in the older firms was by far the greatest, and even though they continued to generate new jobs, the most significant new job generation was in the smaller younger firms. Finally, it is worth pointing out here that all the firms in the sample were operating in areas of high technology. The study therefore represents a comparison of the job-generating potential of 'young' technology-based firms with that of 'older' technology-based firms, and *not* technology-based firms versus 'others'.

Table 12.1   Average annual growth (compounded), 1945 and 1974; mature companies and innovative companies.

	Sales (%)	Jobs (%)
Mature companies		
Bethlehem Steel	4.9	−1.7
Du Pont	8.6	2.6
General-Electric	8.4	3.5
General Foods	8.2	4.5
International Paper	9.2	2.8
Proctor and Gamble	9.6	3.8
weighted average	7.8	1.9
Innovative companies		
Polaroid	14.0	9.0
3M	14.1	9.0
IBM	16.8	10.2
Xerox	24.2	19.4
Texas Instruments (1953–74)	21.2	17.3
weighted average	16.5	10.8

Source: Morse (1976).

A second US study (Morse 1976) compared the rate of growth in employment and sales of several 'categories' of firms in the USA between 1945 and 1974. The three categories employed by Morse were 'mature' companies, 'innovative' companies and 'young high technology' companies. His results are set out in Tables 12.1 and 12.2, and show quite clearly the rather more spectacular growth rate in both sales and employment of the young high technology companies. For the five year period 1969–74, the average annual percentage growth rates, in sales and employment, for the three categories of firms were:

(a)   Mature companies: 11.4 per cent sales; 1.6 per cent jobs
(b)   Innovative companies: 13.2 per cent sales; 4.3 per cent jobs
(c)   Young high technology companies: 42.5 per cent sales; 40.7 per cent jobs.

The study further showed that:

(a)   Young technology companies with sales equalling only 2 per cent of those of the mature industry leaders created 34 369 new jobs, or 34 per cent more than the 25 559 new jobs created by the mature companies.
(e)   Total employment in the mature firms increased by only 3.2 per cent over the five years compared to 23.7 per cent for the innovative companies.
(f)   The younger innovative companies with ending sales amounting to only 58 per cent of those of the mature companies created 106 598 new jobs, or over four times as many as the mature firms.

A third study undertaken by Data Resources, Inc. for the General Electric Corporation in 1977 found, in comparing the performance

Table 12.2 Average annual growth (compounded), 1969–74; young high technology companies.

Date incorporated	Company	Sales (%)	Jobs (%)
1968	Data General	140.5	82.5
1959	National Semiconductor	54.3	59.4
1960	Compugraphic	50.2	24.0
1957	Digital Equipment	36.8	30.7
1964	Marion Labs	24.5	25.4
weighted average		42.5	40.7

Source: Morse (1976).

Table 12.3 Firms with annual average growth rates in the USA (sales 1976–80) of more than 40 per cent.

Firm	Sector	1976–80 average annual growth			1980		
		Sales (in %)	Profits (in %)	Employees (in %)	Sales (million $)	R&D: sales ratio (in %)	Profits: sales ratio (in %)
Tandem Computers	information processing: computers	247.4	284.5	n.a.	109	8.1	10.1
Cray Research	information processing: computers	197.0	126.8	71.8	61	14.5	18.0
Apple Computer*	information processing: computers	144.7	n.a.	11.2	117	6.2	10.3
Floating Point Systems	information processing: computers	120.5	67.0	n.a.	42	10.9	9.5
Intermedics	electronics	111.5	113.4	53.3	105	4.6	10.5
Triad Systems	information processing: peripherals, services	89.5	110.3	n.a.	57	6.6	8.8
Prime Computers	information processing: computers	88.1	132.0	73.8	268	7.6	11.6
Rolm	telecommunications	79.0	101.4	69.7	201	6.7	8.5
Lamson & Sessions	miscellaneous manufacturing	65.3	n.a.	26.8	235	0.6	-1.3
Auto–Trol Technology	information processing: peripherals, services	64.1	96.9	n.a.	51	12.1	7.8
Data Terminal Systems	information processing: peripherals, services	64.0	n.a.	49.5	118	5.1	-2.5
Computervision	information processing: peripherals, services	59.0	116.3	44.7	224	9.9	10.3
Paradyne	electronics	57.9	132.8	51.8	76	8.4	10.5
Siltec	electronics	56.5	64.0	n.a.	57	3.6	5.3
Advanced Micro Devices	semiconductors	56.2	91.0	48.6	226	12.5	10.2

Company	Sector						
Savin	information processing; office equipment	53.7	90.2	33.5	357	2.3	7.8
American Management Syst.	information processing; peripherals services	55.3	57.2	n.a.	59	7.1	3.4
CPT	information processing; office equipment	49.4	55.5	37.9	59	3.4	10.2
Wang Laboratories	information processing; office equipment	48.5	72.1	n.a.	543	6.7	9.6
Storage Technology	information processing: peripherals, services	48.2	58.0	n.a.	604	6.5	7.5
Cornshare	information processing: peripherals, services	47.6	51.4	38.9	70	6.3	5.1
Datapoint	information processing: peripherals, services	47.3	61.8	38.6	50	8.7	10.3
Verbatim	information processing: peripherals, services	47.3	28.5	45.6	319	5.8	2.0
US Surgical Instruments	instruments	46.9	52.8	34.1	86	3.5	9.3
Sega Enterprises	miscellaneous manufacturing	46.8	55.5	9.3	140	1.2	8.6
Parker Pen	miscellaneous manufacturing	45.2	34.8	11.2	664	0.4	6.0
TII/Communications	electronics	44.9	94.3	n.a.	60	2.5	5.0
Kratos	instruments	44.0	44.5	n.a.	56	7.5	5.4
Intel	semiconductors	43.9	43.4	27.5	855	11.3	11.3
Datacard	information processing: peripherals, services	42.6	55.5	n.a.	66	2.6	10.6
Gerber Scientific	instruments	41.6	34.8	32.1	74	7.1	8.1
Data General	information processing: computers	41.0	33.0	31.0	654	10.0	8.4
Computer Consoles	information processing: peripherals, services	40.7	55.8	16.1	44	10.5	11.4
Analogic	electronics	40.3	67.7	n.a.	67	8.9	9.0
Miller (Herman)	miscellaneous manufacturing	40.3	40.0	35.1	230	2.5	5.2
Penin Industries	machinery	40.1	22.8	n.a.	78	1.9	3.8

* For Apple Computer Inc. which only became publicly held in 1980, the growth in sales related only to the period 1979–80.

Source: Calculated from data in *Business Week*, 6 June 1981.

Source: Freeman *et al.* (1982).

of high technology firms with that of low technology firms in the USA between 1950 and 1974, that in the high technology firms, employment grew nine times as fast; productivity grew at three times the rate; output expanded twice as fast; prices increased only one-sixth as rapidly; and they produced a trade surplus of $25 billion in 1974, while low technology products declined from break-even to a $16 billion deficit in 1974 (NSF 1979).

Thus the AEA study, and that by Morse, both provide strong evidence for the high job-generating potential of young technology-based firms in the USA while the Data Resources study points to the superior performance of high technology firms generally. The fact that new technology-based firm formation appears to have increased in the USA following a marked 'low' in 1974–75 (Anon. 1980) might, at least in part, explain the relative success of US manufacturing industry in reducing levels of unemployment from the high level of 8.5 per cent in 1975. Moreover, data presented by Freeman *et al.* (1982) further support our contention regarding the high growth potential of NTBFs in the US. Table 12.3 lists US firms that enjoyed average annual growth rates of more than 40 per cent between 1976 and 1980, no mean feat during a period of world recession. Something in excess of 60 per cent of these enterprises are relatively young new technology-based firms, operating in the general area of 'information technology'.

As a further point it is worth noting that evidence exists from several countries to suggest that, in general, 'innovativeness' in firms is associated with employment generation. Piatier (1981), for example, found from his study of innovation in French industry that innovation was associated with employment gains in 59 per cent of innovative firms, and with employment loss in only 5 per cent of innovative firms. For non-innovative firms operating in the same markets, the figures were 26 per cent and 14 per cent respectively. Furthermore, in a detailed and comprehensive study of innovation in Canadian industry, De Melto *et al.* (1980) found that in the majority of cases innovations were associated with either no change, or with an increase in numbers of both production and non-production workers, although the positive relationship was strongest for product, rather than process, innovations: the introduction of product innovations led to increases in the number of production and non-production workers in 70 per cent and 60 per cent of cases respectively. Comparable figures for the process innovations were 43 per cent and 41 per cent respectively. Further, the introduction of only 20 per cent of all process innovations resulted in a net decrease in the number of production workers in each case, while 37 per cent resulted in negligible changes in numbers of production workers. De Melto *et al.*'s results are summarized in Tables 12.4 and 12.5.

Table 12.4 Proportion of innovations resulting in net increase, net decrease or negligible change in the number of production and non-production workers, by type of innovation.

Type of innovation	Negligible change		Net increase		Net decrease	
	No. of innovations	Percentage of innovations	No. of innovations	Percentage of innovations	No. of innovations	Percentage of innovations
production workers						
product	57	28	139	70	4	2
process	28	37	32	43	15	20
non-production workers						
product	71	37	117	52	1	1
process	41	58	29	41	1	1

Source: De Melto *et al.* (1980).

Table 12.5 Proportion of innovations resulting in net increase, net decrease or negligible change in the number of production and non-production workers, by firm size.

Firm size	Negligible change		Net increase		Net decrease	
	No. of innovations	Percentage of innovations	No. of innovations	Percentage of innovations	No. of innovations	Percentage of innovations
production workers						
0–100 employees	27	25	76	69	7	6
101–500 employees	32	32	65	65	3	3
more than 500 employees	25	47	22	42	6	11
non-production workers						
0–100 employees	39	37	65	62	1	1
101–500 employees	44	46	52	54	0	0
more than 500 employees	27	52	24	46	1	2

Source: De Melto *et al.* (1980).

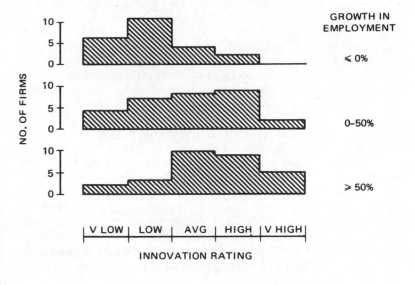

Figure 12.3   Distribution of innovation with growth in employment
1976–79 (Rothwell & Zegveld 1982).

Significantly the employment generation effects are a function of
firm size, i.e. a greater percentage of innovations are associated with
employment gains in the smaller firms.

A more recent study undertaken in the Republic of Ireland, by and
for the National Board for Science and Technology, also indicated a
positive relationship between innovativeness and employment
growth (NBST 1980). The study, which involved constructing an
'innovation index' for each of 120 firms employing below 50 workers
(75 per cent of all firms in Ireland employ less than 50), found that
negative employment growth was correlated with lack of innovativeness, while high employment growth was strongly associated
with innovativeness. The period covered by this research was 1976–
79, and the results relating to employment are summarized in Figure
12.3.

Other interesting aspects of this study are:

(a)   Firms over 30 years old tended to be less innovative than younger firms.
(b)   Innovativeness demonstrated some regional variation.
(c)   Rate of growth in turnover was strongly correlated with innovativeness.

The above three sets of results would once again support the contention that, while new small firms in general can generate significant employment growth in the medium or long term, it is with the formation of technologically innovative new firms that the *greatest* short and long term employment growth possibilities lie. Finally, in concluding this review of the impact of small firms on national employment levels, we argue that there exists considerable evidence to suggest that the rate of formation of new technology-based small firms varies significantly between regions, and we shall discuss this issue in the remaining sections of this chapter.

High technology small firm innovation and regional investment capital sources

In the remaining sections of this chapter we present a selection of relevant survey-based data which investigates the vitality of new technology-based small firms, their propensity for rapid growth and regional variations in subsequent employment. This regional level data will complement the wide ranging results presented above, which generally indicate that small new technology-based firms display growth patterns that are more vigorous than larger or lower technology firms and hence, are more likely to act as significant sources of employment in a relatively short time-span. This detailed evidence also conforms to the general approach adopted in earlier sections of focusing on differences between the USA and Europe, but at a sub-national regional level. Since it is apparent that new technology-based firms have faster growth rates than their less sophisticated counterparts, and clearly since these firms are dispro-portionately located in more prosperous areas, it is likely that such discrepancies will produce differing regional employment impacts. The impacts will be investigated with the aid of relevant data. Concluding comments will focus on possible policy measures for the encouragement of high technology small firm growth in regions that are currently deficient in this type and size of production.

The following evidence is derived from a detailed questionnaire-based study of 174 high technology instruments and electronic engineering businesses in South East England, Scotland and the San Francisco Bay area of California (including Silicon Valley) (Oakey 1984). The research sought to examine the impact of local regional economic resources on internal innovation in totally independent small high technology firms of less than 200 employees. However, the spatial data is preceded by an aggregate comparison of the innovativeness of survey firms with their propensity to seek external sources of investment capital. For it might be hypothesized that highly innovative firms in the highest technology production niches might more frequently need to seek external assistance with which to supplement internal profits.

Sources of investment finance

It is perhaps no surprise to discover, in view of recent high interest rates, that there is an overwhelming tendency in all regions of the study of firms to advance incrementally on the basis of internal resources when funding the *main* investment needs of the firm. For example, 74 per cent of all survey firms funded their capital investment programmes from internal company profits. However, Table 12.6 suggests that it is more frequently the highly innovative firm that seeks external funds, while Table 12.7 shows the tendency for these firms to manufacture high or medium technology output from within the generally high technology study sectors. Both these tabulations are statistically significant. Hence, due to the sophistication and innovativeness of the majority of externally funded firms, external sources of investment capital may have a greater effect on

Table 12.6 Incidence of product innovation, by main source of investment capital.

Source of investment capital (N = 174)	Product innovation		No innovation	
	N	(%)	N	(%)
internal	93	(70.5)	36	(85.7)
external	39	(29.5)	6	(14.3)
total	132	(100.0)	42	(100.0)

Chi-square = 3.86; $P = 0.049$.

Table 12.7 Technological complexity of main product, by main source of investment capital.

| Main Source of investment capital ($N = 174$) | Technological complexity | | | | | |
| | High | | Medium | | Low | |
	N	(%)	N	(%)	N	(%)
internal	34	(68.0)	34	(65.4)	61	(84.7)
external	16	(32.0)	18	(34.6)	11	(15.3)
total	50	(100.0)	52	(100.0)	72	(100.0)

Chi-square = 7.27; $P = 0.026$.

the general level of innovation than its previously noted low incidence would initially indicate. The overall pattern of these results
tends to suggest that innovative high technology firms are more
vigorous seekers of external funding.

These various main sources of external capital are regionalized,
together with the incidence of internal profits in Table 12.8. While
Scotland and the San Francisco Bay area have marginally lower
levels of internal profits as a main source, the breakdown of these
external sources in Table 12.8 indicates that they differ in that the
main external source in the Bay area was banks and venture capital
sources, while the dominant source of external capital in Scotland
was the local banks alone. The residual 'other' category was mainly
comprised of a mixture of various forms of British government
assistance. However, these data are important since they initially
indicate the marginal role of venture capital in the San Francisco Bay
area.

Table 12.8 Breakdown of main capital investment sources, by region.

| Capital sources ($N = 174$) | Scotland | | South East England | | San Francisco Bay area | |
	N	(%)	N	(%)	N	(%)
profit	35	(64.8)	49	(81.7)	45	(75.0)
local bank	13	(24.1)	5	(8.3)	6	(10.0)
venture capital	1	(1.9)	2	(3.3)	9	(15.0)
other	5	(9.2)	4	(6.7)	0	(0.0)
total	54	(100.0)	60	(100.0)	60	(100.0)

New technology-based small firms, investment and subsequent regional employment growth

Sources of start-up capital

Regional evidence on the main source of start-up capital indicates the universal popularity of personal savings as a means of beginning a firm. The 62 per cent average level of acknowledgement for this source is similar to levels observed in other studies of small firm start-up finance (Cross 1981, Storey 1982). While a wide range of other sources are sparsely represented, the only other important origin of start-up funds is private venture capital (Table 12.9). It is also clear that venture capital's status as the second most important source of funds is caused by the San Francisco Bay area sub-sample of firms, from which eight of the ten cases emanated. This is the first sign that the much vaunted venture capital market in the Bay area might be producing regionally different results within the new firm sub-sample. Although numbers are relatively small, eight (30 per cent) of the new Bay area firms founded since 1970 were aided in their birth by venture capital, while this source was insignificant in the British regions. This is a significant marginal regional difference which may aid the birth of small high technology firms in the Bay area.

Subsequent employment growth

It is initially worth noting that small high technology firms are transitory in nature. While there is clear evidence that many small

Table 12.9 Sources of start-up capital in firms founded since 1970, by region.

Start-up capital (N = 73)	Scotland		South East England		San Francisco Bay area	
	N	(%)	N	(%)	N	(%)
personal savings	20	(67.0)	11	(69.0)	14	(52.0)
previous assets	0	(0.0)	2	(12.0)	2	(7.0)
bank loan	2	(7.0)	1	(6.0)	1	(4.0)
second mortgage	1	(3.0)	0	(0.0)	1	(4.0)
venture capital	1	(3.0)	1	(6.0)	8	(30.0)
other	6	(20.0)	1	(6.0)	1	(4.0)
total	30	(100.0)	16	(100.0)	27	(100.0)

firms cease to operate within the first few years following their birth (Gudgin 1978, Storey 1982, Ganguly 1982), it is also obvious that, by definition, firms that grow cease to be termed 'small'. Indeed, if high technology small firms in the sectors of this study grew rapidly between 1970 and the current date, they would not be potential study firms due to the 200–employee ceiling placed on participants. Thus, the following data on employment generated in new firms founded in the five-year period prior to interview are a valid pointer towards the short term job–generating power of the high technology small firms in the environmentally diverse survey regions. Moreover, the employment growth of such new firms can be taken as a general surrogate for profitability and success in the absence of comparable financial data, which are difficult to compute, both because of confidentiality problems surrounding profits and because of difficulties in financial comparisons between Britain and the USA.

Table 12.10 indicates the number of survey firms founded in each region in the five-year period prior to interview, with the total number of the jobs created and the average number of jobs per firm by region. It is surprising that the South East of England recorded a mere three new firms during this period. Given that the sample from which these firms were drawn was randomly stratified by size, and was similar in other respects to its universe and the other regions, it is likely that these new firms are a fair reflection of small firm formation in the South East in the industries and period covered by the study. The other striking feature of Table 12.10 is that firms in the San Francisco Bay area appear generally to grow much faster than their British counterparts. This result bears out observations made during interviews. If the Bay area is compared with Scotland, where the number of new firms is similar, the average size of firm is almost four times as large as the Scottish average figure.

However, the averages of Table 12.10 belie the true explanation for the sharp regional contrasts in employment generation. In fact, the superior performance of the Bay area is largely attributable to

Table 12.10 Jobs created in firms less than five years old ($N = 33$), by region.

	Scotland	South East England	San Francisco Bay area
number of firms	16	3	14
total jobs	251	78	796
average jobs per firm	16	24	57

three new companies which were founded in the five-year period prior to survey and had grown to employ 125, 150 and 200 workers respectively by the time of interview. All three firms had been founded on a new product and had been assisted at birth and during subsequent years by venture capital as a main source of investment finance. The largest growth recorded in Britain for firms in Table 12.10 was 53 employees in a South-Eastern firm. This means that one Bay area new firm generated jobs equivalent to 80 per cent of the total jobs generated by sixteen new high technology small firms in Scotland. Although survey numbers are few in Table 12.10, these minority fast-growing firms in the Bay area did not exist in the other regions, and while the number of these firms may be small, the jobs created by them are substantial. Moreover, there is every likelihood that other fast-growing firms in the study sectors in the Bay area had grown beyond the 200-employee ceiling of this study during the five-year study period and thus do not appear in Table 12.10. Indeed certain recent modifications to the employment figures in the 1982 California manufacturer's directory support this assertion. Firms originally included in the survey on the basis of directory employment figures comfortably below the 200 employee ceiling were subsequently excluded because they had exceeded the 200-employee limit when contacted for interview.

It is generally true that the employment contribution of all small firms to regional economies may be of marginal significance in the short term. However, Table 12.10 hints that in high technology agglomerations such as Silicon Valley, the birth of a small number of fast-growing small firms may have a striking impact on employment. The significance of these minority results at the margin are lent added weight by the known performance of the, now famous, high technology American firms, discussed in the early sections of this paper, that have grown from the type of new firms indicated in Table 12.10 into large world-famous electronic corporations such as Fairchild, Varian, Mostec and Texas Instruments (Morse 1976). All these firms are less than 30 years old – some much less – but their employment capacity in Silicon Valley alone is measured in tens of thousands. With such impressive employment records it is not necessary to generate hundreds of small firms employing an average of 20 employees each for the next 50 years, but merely two or three Texas Instruments-type firms that subsequently become large. Small firms should not be viewed as an end in themselves, but as large firms in prospect. In Britain there is both a noticeable lack of new fast-growing high technology firms, as shown by Table 12.10, and a dearth of currently large firms of the Texas Instruments-type that were small 30 years ago.

Some conclusions

Entrepreneurship and the technology-based small firm

All the preceding data point towards the high employment growth potential of a minority of small high technology-based new firms among firms created in any given year at national or regional level. It is also clear that the term 'picking winners' is largely inappropriate with regard to such firms since they 'pick themselves' through their observed greater propensity to seek external means of funding internal innovation. None the less, this vital behaviour implies that, although identification of such firms may not be a problem, there may be difficulties in meeting the exacting financial needs that their rapid growth dictates. However, in advance of policy considerations, it is useful to place technology-based firms in a conceptual framework in which they are compared with other lower technology firms with less growth potential. This comparison will explain the sophisticated needs of technology-based new firms in terms of the entrepreneurs that direct them. Such observations will provide a useful basis for the subsequent suggestions for specific policy measures designed to aid rapid growth in technology-based new funds.

Success in any manufacturing activity involves a combination of two basic skills on the part of the decision maker (or makers). These are: (a) business acumen and (b) technical ability. In practice a small firm entrepreneur will possess a mix of both abilities, although business acumen will clearly be minimal in many new small firm entrepreneurs. Business acumen may be all important in certain activities, especially in parts of manufacturing industry where the technology is well established and profit margins are low (such as garment making and printing). In such instances business acumen, reflected in optimal purchasing, contract quoting and the organization of labour may be essential to ensure success. In this context technical ability is less important since the technology of the product is already established. However, the lack of technological barriers to entry into the industry because of the widespread availability of the technical specifications of the product means that the resulting growth in competition would bring down prices. However, the converse is true of high technology forms of production. In these industries technical skill may far outweigh business acumen since technical barriers to entry preclude other producers who may have higher business acumen but poor technical ability. Hence high prices may be charged for goods and services that stem exclusively from the personal technical ability of the owner (or owners) of the firm. Thus, inefficiencies in business acumen may be masked by the high prices such activities can command. This principle lies at the heart of the

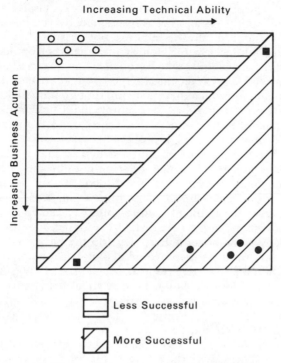

Figure 12.4 An entrepreneurial matrix.

economic viability of high technology industry in general and many high technology small firms in particular.

These arguments are similar to those put forward by Allan Pred (1967) when he advanced ideas on the location decisions of entrepreneurs. With apologies to Pred, his behavioural matrix can be easily adapted to the present consideration of the dynamic attributes of small firm entrepreneurs. Figure 12.4 represents a matrix into which all small firm entrepreneurs might be conceptually placed. As argued previously, a mix of these two abilities exists in all entrepreneurs. The figure shows three main types of businessman. First there is the small firm owner with poor business acumen and little technical ability (represented by the unshaded circles). He has little business acumen to help him reduce costs and his inability to obtain protection and higher prices through the development of high technology products means that he must compete in an area of production with tight profit margins. Although it is not inevitable, firms associated with this type of entrepreneur are most likely to be short-lived.

The second type of businessman is one who scores poorly on one dimension but highly on another (represented by squares in the figure). He would typically be either a businessman with very efficient production but low technology products (bottom left), or perhaps a boffin-entrepreneur who has no idea how to run a business but is blessed with a great technical expertise that enables him to produce a product for which there is strong though limited demand at virtually any price (top right), for example in the field of medical instrumentation. In both instances these entrepreneurs marginally qualify for the 'more successful' half of the matrix.

However, the most successful businessmen in Figure 12.4 are those who, as might be anticipated, develop both business acumen and technical ability (represented by shaded circles). While the absent-minded professor-entrepreneur does exist, logic suggests that in most cases these (mainly white-collar) entrepreneurs with technical proficiency, and almost certainly a higher education, are also more likely to be better able to develop the business acumen necessary to run a business as compared to blue-collar entrepreneurs with little technical knowledge (Johnson & Cathcart 1979). Indeed, Silicon Valley in California, famous for its small-firm growth, has been created by just such highly motivated, technically qualified entrepreneurs who have developed a flair for business (Cooper 1970). Perhaps Hewlett and Packard are the best examples of this phenomenon. However, it is of relevance to the present discussion that it is the small firms with the entrepreneurs of the type indicated in the bottom right of Figure 12.4 that will, over a period of time, show the most vigorous growth and subsequently have the greatest impact on regional and national economies.

The technology-based small firm and regional aid

Previous research has indicated that the depressed regions of Britain do not possess their proportionate share of high technology sectors, and that those firms from innovative sectors that do exist in such regions are proportionately less innovative than matched firms from the South East of England (Oakey et al. 1980, 1982). Nonetheless, it remains true that any depressed region, whether it is the North East of England or a depressed part of the manufacturing belt of the USA, will have a number of new technology-based firms with growth potential. But these depressed regions, by definition, rarely create the wealth from industrial growth that facilitates the emergence of local venture capitalists with industrial experience who are willing to fund such firms. However, government aid in the depressed areas could be directed at these firms, with the specific remit of filling the venture capital gap by providing investment capital for research and development which, in turn, should greatly promote the growth of new products, markets and employment. The evidence from this paper has indicated that venture capital provides a useful service in the San Francisco Bay area of California through the rapid provision of investment capital for fast-growing firms. In this context, it is of further significance that survey evidence from both Britain and the USA has indicated that banks are not particularly forthright in the investment capital funding of small high technology firms. While the gap left by institutional private sector funding in the Bay area is filled, at least in part, by the activities of venture capitalists in various guises, the gap remains in other parts of the USA and in the whole of Britain. Evidence from both Britain and the USA indicates that it is mainly the fastest growing firms with the greatest potential that are most frustrated by an inability to raise venture capital. For example, the most successful British bidder for small firm investment capital in the survey had obtained all the major relevant grants and loans including assistance from the National Research and Development Corporation (NRDC), the Industrial and Commercial Finance Corporation (ICFC) and the Microprocessors Application Scheme (MAP). However, this managing director vigorously asserted that, given more adequate funding, his business might have been three times larger.

Venture capital is important, not only because of its significant marginal importance to innovation and growth in Bay area firms, but also because the behaviour of venture capitalists in funding small high technology firms points to many lessons that might be learned by financial institutions in both the public and private sectors. First, the rapidity with which capital is advanced (or refused) by venture capitalists is enlightening. Because of the short product life cycles common in high technology industry, it is essential that decisions on loans be made in a 'next week or not at all' spirit. Indeed, it is important that a firm not eligible for funds be told of the decision quickly. Venture capitalists compress the decision process to a point where, in many cases, the decision to fund is made virtually on the spot, and funding is extended within days rather than months. Clearly, it is important that the evaluators of proposed investment funding can extend the finance. Here the element of risk is clearly higher than for long term evaluations. However, venture capitalists reduce the risk of individual failures by building up a portfolio of small firms in which various levels of equity stakes may be taken. Thus, the failure of individual firms is more than compensated by other successes and aggregate profits are substantial. Risks are further reduced by the personal experience of the venture capitalist, who is frequently an ex-manufacturer with considerable business and technical acumen.

Much of this behaviour could be replicated by public and private institutions when providing investment capital for research and development in small high technology firms. Government agencies in depressed regions could make considerable advances towards ensuring that the minority of high technology small firms that are born in largely hostile innovation environments are compensated by a locally superior environment for investment finance, with regard both to terms offered and speed of service. Importantly, the level of bureaucracy inherent in such an objective should be kept to a minimum, and the level of risk should be deliberately increased to ensure that worthy firms are not starved of funds for expansion simply in order to maintain a spuriously high success rate for loan approvals. Following the venture capitalist example, risks could be reduced by ensuring that the evaluators possess technical knowledge and by purchasing equity stakes in a portfolio of firms in return for the capital.

To this end, an agency might be established in a depressed area with the sole remit of providing venture capital for high technology small firms. The agency could be established with a lump sum from national or local government, or from combined private and public sources, and be empowered to invest the money in suitable firms, taking an equity stake or an equity stake option in return for the funds. The agency might also develop technical and business 'back-up' services which would assist the evaluation of initial investment in suitable firms, and aid their subsequent growth. This organization would be mainly self-financing after the initial injection of capital, since profits from the sale of equity stake in successful firms would be ploughed back into the central fund. Such an approach would not be politically contentious, since equity stakes in small firms that became established might be sold back to the private sector in order to provide funds for further assistance. Apart from the self-financing nature of this approach to small firms assistance, tax revenue from the growing firm and its employees, and the reductions in unemployment benefit resulting from the expansion of such small firms in depressed areas, would be an added financial bonus.

A further benefit of a government-linked equity stake scheme in the depressed regions would be the protection of these firms from the asset-stripping acquisitions by larger firms from outside the region. There is some evidence to indicate that a number of fast-growing firms in the northern region of England have been acquired in this manner, with a subsequent relocation of the manufacture of their product to another region or abroad (Smith 1982). This is a great loss to a depressed region, both in terms of wasted regional aid and losses in employment. It is imperative that, in seeking to create from various sources a 'critical mass' of high technology industrial production at a growth pole in a depressed region, there should be a minimum of high technology employment leakage to other areas.

One further advantage of a government-sponsored venture capital agency would be the implicit commitment to medium term funding of firms with growth potential. Although product life cycles are short in high technology firms, programmes of research and development on particular projects can easily extend over two or three years. Moreover, the rapid technological advances common to the leading-edge technologies mean that finance for research and development will be a continuing problem that will increase in magnitude as the firm grows. Here grants and loans are of limited value, not only because they are a particularly 'lumpy' form of investment capital flow, but also, and more importantly, because each loan application involves the risk of refusal and, even if successful, does not imply any form of long term commitment to the firm. Clearly, an advantage of the equity stake is that the venture capital agency, as in the case of the private venture capitalist in Silicon Valley, would have a continuing interest in supporting the company.

It is evident that the suggested regional capital investment agency bears many resemblances to the National Enterprise Board (NEB), now merged with the National Research and Development Corporation (NRDC) to form the British Technology Group (BTG). The efficiency of this constantly changing organization has been badly affected by the ebb and flow of government policy since its inception in 1975, but it is notable that the organization has recorded several successes in the funding of high technology small firms, frequently in exchange for equity. While banks always state that no small firm with growth potential is starved of capital, the NEB with its equity option policy and technical back-up service, has been a successful alternative to bank finance for many small firms. Indeed, the prosperity of the now-famous venture capitalists in Silicon Valley, who operate a similar private sector service, is evidence of the inability of local banks to cater for this real investment need in high technology firms, for it is inconceivable that the large profits amassed by venture capitalists in the Bay area would be willingly foregone by bankers. The role of the BTG continues to be revised to conform to the policies of the current British government. But, provided the existing powers of the group are not further diminished, there is a clear scope for an adaptation of the regional branches of the BTG to become the venture capital agencies outlined above, if they are given greater resources and a large measure of regional autonomy.

Conversely, it might be argued that any form of government involvement would be resisted by small firm entrepreneurs. However, the validity of this view is diminished by the success achieved by both the BTG and the Scottish Development Agency in their funding of small firms. This success demonstrates that government assistance to small firms can be effective when it is delivered by credible organizations with proven business and technical expertise. Entrepreneurs will show greater enthusiasm and respect for the agents of government assistance if these agents can prove their understanding of small firm problems and potentials and do not suffocate the aid process with irrelevant forms and unnecessary delays. The respondents to the above questionnaire survey in both Britain and the United States were rarely adverse to government aid *per se*, but merely abhorred the current over-bureaucratic system of delivery. Under the proposed venture capital agency approach, the exchange of equity for finance, together with the acceptance of a nominated agency director on the company board, will be tolerated by the entrepreneurs if they feel that the measures can raise the overall organizational, technical and financial strength of the firm. While not a panacea, the significant potential of job creation from new technology-based firms in any region should ensure that they require specific policy measures as *part* of any overall regional industrial development strategy for all sizes and sectors of industrial production.

References

Anon. 1980. The reindustrialization of America. *Business Week*, 30 June 1980.

American Electronics Association 1978. Written statement before the House Committee on Ways and Means (E. U. W. Zachau, Chairman, Capital Formation Task Force, AEA), 7 March 1978.

Birch, D. L. 1979. *The job generation process*. Cambridge, Mass.: MIT Program on Neighborhood and Regional Change.

Bollard, A. 1983. *Small beginnings*. London: Intermediate Technology Publications.

Cooper, A. C. 1970. The Palo Alto experience. *Industrial Research* May 1970, 58–60.

Cross, M. 1981. *New firm formation and regional development*. Farnborough, Hants: Gower.

De Melto, D. P., K. E. McMullen and R. M. Wills 1980. *Innovation and Technological change in five Canadian industries*. Discussion Paper no. 176. Economic Council of Canada, Ottawa.

Freeman, C., J. Clarke and L. Soete 1982. *Unemployment and technical innovation*. London: Frances Pinter.

Ganguly, A. 1982. Significant surplus of births over deaths. *British Business* **23**, 512–13.

Gudgin, G. 1978. *Industrial location processes and regional employment growth.* Farnborough, Hants: Saxon House.

Johnson, P. S. and D. G. Cathcart 1979. New manufacturing firms and regional development: some evidence from the northern region. *Regional Studies* 13, 269–80.

Kelley, R. 1978. Technological innovation and international trade patterns. In *Technological innovation: government/industry cooperation,* A. Gerstenfeld and R. Brainard (eds). New York: Wiley.

Little, A. D. 1977. *New technology-based firms in the United Kingdom and the Federal Republic of Germany.* Report prepared for the Anglo–German Foundation for the Study of Industrial Society, London.

Morse, R. S. 1976. *The role of new technical enterprises in the US economy.* Report of the Commerce Technical Advisory Board to the Secretary of Commerce, January.

National Science Foundation 1979. *NSF small business innovation research program.* Washington, D.C.: NSF.

National Board for Science and Technology 1980. *Innovation in small firms, preliminary report.* Dublin: National Board for Science and Technology (final report published 1981).

Oakey, R. P. 1984. *High technology small firms: innovation and regional development in Britain and the United States.* London: Frances Pinter.

Oakey, R. P., A. T. Thwaites and P. A. Nash 1980. The regional distribution of innovative manufacturing establishments in Britain. *Regional Studies* 14, 235–53.

Oakey, R. P., A. T. Thwaites and P. A. Nash 1982. Technological change and regional development: some evidence on regional variations in product and process innovation. *Environment and Planning A* 14, 1073–86.

Piatier, A. 1981. *Enquête sur l'innovation: premiers résultats.* Paris: Centre d'Etude des Techniques Economiques Modernes.

Prais, S. 1976. *The evolution of giant firms in Britain.* Cambridge: Cambridge University Press.

Pred, A. R. 1967. *Behaviour and location,* 2 vols. Lund: Lund University.

Rothwell, R. 1984. The role of small firms in the emergence of new technology. *Omega* 12, 19–29.

Rothwell, R. and W. Zegveld 1982. *Innovation and small and medium sized firms.* London: Frances Pinter.

Smith, I. J. 1982. Some implications of inward investment through takeover activity. *Northern Economic Review* 2, 1–5.

Storey, D. 1980. *Job generation and small firms policy in Britain.* Research Series II. London: Centre for Environmental Studies.

Storey, D. J. 1982. *Entrepreneurship and the small firm.* London: Croom Helm.

Notes on contributors

Ash Amin is a Research Associate in the Centre for Urban and Regional Development Studies, University of Newcastle upon Tyne. He has written on industrialization in the Italian south and is currently engaged in a project financed by the Economic and Social Research Council, on the spatial implications of internationalization in the UK car components industry.

Keith Cowling is Professor of Economics at the University of Warwick. His most recent book is *Monopoly capitalism*. He is currently editor of the *International Journal of Industrial Organization*.

James Curran is Reader in Industrial Sociology at Kingston Polytechnic. He has been involved in several research projects on various aspects of the small business and has written extensively on the subject.

Christopher Freeman is Deputy Director of the Science Policy Research Unit, University of Sussex. He has written extensively on various issues related to technical innovation and is currently working on technology policy, technical innovation and diffusion.

David Gibbs was until recently a Research Associate in the Centre for Urban and Regional Development Studies, University of Newcastle upon Tyne and is now lecturer in Geography at Manchester Polytechnic. He has been involved in a number of research projects investigating the interrelationship between technological change and regional development. Other interests include work on the restructuring of the British clothing industry.

John Goddard is Director of the Centre for Urban and Regional Development Studies at the University of Newcastle upon Tyne where he holds the Henry Daysh Chair of Regional Development Studies. From 1980 to 1985 he was editor of *Regional Studies*. He is co-editor of *Urban and regional transformation of Britain* (with A. G. Champion). His main research interest is in the location of office activities, particularly the impact of technological change and corporate restructuring on the distribution of non-production functions.

Bernard Leach is Senior Lecturer in Science, Technology and Society at Manchester Polytechnic, and Chairman of the Manchester Employment Research Group. His research interests in employment and new technology are based on work done with trade unionists in the food manufacturing sector.

Kevin Morgan is a Research Fellow in the School of Social Sciences at the University of Sussex. He is engaged with Andrew Sayer on a research project on the role of the electronics industry in British regional development and is the author of a forthcoming book entitled *The politics of regional development in Britain*.

284

Ray Oakey was until recently a Senior Research Associate in the Centre for Urban and Regional Development Studies at Newcastle University and is now a lecturer in the Department of Business Organisation at Herriot-Watt University. His current research is concerned with technological change in small high technology firms and their impact on regional growth.

Roy Rothwell is a Senior Research Fellow at the Science Policy Research Unit, University of Sussex. He has co-authored books and written articles on industrial innovation factors, the role of small firms in innovation, and public policy towards innovation.

Andrew Sayer is a Lecturer in Human Geography in the School of Social Sciences, University of Sussex. He is interested in industrial geography and methodology and is currently engaged in ESRC funded research on the electronics industry and British regional development.

John Shutt is Senior Research Officer in the Employment and Economic Development Department, Sheffield City Council. Previously he was involved in research on multinational corporations and industrial restructuring at the North West Industry Research Unit, Manchester University. He was involved in the Community Development Projects research on inner city decline in the 1970s.

Ian Smith is a Senior Research Associate in the Centre for Urban and Regional Development Studies, University of Newcastle upon Tyne. His current interests include the spatial implications of foreign direct investment and industrial restructuring through takeovers in the United Kingdom.

John Stanworth is Professor and Director of the Small Business Unit at the Polytechnic of Central London. His most recent research has been on the franchised small business and he has published widely on this and other subjects related to the small business in Britain.

David Stewart is Associate Professor in the Faculty of Business Administration at the University of Newfoundland, having formerly worked at Paisley College of Technology. His main interests concern the application of statistical techniques in marketing and economics.

David Storey is a Senior Research Associate in the Centre for Urban and Regional Development Studies, University of Newcastle upon Tyne. He is author of *Entrepreneurship and the new firm*, and co-author of *The small firm: profits, jobs and failures* to be published in 1986.

Morgan Thomas is Professor and Chairman of the Department of Geography at the University of Washington in Seattle, USA. He has long been concerned with the conceptualisation of regional economic growth and structural change. His current research is on the role of innovative firms and industries in the process of regional economic development.

Alfred Thwaites is Deputy Director of the Centre for Urban and Regional

Development, University of Newcastle upon Tyne. His research has concentrated over a number of years on various aspects of the regional dimension of technological change, especially in the UK manufacturing industry.

Stephen Young is Senior Lecturer in the Department of Marketing and Co-Director of Strathclyde International Business Unit at the University of Strathclyde. He is the author of numerous books and articles on the topics of multinationals and foreign direct investment, and recently has been involved in work on industrial policy.

Index